LIBRARY INFORMATION SERVICES AND SYSTEMS

Library Information Services and Systems

P. Kaushik

ANMOL PUBLICATIONS PVT. LTD.
NEW DELHI - 110 002 (INDIA)

ANMOL PUBLICATIONS PVT. LTD.
H.O.: 4374/4B, Ansari Road, Daryaganj
New Delhi - 110 002
Ph.: 23261597, 23278000
B.O.: No. 1015, Ist Main Road, BSK III Stage
III Phase, III Block
Bangalore - 560 085 (India)
Visit us at: www.anmolpublications.com

Library Information Services and Systems

First Published, 2006

ISBN 81-261-2625-6

PRINTED IN INDIA

Published by J.L. Kumar for Anmol Publications Pvt. Ltd., New Delhi - 110 002 and Printed at Mehra Offset Press, Delhi.

Contents

Preface

"Library Information Services and Systems" as a paper is being taught at B.L.I.Sc. and M.L.I.Sc. in 'Library Science' at various universities and institutions. This book is designed as an introductory text to the above paper, encompassing vital information on all pertinent aspects. Thus the material presented here would be of interest as well as of great use to the students, teachers and professionals of Library Science. This book will provide complete knowledge of the information services, system approach in library, technical services, librarianship, computer information, online information etc. to the students.

The major topics dealt in this book are—Information—An Introduction; Systems Approach in Library; Information Alerting Service; Technical Service in Library; Librarianship and Information Centre; Computer Based Information; Online Information Service; Library Information Networking etc.

It is hoped that all those will benefit from the contents of this book for whom it is meant. The author will feel amply rewarded, if motive is achieved.

Editor

1

Information—An Introduction

Information is one of those misunderstood concepts. Yet it is at the same time one of the most used. We go to the bus station to seek information from timetables. We obtain information from government offices such as the DSS and the DVLC. Banks, supermarkets, leisure centres, libraries and even the police ply us with more. Newspapers, television and the radio present us with their own ideas of what information should be. In many instances, however, we may not agree with their conclusions. McLeod termed its subjectivity as being one person's junk and another's treasure.

We all understand and deal with this accordingly when extracting news from the media, for example. Yet many of our organizations consider information to be something more. They see it as a vital resource, to be managed like any other valuable resource. How it is used and disseminated through the available technology can determine how efficient, and indeed effective, an organization is Peter Drucker sees' information acquired in a systematic and purposeful way as enhancing an organization's productivity.

Information is important, we cannot operate without it. But more than this, we are discovering that our ability to process it by increasingly sophisticated technological means is fundamentally changing the way that employees perceive their organizational environment. The consequences of this could be either to break down established functional controls or indeed to enhance them by becoming super-efficient. Much will depend upon the characteristics of the organization before implementation.

As firms become increasingly 'information dependent' we need to identify the perceptual relationship between ourselves and the information we use. How, for instance, can we possibly design an adequate information system if we do not understand the nature of information? The answer to this lies, in part, with the conventional wisdom of the day. Managers, like everybody else, develop their views through exposure to established ideas. Thus, the way in which they understand information will influence the way in which they treat it. Such conventional wisdom is coloured by the technicians, on the one hand, and the user's own experience on the other.

Anecdotal prescriptions abound as guidelines to the way presented for all who care to listen. These arise from a blanket of professional and academic thinking which surrounds the business environment and provides remedies for action. We could categorize all these ideas into two bodies of thought, two paradigms. The first could be termed the resource-driven paradigm. This is because its central theme in understanding information is the continuity and consistency of the information itself. It is very much in vogue at present.

The second body of thought is the perception-driven paradigm. Information is seen as an abstract concept, the product of individual perception. It is a temporary phenomenon and as such belongs only to the receiver. The difference is not merely one of academic debate. Managements adopting one or the other can affect the design of their organizations. If information is considered to be a resource then resulting systems are usually more centrally controlled, the assumption being that all information is corporate property. Whereas information considered to be personally owned is seen as being outside the formal structure.

Within the framework of this paradigm the view of information is c:oloured by its use as a resource. Like any other resource it can be tapped at any time with the certainty of achieving a predictable value from it. Information is regarded as unchanging, and therefore can be easily accommodated into a firm's formal procedure. There are a range of propositions available which seeks to explain information. Each proposition has a consequence for organizational design.

Herbert A. Simon took the view that information, along with energy, constitute the two basic currencies of our society. We need energy to breathe, to move, to think, to live. But this alone is not enough. We need to know when to breathe, when to move and how to think. Information provides us with that knowledge. To adopt this perspective is to interpret information as an independent entity. It is all about us waiting to be picked up and used. There may be minor variations in its ir erpretation by different individuals, but consistency can be easily achieved through better training.

Specific sets of information, such as finance information, are given a unique value by organizations which are usually based upon departmental rather than individual needs. Particular information is thus attached to particular departments. This allows information to be generally accessible because perceptions of it are bound by the formal departmental framework. Information is then tied into that framework and cannot be used legitimately within any other context, thus guarding its consistency. What is excluded, therefore, is an important role for the individual receiver. This is not to suggest that information cannot be perceived by individuals. Psychologists such as Anderson and Bower have long been aware of the importance of information reception in determining an individual's behaviour.

However, information can be received automatically without an individual having to understand it. For example, through training an employee could process production statistics without knowing what they mean. In this case it is the functional process (through its formal procedure) that is acting as the receiver rather than the individual. An accounting process, for instance, responds to specific inputs without anyone having to understand them. A motor car responds to certain information transmitted through mechanisms such as the throttle, steering wheel or brake. Both of these examples are designed to act as receivers to specific information.

By implication, information can be transmitted to any receiver that logs into the particular transmission. In the same way as a radio picks up a station when it is switched on, the right form will pick up the right information. And like radio waves, information is omnipresent, only needing the correct tuning. Such a view allows information the continuity and consistency required to be regarded as a resource. It also allows a further proposition.

The design of any formal information system must assume that information does not change during transmission. It can, however, be transformed from data or other information sets before transmission. Within such a framework it is the transmitting functions (departments, processes, etc.) which are considered to be the main determinants. The information receiving functions (also departments, processes, etc.) are designed to link into the operational needs of the transmitter functions.

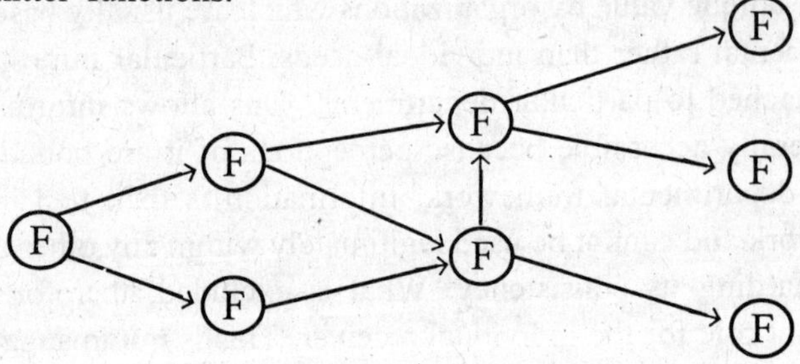

F = functions

Fig. 1. An information network between functions

Each function, however, can be both transmitter and receiver of information, and together with other functions will form part of an integrated network (Figure 1). The functions are tied by their simultaneous roles as information receivers and transmitters, thereby being prevented as much as possible from deviancy in their information usage.

Consequently, business organizations are driven by those functions which transmit information. The higher the value that a particular set of information is given, the more important will be its relating transmitter function. For example, the finance department could both transmit and receive information. Indeed, each job function within that. department could also do the same. A cost clerk, for instance, receives information from the factory floor which he then processes into other information and transmits to some other source, perhaps management. The value of the information he processes will depend upon the utility his organization has placed upon it. If the utility is high, then the prestige attached to the transmitting function will also be high irrespective of job complexity. In the same way, if a department has a great number of important information transmitters within its control, then it too will be prestigious and possess influence.

Perception-driven Paradigm

The perception-driven paradigm does not consider information to be a resource. Individuals or groups are seen to own their information. What belongs to the organization are the data sets, the facts and figures specific to certain functions. For instance, data on how an organization is performing in its market quite obviously belong to that firm. How well that data is used is dependent upon the individual's own competence in interpreting it. Management can control this indirectly through training, but they cannot directly control the thought processes which turns data into information. Once again, there is a collection of propositions or ideas about information which formulate a general approach.

Adherence to this paradigm, as in the previous paradigm, may not necessarily be by conviction but rather by default because people not treating information as a resource automatically form part of this group. However, there are others who are members by conviction. Information is said to be receiver-dependent, in that, any set of information can be considered to be information only if it is recognised as having value by a particular individual. Thus, a river flooding may be information to someone who lives on its banks but of no consequence to someone living several miles away.

It would be difficult, therefore, to understand information as a group or organizations property since its determination is subjective. Management teams have implemented computer technology and in so doing also developed their information sets into a resource. They experience problems, usually some time after a successful launch, and then abandon using their technology in an integrative manner, returning to the 'islands' approach (that is, a computer system, perhaps physically integrated through networks, etc., but perceptually segregated into different functional areas). Information is no longer seen as a resource; indeed its treatment as such is often seen as the culprit and not the technology itself.

Both paradigms recognize a difference between data and information. Computer personnel, for example, have long known of the distinction. Information is seen by them as processed data. The two are interrelated, data being the input to a process, and information the output. In the same way that an output of one system can form the input of another, information from one system can form the data of another. This is consistent with treating information as a resource. Perceptually-conceived information on the other hand is not the consequence of a formalized process. Data are a factor, but then so are other aspects such as individual traits, culture, structure and political processes. The relationship between data and information is, therefore, not so strong. This contradicts the objectives implied by the creation of management information systems and data processing. The former allows the individual access to established information, whilst the latter converts data into information. Since the production of information cannot be formalized there is no point in trying to achieve it. Systems should, therefore, be designed to produce the most accurate and readable data in order to enhance easy conversion into information.

When Ligomenides describes information as a fundamental force, he should be referring to data. Levitan, on the other hand, is correct in claiming information to be dynamic and continuously evolving. The logic of these two views can be seen when data and information are differentiated. It is only data which is time-independent, and therefore unchanging and static—a fundamental force. By this we mean that data retains a constant empirical value: a fact is a fact and cannot be altered. Information, on the other hand, can be altered and changed. It is time-dependent and thus its value can alter from one moment to the next. It is dynamic and evolving because it is determined by an individual's perception.

It is, indeed, time and utility which transform data into information. If at a particular time a set of data is useful to an individual then it can be described as information. Equally, at another time the same set of data may not have utility and therefore not be information. The data themselves have not changed in any way, remaining always constant. What has changed is the individual's perception of those data. Information is in reality the consequence of a complex psychological process which transforms perceived data, into usable thought inputs.

It is, therefore, data which the individual receives from the environment, the brain which transforms these data into information. No formal system can directly pre-empt this stage; thus no formal system can transform data into information.

Data can be transformed into different data, transmitted and received. For example, production data submitted to the cost department and processed into second generation costed production data, which are in turn submitted to the financial director. Information is transformed, in part, from data; it can only be received and never transmitted. The financial director may attach value to costed production data and thus receive it as information. If he/ she passes it on, it will once again be as data, perhaps refined into third generation data. There cannot be information systems because information is so transient.

The individual's subjectivity, which can be developed by training and formal procedure, determines what is information. At another time that perception may be different. Information systems cannot work in this way. Their assumption must be that information is not transient but consistent.

Quite obviously information systems do exist in one form or another. They may not be what they claim to be but they are nevertheless working. Is it worth arguing the difference? The answer to that lies within ourselves. Our actions and behaviour, and consequently our organizations, are governed by our perceptions. If, therefore, we understand information to be permanent rather than transient then how we organize ourselves will be coloured by that.

Structural Implications

The difference between these two paradigms may seem subtle, and in terms of information usage it may well be. However, NBS research indicates that the effects upon organizational design can be major. Structural characteristics consequent upon individually-owned information, for instance, can adopt two extremes. On the one hand they can be organic and informal (adhocracies) whereby all members are seen as contributing equally, each possessing a particular range of techniques to interpret data, whilst at the other extreme there are formal and mechanistic organizations (bureaucracies). The rigidities of structure stifle any use of information as a resource, so by default such processes are left to the individual. These contrast with the resource-driven paradigm in which the structural characteristics of organizations are seen to be centrally orientated, with spheres of influence at the periphery, their importance dependent upon the perceived value of particular sets of information.

Wider Implications of Information

The development of an organization oriented toward the resource-driven concept of information is well known, and many large firms are aligned in that direction. A sophisticated network is established, more than likely computerized, accessing and distributing information. Particular attention is paid to ensuring standardization of information sets. For example, a piece of costing information is so devised that it can be used by accounts, marketing and production. These organizations treat all information as their property, attaching to it a value like any other asset. This denies the employee any sense of ownership and tends to detach them from the work process with consequential inefficiencies evolving. It is asserted, that a motivated staff is a contented and efficient staff.

One important way to motivate is to give the individual responsibility within their job. Such responsibility is manifest in how much ability a person will be given to determine the information need of their particular function. To standardize information in the way that many corporate systems do, takes away that fundamental element of responsibility. Levitan, on the other hand, would claim this to be an inevitable consequence of increasingly sophisticated corporate structures. In addition, Karen Levitan and others imply that information which is not used as a resource is inferior. On the contrary, one could argue that giving the individual ownership could result in a greater entrepreneurial drive.

It has been suggested that there is a relationship between the way in which a firm uses its information and its structure. A matrix can be established differentiating organizations in terms of how they treat their information and the consequential structural characteristics. If, for example, information is plotted against size (another important contingent of organization) four major structural types could be identified. Each is the outcome of the way a particular firm uses its information.

On the vertical axis of the matrix are the two extremes of information. On the horizontal axis are the two extremes of organizational size (Figure 2). Both information and size are considered to be contingents, that is variables which affect the characteristics of an organization. The four possible combinations of these two variables determine four organizational structures. Thus, each structure is an ideal for each of the four combinations. For example, a managerial structure is the appropriate structure for a large firm using information as a resource.

Resource	Managerial	Technical/ Professional
Treatment of information	Bureaucratic	Entrepreneurial
Perception	Large	Small

Structure parameters

Managerial	:	larger in size with central/top control but with more departmental integration
Bureaucratic	:	larger in size with formal structure and a diversified control

Technical/professional	: smaller in size with a professional body and formal structure
Entrepreneurial	: centrally controlled but with less formal structure and smaller in size

Figure 2: Information/structure matrix

Research into the validity of such a matrix is by no means complete. There is evidence from the NBS regional survey, for example, that such a correlation does indeed exist. In general, the more successful managerial-style firms tend to treat their information as a resource, whilst the more successful entrepreneurial organizations tend to treat their information as a perceptual phenomenon, and so on. It is not yet certain whether the matrix is predictive, that is implying combinations which are not successful. There is sufficient evidence, however, to support the claim that information usage affects organizational structure.

The issue of information is much more than whether or not it is a resource. Information is indeed the essence of an organization, shaping and determining its structure.

For example, bureaucratic organizations could hot effectively treat information as a resource because their mechanisms could not control it that way. A technical/professional organization, on the other hand, is better able to handle its information as a resource because of its structural characteristics.

The implication is that there should be a natural balance between the design of an organization and its information structure. Where this has not been achieved it is because managers are not matching the structure of their organizations with an appropriate usage of information. NBS research has also shown that the implementation of computer technology can worsen any potential for imbalance. This is perhaps because of two factors.

Firstly, the characteristics of the technology itself do tend to enhance resource-driven rather than perception-driven information. Secondly, the greater volume of information generated makes the problem more apparent.

If the matrix in Figure 2 is valid then there is neither a right nor a wrong way to control information: much depends upon the individual circumstances. Resource-driven information and perception-driven information are opposite extremes of one continuum.

Management teams were grasping eagerly at the new computer technology as a solution to their efficiency problems. There were at that time forces in the environment-market, political, social or economic-with which the traditional methods of organization could not cope; it was believed that the computer would provide all the answers. In the space of that time many colleagues began to discover that the impact of computer technology seemed to be contradictory. On the one hand, it did tend to improve efficiency, whilst on the other it was not always so certain that an improvement in effectiveness followed. It seemed that underlying, and as yet not understood, forces were at work.

Departments employing the same technology were more or less successful than others. Business organizations with all the ingredients of success and implementing computers to further fuel their growth quite often experienced failure a few years later. Since those early days there has been considerable discussion and research on the impact of information technology. It seemed that the perceptual aspects of organization were not merely misunderstood but often ignored, and thus we were not able to understand fully the implications of introducing information technology. We now realize that not only does it have an impact on the way we run organizations, it also has an impact on our behaviour. There is a readily understood physical aspect of any firm and a more abstract, perceptual aspect which arises from the way that people behave as a collective. Information technology is not the only agent in this process, but because of its particular characteristics it can have an extraordinarily powerful effect on both these aspects.

The two are inseparable. Models that seek to understand either technology or organization must do so within the framework created by this relationship. Otherwise an essential factor leading to an appropriate analysis will be missed. The other main objective is to produce a model which can do this. Unlike many of its predecessors, the model will not concentrate on the functional or hierarchical nature of organizations but rather on the dichotomy between the physical and perceptual aspects. This exists whether or not there is information technology present, but in many cases the implementation of such technology can exacerbate potential dysfunctional forces existing between the two. In effect there are two organizations—a physical organization and a perceptual or virtual organization.

The impact that information technology can have on the sometimes tenuous relationship existing between the two can be quite profound. The model explores thoroughly this relationship. It proposes virtual organization as the antithesis of physical organization. That is abstract, unseeing and existing within the minds of those who form a particular organization. The point being that because the framework of virtual organization is often subjective and open to many different perceptual interpretations, it is difficult for anyone to establish an appropriate response to it. This makes it no less real; nor does it reduce the need to respond to it. Left unattended the effects of virtual organization can be quite catastrophic, especially if stimulated by the impact of information technology. This has considerable significance for the practitioner, especially those who have introduced, or are thinking of introducing, information technology. The model suggests that for a firm to survive there would ideally exist a dynamic equilibrium between the two organizations which has been termed the organizational balance. Anything which upsets this balance, such as the introduction of information technology, has to be compensated for by proactive action of management. If managers do not understand, nor indeed perceive the existence of virtual organization, then they will not be able to take the appropriate measures.

Demonstrating the existence of virtual organization can be problematic. By definition it cannot be observed directly since it exists only in the mind. At best one could ask a selection of staff for their impressions and make certain deductions, but these are likely to be dubious and tainted with the researcher's own perceptions. As such there has deliberately been no direct empirical research to establish the foundations of this model. Support for its validity has been sought in three other areas. Firstly, there is indirect empirical data gained from several research projects conducted at the Newcastle Business School. This comprises a study over two years by Stuart Maguire and myself into eighty-five small to large firms in all sectors of the North East. We examined particularly the strategy that firms employed to implement and control their information technology.

The data were gathered through a series of observations, interviews and involvement in the process. Other data were obtained from one or two firm studies on the impact of information technology by a group within the Newcastle Business School called AMBIS (Advanced Manufacturing and Business Information Systems). The argument for using these data rather than dedicated data is that they should be less contrived. Secondly, there is support to be gained from relevant personal experience. Although many would find this approach invalid because it does not comply with traditional or conventional ideas about research data, there is an increasing acceptance that such data can prove useful. In the social sciences, for example, Duke argued that such an approach (amongst others) would make a valuable contribution to the understanding of social experience. It is accepted that it cannot provide the only data, but the data that it does provide should be considered no less valid than any other.

We return to a more traditional style in support of the main arguments. That is, rather than gathering empirical evidence first and then developing a model, we should develop the model first from experiential instincts and then support it with data. This is put forward in the belief that to pursue the traditional methods of data-first research would not produce the generic model necessary to achieve the objectives set above. We have become unimaginative in our ideas about organization because we have been blinkered by too many sets of data.

How the book is structured in terms of presenting a logical argument takes on a greater significance than if it were based merely upon direct empirical data. It requires presentation of basic argument, counter-argument and a compromise position which leads the reader forward to the logical conclusion. This is the dialectic which involves thesis, antithesis and synthesis.

This overview, therefore, should not only cover the background to the book's major arguments and supportive material, but also provide the reader with a basic chapter plan.

To explain the impact of information technology we must look beyond the functional aspects of business organizations. The importance of information is reflected in its ability, through the appropriate technology, to corrupt departmental boundaries. This chapter, therefore, proposes that it is better to understand an organization as a network of information flows, which is itself set within other network flows of region, market, industry, and so on. Such a perspective is underlined by many firms accessing information beyond their established functional boundaries. Within the organization, this could involve different departments accessing a common pool of information from the company database.

Externally, employees can gain entrance to public databases such as Prestel, which are run by autonomous bodies. The drive is towards centralization and hence better management control. Paradoxically, the opposite is being encouraged, whereby every user has the potential to access information which enables them to operate more efficiently, and also to do so outside the control of their manager. Under these conditions it is difficult for managers to control not only who reads and writes what but also, and perhaps more importantly, who knows what.

Large amounts of information can be processed and communicated via a network without managers ever being able to determine whether it runs contrary to their own policy. Security has, as a consequence, become an extremely important issue. The more the dissemination of information is allowed, the more likely control mechanisms will become corrupted.

In simple terms, data are facts, whilst information is the consequence of interpretation. What is information to some is not to others, and it is the subjective interpretation of what is and is not valuable which has caused managements considerable problems. The control parameters on the organization's database are based upon managers' own perceptions of its value as information which may not coincide with that of a potential intruder or misuser. But more than this, individual employees' perception of their information stock widens-because of their greater accessibility to the information network. As a consequence, their perception of their own job parameters also widens beyond what management might think desirable.

INFORMATION, THE LIFE BLOOD

Information is the life-blood of a community information service and the information file is at its heart. Unless the heart is sound and continually pumping a supply of regularly renewed and fresh information into the system, it will not function at its best. Therefore, it is important to give extra care and attention to planning the resources needed to set up a sound information base and a workable system for keeping it up to date.

Some basic things you will need to consider are as follows:

(a) How is the information to be collected?

(b) What method is to be used for processing and storing information?

(c) How is the information to be retrieved?

(d) What size is the file likely to be?

(e) What areas, geographical and subject, is the file to cover?

In addition, you will need to consider how the information is going to be disseminated, if it is not just for internal use; but that is the subject of the next chapter. The kind of system you choose and the degree of its sophistication will depend on the nature of your information service, the size and complexity of the information you need to store, the staff, and the financial resources available. When designing a system, make sure it is readily understandable to all those using it-volunteers and public included-and not just to professionals.

Coverage

In identifying the need for your community information service, you should have reached a decision already on the community to be served. This may be either a geographical community or a community of interest or both. Either way, you will still need to make a decision about the extent of your information base. For example, a neighbourhood information service must decide what information to collect on the wider area-town, county, region, nation-outside its local community. An information service aimed at a fairly wide area may need to limit its interests to a particular sector of the community or to a particular range of subjects, *e.g.* the low paid, those receiving income support, or those with debt problems. Even an information service in support of a local campaign may benefit from collecting information on similar campaigns in problems country-wide.

Types of Information

The information base of your service is most likely to include the following types of information:

Soft information—details of clubs, societies, organizations and services; individuals; events, etc. Usually this information will not be available in a published form, or at least not in sufficient detail, and it will be necessary to make a conscious effort to collect it. This information may comprise the major part of the resources file.

Hard information—factual information on a specific subject *e.g.* benefit rates for single-parent families, how to get legal aid, how to change your name. This information will be available in a variety of Banns, some ephemeral such as leaflets, pamphlets, booklets, broadsheets, posters, periodical articles, etc. Such items are usually kept in a vertical file, in storage boxes or similar receptacles and accessed *via* some form of index or classification scheme. Other hard information may be in the form of books, multi-volumed reference works, law books, or even audiovisual forms. If there are many items of this type, they will need to be classified and shelved.

Supplementary information—information already produced in a particular format-directories, handbooks, diaries, annual reports, constitutions, newsletters-of organizations appearing in your information file.

'Soft' Information

It is highly unlikely and undesirable that an information service should need to 'go it alone' in the collection of information. Such is the volume, complexity and variety of sources of information in present-day society that, unless your service has very narrow terms of reference, it will be virtually impossible for it to collect and keep up to date all the information that is required.

Therefore, it is important that you first of all identify the information providers, support services and' gatekeepers' in your community and establish effective contacts with them. These links may already have been forged in the process of conducting a community profile. They now need to be fostered and strengthened, so that there can be a mutual exchange of information. These contacts will also be able to provide you with useful feedback from the community as to the success or otherwise of your service. The network of contacts can be maintained on a fairly casual basis as the need arises, or you might want to formalize the arrangement. Some ways of doing this include irregular 'get togethers', informal luncheon clubs, regular meetings with agendas and minutes, or the circulation of a newsletter or bulletin. Other activities that could develop out of such meetings are joint collection of information, shared publicity, compilation and publication of directories, information handbooks and leaflets, training, and general discussion of common problems. Collecting information is a time-consuming process and there is no one method of going about it. You will probably have to use a combination of several techniques to build up a satisfactory information base. One thing definitely to be avoided is duplicating work that has already been done. 50 first of all identify the following:

Existing Information Files. Contact all the other community information services, council departments and organizations who are likely to maintain information files and ask if they would be willing to share this information. Try to offer something in return, either an exchange of information or some other help you can provide.

Local Directories. There are several types of directories that may be available in your area and which are useful sources of soft information: *(a)* local government authorities often produce directories or town guides of their area which contain a certain amount of local information or they may produce a guide to council services; *(b)* telephone directories, especially Yellow pages which have an alphabetical subject arrangement; *(c)* area directories, such as those produced by Thompson's Newspapers, which are similar to Yellow pages but also contain a section of community information-your local newspaper may produce a directory of local services, sometimes m conjunction with local information groups; *(d)* citizen's guides may also be produced by the local newspaper as a supplement to an existing newspaper; *(e)* CVSs or RCCs sometimes produce directories of voluntary organizations in their area or you may find these listed in your local CVS/RCC annual report; *(f)* directories covering a special subject, such as accommodation, halls for hire, etc.; *(g)* directories aimed at a particular interest group or groups *e.g.* people with disabilities or senior citizens.

National directories are useful not only for the wider network of services but also for identifying local offices of a national organization.

Other methods to use in building up your information base and maintaining its currency include:

Looking and Listening. A lot of information can be gathered by simply walking around your community, looking at notice-boards, picking up leaflets, or attending open meetings, fairs, fetes and other community events. This method of collecting information is unpredictable and requires more than a 9-to-5, five-day week.

Contact with Individuals. People are a major source of information in any community and there are always those to whom others naturally go for information. Try to identify such people and enlist their help, possibly by offering something in return-bartering is a time-honoured system! Direct contact with individuals in other information services and organizations is often a better way of ellciting information than impersonal methods and also paves the way for further cooperation. Pay regular visits to such centres.

Scanning newspapers, magazines, newsletters, etc., can turn up details of new organizations; changes of personnel, premises or hours of opening; new services introduced; and may highlight problem areas where information may be needed.

Other documents, including council minutes and agendas, planning regulations, annual reports (ask to be put on mailing lists for these), leaflets and manifestos.

Media publicity Local press, radio and cable television stations may be prepared without charge to put out a call for organizations to contact your service. If not, then consider inserting an advert or, where there is, a local directory produced, have a tear-out slip included for organizations to fill in and return to you. As a result of these various methods, an amount of raw material will have been obtained which may be of use to your information service. How accurate, up to date and complete the data is will depend very much on the reliability of the source. In most cases, unless you have every confidence in the source, the information will have to be checked before it is entered in a more permanent form in your resource file. So, at this stage, simply record it onto say a scrap 5in × 3in . card and put it into a temporary file.

The information you have obtained will be of several different kinds but the most common will probably be that relating to organizations, clubs and societies. This is the most difficult type of information to collect since it is ever changing and therefore unrelenting effort will be required to achieve even reasonable completeness or accuracy-100% will be impossible. However, with a good system for collecting and updating the information, you should be able to build up and maintain an acceptable file.

A lot of staff time will be needed to carry out this work, so first of all investigate whether there are other local information services that need this type of information and would be willing to help in its collection. It may be possible to collect the information through an umbrella group, where the work can be framed out so that it is not too great a burden on anyone organization. Alternatively, a joint approach can be made on behalf of a number of organizations.

Ideally, the most effective way to collect information of this kind is to pay a personal visit to each organization or service, but rarely will that be possible without extensive staff resources or a very small community. The cheapest and quickest way to collect this information is by telephoning. Prepare a standard list of questions to ask so that entries in your information file follow the same format.

If it can be afforded, include with your questionnaire some means of returning it free of charge, as this will significantly improve the response rate. Separate forms may be required to collect different kinds of information. The following is a suggested list of headings which you might need to include on forms for collecting information from two of the most common types of organizations.

Clubs and Societies

(a) Name: the name by which the club is best known, plus the full name if different. Indicate relationship to larger body, *i.e.* branch, regiment, lodge, etc.

(b) Secretary's name, address and telephone number or those of a similar person if the organization has no secretary.

(c) Purpose of organization if not self-evident from the name.

(d) Eligibility: any restrictions by age, sex, ethnic group, occupation, status (single, divorced, widowed) etc.

(e) Place, day and time of meetings.

(f) Subscription: any charge to become a member or to attend meetings.

(g) Other officers: names, addresses, telephone numbers of treasurer, president, chairman, publicity officer, membership secretary, etc.

(h) History of the organization including special events or persons associated with it.

(i) Annual general meeting: the date of an organization's AGM can be a useful indication of when to send out update forms as this is when officers or policies are likely to change.

(j) Publications: newsletter, diary, commemorative brochures, annual report, etc.

(k) Date the information was obtained and/ or last updated or checked.

Agencies and organizations providing a service;

(a) Name: popular name and full name, *e.g.* CHAT (Come Here and Talk), SHAC (Shelter Housing Action Centre), plus relationship to parent body where necessary.

(b) Address: street address and postal address, Post Office, box number if used.

(c) Contact person: personal name, title and address, if different from above.

(d) Hours of opening: days and times; note if seasonal, *e.g.* holiday period, term time.

(e) Telephone and fax number, including-service number, administration number, after-hours or hotline numbers.

(f) Services provided: advice, counselling, practical help, etc.; types of enquiry the service would like to have referred to them.

(g) Eligibility: age, income, sex, residency, status.

(h) Cost: free, fees, means-tested, donations; any facilities for payments to be spread over a period; help available from local or central government, charities, etc.

(i) Geographical area served: neighbourhood, city, county, region, adhoc area; no geographical restrictions.

(j) Application procedures: walk-in, appointment or waiting list; what papers or documents need to be brought.

(k) Branch offices: extension bureaux, mobiles, surgeries, etc.; include hours of opening, routes and times of stops.

(l) Director, administrator or executive director of the service; name and telephone or extension.

(m) Volunteers: does the service use volunteers and for what purposes? Method of recruitment.

(n) Transportation: how to get to the service, *e.g.* bus route numbers, underground line and station, etc.

(o) Date information was obtained and/or last updated or checked.

(p) Publications: directories, handbooks, leaflets, annual report, etc.

(q) Special facilities: foreign languages spoken, access and facilities for people with disabilities, photocopying or fax service, escort, advocacy, etc.

(r) Funding: local government grant-aided, donations, etc.

These two lists represent most of the facts that a community information service might need to know about an organization or service. In practice, depending on the scope of your service, it may not be necessary to include all the fields in the questionnaire. It is a good idea to get the person filling in the questionnaire to sign it, thereby giving the information service some protection against claims of giving out wrong information a not uncommon occurrence, especially when the information is committed to print.

There are other types of 'soft' information that your service might need to collect, for example halls for hire, places of local worship, accommodation, 'What's-on' events, local industry. The procedure is much the same:

(a) Decide what information you need to know.

(b) Devise a standard format or list of questions to ask.

(c) Identify possible sources of information.

(d) Decide which method or methods to use to collect the information: telephone, personal visit, postal questionnaire, press advert, etc.

How to Store 'soft' Information?

There are various methods that can be used for storing information:

A list is easy and quick to consult, can be photocopied for clients to take away and can be faxed, but has very little flexibility for inserting and updating information.

A strip index provides flexibility, can easily be photocopied, and is available in various forms: large binders holding many pages, smaller folders containing just a few pages, address books, wall-hung panels, rotunda units, etc. Strips are available in several colours, which allows for a simple categorization, and various widths. Even so, they are limited as to the amount of information that can be contained on them. It is also not quite as easy to insert new strips as the manufacturers claim.

Cards are still one of the most commonly used systems for storing information. They are infinitely flexible, easy to insert and update, can be sorted into any preferred order, and require very little technical know-how. The most popular sizes are Sin x 3in, used mainly for indexes or temporary information waiting to be checked, 6in x 4in, and Sin x Sin, which are large enough to contain sufficient information about most organizations or services and to be preprinted with a standard grid for recording the information. There are more superior types of card files available, such as the Rondofile or Rotadex systems which use custom-designed stationery and therefore tend to be more expensive. With systems that use standard cards, you can—if you are hard-up or want to save trees-use the reverse of scrap cards. Card files have a number of disadvantages: they are not so easy to carry around, they are not easily reproducible if someone wants a copy of a particular section, multiple access (*e.g.* by name, subject, area, service, etc.) requires duplication of cards, and the updating process can be tedious.

Loose-leaf binders with one sheet for each entry, sometimes called 'sheaf' binders, have a similar flexibility to cards. They are slightly slower to add to and amend but are more portable. They are suited best for alphabetical arrangements as they are difficult to guide.

Microcomputers now have the capacity to handle immense information files that can be accessed by any number of predetermined variables or even free-text searching by keyword, depending on the software used. With a printer attached, all the information or sections of it can be printed out on demand or to provide a master for printing by conventional methods. Personal computers now begin at prices that bring them within the range of most community information services. However, there is danger in automatically seeing the computer as the best solution for maintaining your information file, as this may not always be the case. A lot depends on the size of your file and its complexity, what you want to do with the file, and to what other uses you want to put the computer.

Filing System

Whichever method is chosen for physically storing the information, except for that by microcomputer, it will be necessary to decide the best way of arranging entries so that the information can be retrieved swiftly and accurately. In order to ensure that the total resources of your information service are used to the full when answering an enquiry, it will help if the system used to organize the information file can be integrated with that for the vertical file and the book-stock. This point needs to be borne in mind now, although it will be dealt with more fully later.

The bulk of the information file is likely to comprise 'soft' information which you have collected about organizations, clubs, societies and services and, to a lesser extent, about individuals who are a valuable source of information or advice, plus items of 'hard' information not available or conveniently available in printed form. There are several ways in which you might want to retrieve this information by the names of the organizations, by subject (*i.e.* area of interest), by clientele, by the type of service (*e.g.* counselling), or by place. In practice, the 'clientele' and 'type of service' approaches are usually catered for through the subject file rather than, as separate files.

Organizations File. The master file for the whole system will usually be an alphabetically arranged sequence of entries by name of organization. It is generally recommended that the full, official name of the organization is used, with references from other forms of the name. In practice, it does not really matter as long as there are references from the alternatives to whichever form is chosen. There is a good argument for putting the main entry for an organization under the form of name by which most people refer to it, even if this differs from or is an abbreviation of the official name. This is especially so where the file is to be used by the public.

In addition to details of organizations, each entry in the master file may also contain certain 'housekeeping' details relating to the maintenance of all the information files, plus references to appropriate headings in the subject file, where relevant information can be found, and a classification number.

Subject File. Most enquiries received by a community information service are likely to be about the need for a service or activity or for help with solving a problem, rather than for information on a specific nam.ed organization. So the information you have collected about organizations, services and individuals will also need to be accessible by the services and activities they provide. There are two ways this can be achieved, by either using a subject index or having a subject file of organizations.

If you are compiling your own list of subject headings, choose terms that are in common use by your clientele, especially if they will be consulting the files directly, rather than the 'official' term, *e.g.* OUT OF WORK or ON THE DOLE instead of REDUNDANT. Always refer from alternatives not used to the chosen term.

A subject index is rather like the index to a book. It is an alphabetically arranged file of subject heading cards on which reference is made to where information on that subject can be found. The cards themselves do not contain information. The subject index can contain references to organizations, individuals and other supplementary material such as pamphlets, periodical articles, audiovisual material, books, etc.

A subject file consists of an alphabetically arranged set of subject heading cards behind which are filed copies of the organization cards appropriate to that heading and possibly cards containing items of 'hard' information. An alternative is to arrange cards according to a classification system either devised by yourself or adopted from another service, such as the NACAB classification scheme.

Place File. Where an information service covers a number of distinct towns, villages or neighbourhoods, each having a similar range of organizations, it may be helpful to have a file that can be accessed by place. There are a number of options. You could sort the organizations file initially by place, especially if it contains few organizations whose responsibilities extend to the whole area covered by your service. Alternatively, if most of the organizations are prefixed with the name of the place (*e.g.* EXVILLE ATHLETIC CLUB, EXVILLE COUNCIL FOR THE DISABLED), the alphabetically arranged master file will automatically bring together those from the same location, provided inverted headings have not been used.

Some arrangements will have to be made for organizations which do not conform to the pattern, either because the place-name does not feature at the beginning or because it is not contained in the name of the organization at all. In these cases, an additional card can be made out with either an inverted heading (*e.g.* EXVILLE, ROTARY CLUB OF) or the place-name can be prefixed.

The third option is to have a separate file of organization cards arranged initially by place and then alphabetically by name of organization or by subject.

Filing Alphabetically

Filing alphabetically is not quite as simple as ABC, as any librarian will tell you. There are two recognized methods, known as 'word by word' and 'letter by letter'. In word by word, entries are initially sorted by the first word in the heading, then headings that begin with the same word are sorted by the second word, and so on. Another way to describe this method, which may be more helpful, is to treat spaces between words in a heading as an imaginary letter coming before 'a' in the alphabet, then sort letter by letter.

In letter by letter, you simply ignore any spaces in the heading and sort one letter at a time from left to right. Here is how a small group of headings would look sorted by the two methods:

Word by word	*Letter by letter*
DO SOMETHING! BOYS CLUB	'DOG AND BONE' DARTS TEAM
'DOG AND BONE' DARTS TEAM	DOGSBURY RESIDENTS' ASSOCIATION
DOG SNIFFERS ANONYMOUS	DOGS HOMES
DOGS HOMES	DOG SNIFFERS ANONYMOUS
DOGSBURY RESIDENTS' ASSOCIATION	DO SOMETHING! BOYS CLUB

There are several other niceties to do with filing alphabetically but we only need mention here that hyphens are treated as spaces in word-by-word sorting and numerals are spelt out as said, so that 1900 (the year) is considered for sorting as Nineteen Hundred and 1,900 as One Thousand, Nine Hundred.

File 'housekeeping'

In addition to the information needed to answer enquiries, there are other items of information to do with the maintenance of the file which may usefully be included on each entry, such as the following:

(a) the date the information was obtained, last updated or last checked, hich will indicate not only the degree of reliability to be placed on it but also when to update;

(b) the date a questionnaire or update letter was sent—a check for chasing up non-returned forms;

(c) additional contacts or other information which does not fit into the main part of the entry;

(d) subject headings used in the subject file;

(e) place headings used in the place file, if not obvious from the name of the organization;

(f) feedback-comments from users of the service;

(g) 'tracings', *i.e.* a list of other cards that refer to they can be traced and amended or withdrawn when necessary.

The amount of this 'housekeeping' information you need to include will depend on how sophisticated you need your file to be. The bigger the information service and the larger the file, then the more likely it is that you will need to introduce a systematic procedure for processing information. In such a case it is usual for the housekeeping information to go on the reverse of each entry, using a standard grid like the one illustrated here. It is arguable that if your information file requires this degree of sophistication, you ought seriously to consider keeping it on computer.

Updating

By their very nature the entries in your database will be changing continually. Hours of opening, meeting places, officers, membership fees, subscriptions, charges, etc., are all susceptible to frequent change. Therefore, it is important to have a system for regularly updating each entry in the database. There are several ways of achieving this but, whichever method you adopt, it must be regular and ongoing.

Interim Updating

All the entries for organizations should be checked at least once a year to ensure they are still correct. In between times, however, new information will be brought to your attention by various means, including word of mouth, newspaper reports, organization newsletters, company reports and by direct contact with the organization itself. If the source of information is reliable, it can be substituted immediately for the out-of-date information in the database but, if not, it should be noted and a further check made to verify its accuracy. A simple way to add new information to an entry in a card file is to write it onto self-adhesive labels or slips (obtainable at most stationers) which can be stuck over the original information. Even though an entry has been updated in between times, it should still be checked formally once a year.

Annual Updating

Once a year is probably a reasonable time-span for updating your database but a shorter interval may be necessary if the information content changes frequently. You will need to decide how the annual update is to be carried out. Some organizations like to update the entire file at the same time, so that they can say the file was as accurate as possible at a particular date. However, this does create a tremendous amount of extra work for a period of several weeks and you may feel it necessary to get extra paid, work-experience or volunteer help. Another disadvantage of this method is that it captures a picture of organizations at a set moment in time. Some organizations may be just about to make changes, and your records for these would be out of date for almost a year.

Alternatively, you may decide to update on a continuous basis by using either the date the record was added to the database or the organization's Annual General Meeting (AGM) date as a trigger. This is easy to do if your database is kept on a computer, since a date field can be used to produce a subset of records and, by linking the database with a word processing package, a personalized standard letter can be printed out for sending to each organization. It is less easy with a card or any other kind of file. You can get little coloured metal tags to clip on to the top edge of cards, a different colour for each month, or you could use an appropriate symbol on the heading of the card, such as a coloured dot, a letter or number. Tags can make the file look a bit messy and are easily knocked off if it is in constant use; symbols require the whole file to be checked through.

It is better to update records shortly before or after each organization's AGM, since most organizations, if they are going to change their officers or constitution, generally do it once a year at the AGM. This is so because many organizations do not know their AGM date a year in advance, it is enough just to indicate the month in which the AGM is usually held. For those organizations and services which do not have an AGM, you will need to use the date the information was added as the trigger.

When writing to organizations to update their information, it is better to send them a copy of their record with a request to indicate any changes, rather than sending a blank questionnaire. This saves the secretary unnecessary time in repeating information that has not altered.

An alternative to writing to each organization is to phone, but this is time-consuming and costly, and only feasible if the number of organizations to contact is fairly small. Avoid sending out updates at times when people are likely to be away, such as during the summer. There are certain times when it is more appropriate to update other kinds of information, *e.g.* social security benefit rates (which usually change in April and September), adult education classes or school, college and university courses which change term-wise.

'Hard' Information

As well as the database, most information services will need a certain amount of 'hard' information to answer enquiries. Short, unrecorded or inadequately recorded items of 'hard' information, as we have already seen, can be incorporated into the database. However, the majority of hard information will usually be found in one or more of the vast range of print forms, starting from locally produced free broadsheets to extremely expensive multi-volumed loose-leaf reference works.

Within the scope of this book, it is not possible to go into detail about the sources of this material, since they will vary considerably. according to the type and subject range of the service you are operating. Community information changes rapidly so any printed sources should be treated with care. However, you might find useful a chapter on the sources of community information that I contributed to Printed reference material and related sources of information, 3rd edn, Library Association Publishing, 1990, which concentrated on organizations and on those items which are regularly updated.

The following framework for collecting community information was originally devised by Grainne Morby, who at the time was working for the Community information Project, with some additions of my own:

Distinguish Between Subject Areas

In other words, identify the main topics into which the subject scope of your information service naturally divides. Throughout this framework I will take as an example an information service for which the main area of interest is housing. It is sometimes useful to apply a consistent criterion when dividing up a subject, although obviously this would not be so easy for an information service whose scope covers as broad an area as, say, 'community information'.

However, taking housing as our example, you could decide to divide it by type of accommodation, *e.g.* owner-occupied, private-rented, council-rented, New Town, Housing Association, institutional accommodation, tied accommodation, mobile homes, etc. In most cases you would probably need an additional category for subjects that cut across all or more than one category. In the case of housing, this might be 'squatting' or 'homelessness'.

Since the material you want to collect will usually be written to meet a particular need or needs, it is advisable to collect information around those needs rather than for fitting into a theoretical framework. The kind of broad client groups that might be identified in the field of housing are landlords, tenants, owner-occupiers, squatters, transients, elderly people, people with disabilities, the homeless. Then, one could identify client groups who share a common problem or need associated with their particular type of accommodation, such as eviction, dampness, house repair, renovation, harassment, mortgages, rent arrears, planning permission, redevelopment, etc. Once these subject areas and client needs have been identified, it should give you clearer guidelines when you come to select material from the various sources identified in the next part of the framework.

Print Sources

Official

(a) National

— *pre-legislation:* political party manifestos and policy documents, speeches by Ministers, the Queen's Speech at opening of Parliament, White Papers, Green Papers.

— *Legislation:* Bills, Hansard reports of debates in both Houses of Parliament, Acts, Statutory Instruments.

— *Guidance to local statutory bodies:* circulars and letters from Ministers, guidance notes, reports of Inspectors.

— *Reference books:* collections of legislation, *e.g.* Statutes in force, Legal aid handbook.

— *Periodicals:* from government departments and agencies, *e.g.* Department for Employment gazette.

— *Guidance to the public:* leaflets, posters, videos and other A/V material.

— *Ombudsmen.*

(b) Regional

— Health authorities, British Rail.

— Privatized utilities: gas, water, electricity, telephone.

— Consumer watchdog bodies: Post Office Users' National Council (POUNC), Office of Gas Supply (OFGAS), Office of Electricity Regulation (OFFER), Office of Telecommunications (OfTel), Office Of Water Services (OFWAT).

(c) Local

— Local authority policies and decisions: agendas, minutes, standing orders, bylaws and regulations.

— Guidance to the public: handbooks, leaflets, etc. from local authorities, area and district health authorities, Community Health Councils, local offices of government agencies.

2. Non-official

(a) National

— Reference books and handbooks from commercial publishers. Voluntary organizations.

— Pressure groups, self-help groups.

— 'Umbrella' organizations, *e.g.* National Council for Voluntary Organizations, Federation of Independent Advice Centres. Professional bodies, *e.g.* The Law Society.

— Trade associations, *e.g.* National Association of Retail Furnishers. Educational bodies, *e.g.* National Extension College, Open University.

— Trade unions.

— The media.

— Practitioners in the field who publish.

(b) Local

— Claimants' unions.

— Law centres, other specialist advice centres.

— Neighbourhood and generalist advice centres, resource centres.

— Local 'umbrella' groups.

— Pressure groups, campaigning groups, action centres. Voluntary organizations.

— Local media: newspapers, community newspapers, radio, cable television.

(c) New Technology

— Video-text systems: Prestel, teletext, private viewdata.

— Online computer databases, *e.g.* Volnet

— CD-ROM, videodiscs, etc.

This list is not intended to be exhaustive but will give you some idea of the range of sources in which to look for information. Howard Matthews, in his book *Community Information* has drawn up a set of criteria for selecting community information materials. It is aimed particularly at library community information services but may be generally helpful for anyone setting up such a service.

1. Selection should be done by those who know the community best.
2. Material should relate to specific, local, identified needs.
3. All material should be current.
4. All material should be written at a level appropriate to its intended use.
5. Material should be concerned with the practicalities of problem solving.
6. All new material should either fill a gap, offer a new viewpoint, or promise something better.
7. Material should take into account the level of use the client will make of it.

Obtaining Publications and Other Material

Once the material you require has been identified, you will need to obtain it. Some material will be priced, in which case you will need to order it, and some will be free.

Priced Publications

The procedure for obtaining priced publications, particularly in the field of community information, is not as simple as you might suppose. Since a lot of the material may well be fairly cheap and the small or community publishers, booksellers and library suppliers are reluctant to obtain it as the profit margin is likely to be too low for the amount of effort involved. The alternative is to order direct but this also has its difficulties as many small publishers now insist on money with order, and this can cause problems for some organizations through the need to raise a cheque or limitations on the amount that can be spent from petty cash.

A few national voluntary organizations, *e.g.* Age Concern England, operate a standing-order system for their publications—this is one solution, although you may need to accept blanket coverage of the organization's output. In the larger cities, you may find a community or alternative bookseller who is prepared to supply this material to order. A directory of alternative bookshops is published annually by the magazine Radical Bookseller. Whatever the method of ordering, it is important to keep a record of what has been placed on order and from whom to avoid duplication of titles and as a check on supply. For each title make out an order or slip. This can be either a scrap 5in x 3in card or one specially printed with a standard grid. The following indicates the kinds of information that need to be recorded:

(a) title of publication-more important than author for this kind of material, since authorship is often unclear;

(b) author-might be an individual or an organization;

(c) price, date of publication and, if a periodical, frequency; supplier-this may be a bookseller, library supplier or the address of the producing body;

(d) date of order;

(e) source of information about the item;

(f) location, if you are ordering for more than one centre.

You may find it helpful to use the order cards later as the basis of a catalogue of the publications in your information centre; in which case, leave space at the top of the card for either a subject heading, classification number or filing code. After an order has been placed with a supplier, the order cards are filed, preferably by title, in one alphabetical sequence known as the 'order file'. When a publication is received, the order card is removed from the file and accompanies the publication to the next stage if it is to be used later as the catalogue card. If not, you may find it useful to file the order card in a 'publications received' file, until such time as the publication is permanently recorded in the system, after which the card can be thrown away.

Periodicals

Publications which arrive at regular intervals-weekly, fortnightly, monthly, quarterly-will not require an order card but you will need to keep a record of each title taken. This should include the following items of information:

(a) title of periodical;

(b) frequency;

(c) supplier;

(d) when subscription is due for payment;

(e) a grid to record receipt of each issue;

(f) instructions for disposal of back copies.

For those using computers, there are software packages available for periodicals management but these are aimed at organizations who take an extensive range of periodicals and such packages are not cheap. If you have a database management package on your computer, you would do better to devise your own periodicals database.

Free Material

This can vary from quite substantial loose-leaf binders plus updates to leaflets, posters and bookmarks and may be required in bulk for clients to take. Since this is likely to be a frequent type of request, it may be quicker and simpler to duplicate a standard letter to send to organizations, with space left to fill in address, title of item, format (leaflet, booklet, poster, etc.) and number of copies required. It is advisable to keep a record of what is requested, if only as a check on whether it has been received or not.

A lot of the sweat has been taken out of identifying free materials, and addresses from where they can be obtained, through the setting-up of Camden Libraries' Free Leaflets Information Service (FLIS). For an annual fee (E120 in 1992) subscribers receive a copy of the Frills directory of free information leaflet suppliers, a monthly batch of new and updated leaflets and amendments. to the Frills directory, and details of a model system for organizing leaflets. Details of this service can be obtained from Community Information Services, Camden Leisure Services Department, St. Pancras Library, 100 Euston Road, London NWI 2AJ. A similar, but not so extensive, service is provided by the NACAB as part of its Information Service, but you would need to have approval to subscribe to the full pack.

Organizing Hard Information

We have already seen that hard information can be found in a great variety of forms. For the benefit of organizing it, the following categories can be identified:

Material in book form for use by clientele or information workers will be best arranged on shelves in the broad subject groups identified when acquiring the material or according to a classification scheme.

Ephemeral material for use by information workers is best stored in a vertical file using the same subject headings as those in the subject sequence of the information file, though probably with more sub-divisions, or using a classification scheme. Alternatively, the material could be kept in file boxes on shelves using broad subject headings.

Ephemeral material for use by clientele on the premises is best kept in file boxes, ring or display binders and ideally interfiled with books. Vertical files are not recommended for public use as they tend to be a deterrent. Another way of dealing with ephemeral materials is to gather them together in packs on particular topics and, for maximum impact, to display them face outwards on sloping shelves.

Ephemeral material for the public to take away can be displayed in special leaflet dispensers, on a sloping surface or on tables. Ideally, they should be displayed in broad subject groups or by originating organization, *e.g.* Benefits Agency, Department for Employment, but this is rarely possible because even within organizations leaflets are produced in varying sizes.

Supplementary Information

Many organizations produce printed material in the course of their work or activities. The most common types of material are directories or address lists of members (individuals or constituent groups), newsletters, events sheets or cards, annual reports, constitutions, posters, leaflets, funding appeals, campaigning literature, advertising brochures, balance sheets and commemorative booklets (anniversaries, etc.). All this material is potentially useful as back-up information to the database but there is no sure way of obtaining it. When sending out the original questionnaire to organizations, you can ask to be put on their mailing list for this type of material, if one is maintained.

Some organizations that operate on a shoe-string budget may make a small charge for their mailing list facility. Even when you are put on a mailing list, regular receipt of material may depend very much on the enthusiasm or efficiency of the secretary of an organization. Often the best solution to obtaining material is to maintain regular contact with organizations and to pester them continually. When material arrives, it should be dated, so that you know roughly how old it is, and carefully filed for future use. The simplest method is to have an envelope or folder for each organization. Write on the outside of the envelope the name of the organization as used in your database and arrange envelopes alphabetically in boxes or a vertical file. You should also add to this file any cuttings from newspapers or magazines concerning those organizations. The file should be checked regularly, at least once a year, to remove out-of-date material. When writing to organizations for updated information for your database, ask them for any new literature.

Before throwing away the withdrawn material, check to see if it would be of use to some other organization or section of your service which collects material on local history.

Classification

It is not my intention to go into any great detail about the classification of community information materials. For most small information services, it will be quite adequate to arrange material by broad subject groups subdivided according to the form in which the clientele's needs and problems are presented. For ease of labelling vertical files, book spines and boxes, a simple notation can be used based on the initial letter or letters of subjects. For example, Cambridgeshire Libraries' community information service covers 21 categories:

Ben	Benefits	Gov	Government
Bus	Business	Hea	Health
Car	Careers	Hou	Housing
Com	Community	Law	Legal rights
Con	Consumer	Mon	Money
CR	Community relations	SC	Senior citizens
Dis	Disability	Tra	Transport
Edu	Education	Ump	Unemployment

Emp	Employment	Wom	Women
Env	Environment	You	Youth
Fam	Family		

Some libraries also include as separate categories: Death, Equal opportunities, Fuel (or Energy), Gay rights, Leisure, and Trade union rights. These categories can then be broken down into smaller sub-categories as necessary. Taking the earlier example of Housing, a possible range of sub-categories with a mnemonic notation might be:

A	Agricultural accommodation	Re	Rented accommodation
H	Homelessness	ReC	Council housing
I	Institutional accommodation	ReH	Housing Association housing
M	Mobile homes	ReP	Private rented
O	Owner-occupied	S	Squatting

Numerals could be introduced for more detailed sub-divisions, *e.g.* Ol-Buying and selling a house; O2-Home insurance; O3-Planning applications; O4-Development; etc.

An effective method that can be used where you have only a small number of broad categories (no more than ten and preferably less) is colour coding. Allocate a colour to each subject and attach an appropriate coloured sticker or tape to the spine of each book or file box. Colour coding can be used in conjunction with notation to provide more detailed sub-division of a subject. When a community information service grows to a size where broad categories are not adequate to contain all the material and allow efficient retrieval, then it may be necessary to consider using a classification scheme.

❐

2

Systems Approach in Library

Management of any organisation has become more complex because the world outside the organisation intrudes much more than used to be the case. Legislation controls many aspects of employment, conditions of service and the working environment. Users are often encouraged by pressure groups within society to demand better, or different, services. Those responsible for allocating funds have to justify expenditure to taxpayers or investors. Staff are aware of job opportunities elsewhere and are able to compare working conditions and rewards. Libraries and information services are no exception to these intrusions.

The early history of the public library movement contains many accounts of dispute about the necessity of providing services and much time was spent in statistical comparison between rival library authorities. The debate has continued, though sometimes at a muted level, to the present day. Similar instances of disputes about the value of services can be found in the academic library, special library and information service sectors. The pressure to justify may not be new but its origin in manifestation are changing. Information technology is multiplying the channels through which information can flow from the originator to the user and some channels can circumvent libraries and information services as traditionally conceived. The provision of information on databases is a goon example: a glance at popular computer and business journals will reveal many articles explaining how to use networks to establish contact with the host services providing the databases and how to select and search an appropriate database. Those providing the services are aware of the growing number of 'end-user' searchers and are gradually adapting the query languages and retrieval methods to make them more readily comprehensible. Libraries and information services are no longer a necessary feature of life for all information users, if they ever were. Society has changing expectations too. The multiplication of media has obviously increased the ways in which people can satisfy an information need or simply enjoy themselves. Most libraries and information services have responded by stocking audiovisual and other media; some have promoted their use in advance of great public awareness interest. The power and uses of information are also more in the public eye: the rise of the 'customer society' has fostered an increase in the demand for information related to the rights of individuals. Professionally, the nature of work in library and information services has changed and is continuing to change. There can be few information workers who will not at some time in their professional lives, make use of computers or of the products that the computer revolution has spawned. For many, the use of computers is an everyday occurrence: wordprocessing, gaining access to information on databases, electronic mail, and the use of facsimile transmission are a few examples of the uses to which this technology has been put. It is interesting to note that many of these uses do not constitute novel approaches to the provision of services, though technology may enhance or increase the speed of them. Electronic mail is a new way of sending messages using technology but its use still results in a message arriving in a mailbox, albeit electronic. The essential nature of the service, passing information from one location to another, is not changed: the new technology frequently complements rather than replaces, the existing.

The temptation for the manager introducing a new technology may be to assume that the previous pattern of services can, and should, continue without change apart from a welcome increase in speed, reduction in costs or other tangible benefits. There are dangers in giving in to this temptation. First, to assume that past practices represent satisfactory service and good value is quite unwarranted without some investigation. Secondly, the use of new technology may afford opportunities to offer something new. The development of online information retrieval, for example, could have been seen as the need to automate searching under authors, titles and subjects in an electronic form of catalogue or index, Instead, an opportunity was recognised: the use of computer could enhance the range of retrieval key far beyond that usually considered feasible or economic in card catalogues and printed indexes, to include such novelties as word proximity searching and searching on publication dates.

A third danger in using the past as a model for the future is the perception of the service by the user. When computer were an uncommon and suitably impressive sight, there use by an organisation was often publicised. Some firms but computer suites on the ground floor of their offices and put the machines and their operators on public view. Advertisements might include some reference to computer use. It is apparent prospective customers were being invited to enter the modern world by association with the organisation and its products. The expectations of such customers were raised and they might assume that the improvements of which the organisation boasted should extend to all the services provided. In the mind of the customer the nature of the service, that is package of benefits, goods, and feelings associated with using organisation had changed. The technology in use and on public display enhanced the image of the service.

To the customer, the conjunction of bright, sparkling, new technology and a level of service litter better than in the past could lead swiftly to disillusionment and discontent. To the staff having to deal with customers, the raised expectations could lead to frustration and lowered morale because of their inability to provide an enhanced level of service. Although the computer is now a commonplace item in libraries and information centres the problem of user expectations often remains unsolved, and sometimes, unrecognised. Despite many anecdotes about the failures of modern technology, users tend to assume that a service will be improved with its use. Staff may also share such expectations before having full working experience. The changes to library and information services consequent upon the development and use of new technology are complex and involve alterations to working practices, working relationships, attitudes and levels of expertise as well as technical changes to processes and equipment. Thus, it is best to view them as manifestation of 'socio-technic' change since this should remind the manager that technological changes, however small, will also have an effect on the social aspects of the working environment. Both aspects, the technological and the social, are the subject of change. The discussion so far has centered on the use of new technology but the pints made could apply, equally well, to any change in an organisation: a change of personnel, change of method, change of building, even a change of name. There is an increased pressure on the manager to justify and account for what is done. The manager is thus confronted with a difficulty: there may be pressure from without and within the organisation to change to meet the challenge offered by competitors and to achieve new targets for the beneficial use of resources. Change can lead to enhanced services and improved efficiency but it also brings problems. Such problems are rarely confined to one aspect of a service but are likely to affect staff, users, competitors, suppliers, organisational arrangements and structures and so on. Yet, change can hardly be avoided if an organisation is to remain vital and healthy.

The greatest task for modern management of all kinds of enterprises is the productive management of change. The systems approach to management provides a framework and body of techniques for accomplishing change which also recognise its inherent difficulty and the problems which change may create. Change can also offer opportunities and the systems approach provides a means of encouraging managers to identify, investigate, evaluate and promote such opportunities. Use of the systems approach should include an active style of management: one which seeks to develop the organisation and constantly explores avenues for this to be achieved. Management of libraries and information centres in the modern world is more complex because they are more complex as organisations and because the environment in which they are found is itself more complex. More is demanded of them by society and there are many ways in which some of the information and cultural needs of society can be met. This complexity and the pressure to satisfy needs in an efficient manner has increased the challenges of library and information service management. Meeting this challenge calls for certain key qualities.

First, technical understanding: that is, a knowledge of how, in a particular enterprise, resources and processes are utilised to complete tasks. An astute manager recognise that the right of access to resource will ultimately, have to be justified: some attention must be given to the questions 'why do we need these resources?', 'do we still need them?' And 'could greater benefit be derived from using them in some other way?' Greater attention has been given by library and information service managers to these questions recently because assumptions about the work of such services to society have been challenged. Being accountable also encourages a manager to pay attention to the way in which resource are used in the various processes of the enterprises. The efficiency with which resources are used and the effectiveness of the resultant service in meeting the needs of users have become important preoccupations.

The second characteristic of the successful manager is an understanding of the basic ideas and principles of management. These form part of the core of professional studies for librarianship and information science. There is a danger, though, in assuming that pursuing such studies will produce managers. There is a limit to the amount of theory which can be included within the curriculum of a first qualification course and sound arguments for limiting that exposure to what is likely to be useful during the early years of a professional career. In any case, absorbing a body in theoretical knowledge and practical techniques will not turn the student into a manager of a library or information service unless significant time is given for the new professional to develop confidence and experience. Training is a vital adjunct to professional education and an essential part of the training is the inculcation of the belief that every professional is, in some sense, a manager of resources, shares a collective responsibility for the success of the service and is accountable for resource usage.

An interpersonal style which enables the manager to get things done through other people is the third characteristic. 'Getting ordinary people to do extraordinary things', a phrase coined many years ago, describes the art, as distinct from the science, of management. Part of that art is the skill of leadership. Leaders are not always good managers but they can convey a sense of enthusiasm and urgency to those who do possess the necessary management skills. However, for any manager the ability to lead, when necessary, is an essential, skill, the successful exercise of which depends on having decided in what direction it is preferential for the organisation to go. Interpersonal style then becomes an important qualify if others are to share in the process of change. They must be convinced of the need for change and that the proposed direction of change is apposite and within the competence of the organisation.

Fourthly, a manager must possess an ability to plan in the long and medium terms as well as being able to react to short term and urgent matters. One of the difficulties of managerial life is learning to set priorities; so many matters present themselves as being 'urgent' that it is easy to spend the majority of the available time on dealing with them. Such behaviour many, indeed, appear to be approved by senior people responsible for the funding of the organisation; the service appears to be responsive and efficient because action follows on closely after 'urgent' matters have been raised. What is concealed by this responsiveness is that it is essentially a reaction to events which is devoid of much, if any, consideration of longer-term effects. Such a fire-fighting approach to management will work for a short time: the blaze will be extinguished but the deep-rooted, smouldering, fire will continue to burn and erupt in unexpected places.

These qualities need to be present for the development of most organisations, but it is probably too much to expect that one person will have them all or that they will be equally important in every enterprise. For example, the pace of change experienced by a small library or information service attached to an organisation concerned with research might be great: the need to match the collections and services to emerging research areas would predicate the need for a close involvement of information workers with the appropriate research teams. The managerial emphasis should be on planning to accommodate such changes are quickly as possible. There might be less need to emphasise leadership skills because of the small number of information workers involved. A converse example would be an academic library providing services top faculties teaching a traditional pattern of studies: the pace of change experienced by the library could be slower and there might not be the need to emphasise close involvement of library staff with teaching teams. The need to facilitate change would, however, still be an important role for the manager and would require a concentration on the task of leadership.

To explore these ideas further consider an aspect of psychology. A person's perception of the world is thought to be formed by beliefs, attitudes and the surrounding culture during the formative years of life. Changes in the environment and the acquisition of experience lead to modifications of perception, but this is a fairly low process. Perception tends to predicate the type of response the person will offer to new circumstances which daily life presents.

Some people for example, respond more strongly to challenges about how to do things than others: such people tend to be 'task-oriented' and may be rather more interested in completing some work than in the reactions of people around them. Others have a strong response to people: for them, the task is almost a vehicle for watching and participating in the complexity of human behaviour. There is a strong similarity here in the contrast between the early twentieth-century preoccupation with 'scientific management', which emphasised careful design and measurement which emphasises the need to foster motivation of individuals through jobs designed to meet their needs for social satisfaction and a degree of autonomy. The contrast has been well explored by Jones.

The idea has been elaborated by Blake and Mouton in their Managerial Grid, which was developed as a training aid for managers. The Managerial Grid method depends on analysing the characteristics and behaviour to be expected from various management styles, comparing them and then seeking to define the behavioural requirements for shifting from one style to another.

A particular focus is the distinction between concern for people and concern for task completion. The aim is to increase the range of styles a manager can employ rather than enforcing a permanent change from one to another. The Managerial Grid thus recognises that the appropriate style depends upon the problem being faced. The greatest aid in this kind of personal management development is to know what one's own characteristics are and to what factors one tends to respond strongly or weakly.

It is also of value to know this when trying to build a management item. In a service managed and run by one person much of success will depend on the willingness and ability of that person to balance the various demands inherent in the job. Management style in such circumstances will inevitably result in a service with a distinctive character-one which some customers will favour and others will reject. With a team, however, because there are several personalities involved, there is the potential for creating a service which is bland but more broadly acceptable.

Enterprises are manifestly different as to their technical content, their economies and organisation sizes, the degree of contact with customers, their environmental impact and so on. Studies suggest that differences in managerial style can be linked. to difference in the culture of enterprises. Research tends to show that, for example, in a successful manufacturing company the type of technology used, the degree of uncertainly and the unpredictable nature of the production task determine the kind and level of control needed. This level of control, in turn, effects the organisational structure, management style and behaviour. Additionally, there seems to be no best way to organise an enterprise. Thus, it may be concluded that successful management involves recognising what style tends to be most suitable, most of the time, for the kind of enterprise being run, but there must also be a recognition that other styles may suit particular circumstances: their selection is, in other words, contingent upon the circumstances. There is no reason to suppose that variant styles are not also important in libraries and information services and. considerable variations in style are, in practice, to be found. Much library and information work forms part of what might be called a 'service enterprise': that is to say, there are not many librarians or information workers who rely directly on the sale of information or information-related products to earn a living. Instead there is a reliance on using resources, including skills and talents, to enhance or facilitate the use by others of information.

The word 'information' here includes anything that might be thought of as a legitimate sources: novels, reference books, databases, catalogues, computer software, audiovisual material and so on. Librarians and information workers are intermediaries and their services are of value because users recognise that life can be made easier or more pleasant through the use of these services.

Library and information work rarely constitutes the whole, or even the major part, of the work of an organisation. Certainly it is possible to think of a university library as functioning as an autonomous unit. One could perceive it as receiving an input of money and a set of goals from the environment of, say, the university authorities, but how it sets about achieving those goals and spending the money might seem to be largely under its own control. This is something of an illusion: the degree of autonomy is severely constrained by external factors, such as the policy of the university, auditing and legal requirements, professional and social acceptability, and internal factors, such as levels of staffing and the expectation by users and staff that existing services will be largely maintained as before.

A similar argument prevails for the commercial or 'special' library, through the more precise definition of the target user group, means that the external factors may exercise an even greater influence because the range of needs may be considered to be fairly tightly determined. The operating environment, than, as well as the internal environment, is of major importance for a service enterprise. So far, it has been suggested that, as a manager, the librarian or information worker will have to cope with a considerable degree of complexity in running a library and information service. Information or the kind of feeling that can be engendered by using information is an intangible product; it is supplied to a user who may be aware or unaware of need; the service is usually maintained against a background of some external financial and other control.

The result is an environment which has become increasingly challenging to conventional library and information services because there are several pathways to apparent satisfaction. Consider, for example, the inhouse company information service providing specialised information to employees of the firm. Over the years some expertise in online searching may have been developed and an internal company information datable may also have been established as part of its work. Installation. of as a computer-based data communications network throughout the company premises makes this database accessible to company research staff from their own terminals, if they so wish. Perhaps they also become aware of external databases and begin to use them. The role of the information service manage response? Perhaps they also become aware of external databases and begin to use them. The role of the information services manager respond? Perhaps by protesting about a possible explosion of costs because of inefficient searching by endusers? But what proof is there that experts in searching provide a better and more cost-effective service?

Another possibility would be for the information service to become involved in the specification and design of an intelligent link to databases, to facilitate searching by relatively unskilled end-users, coupled with a cost-recording function. Such approaches build positively on a perceived challenge or threat, turning it into an opportunity. The manager of a library or information service, then, is concerned with objective consideration of the future which recognises the importance of revealing the expectations and assumptions of the organisation. and integrating them with a careful analysis of the operating and international environments. This analysis must extend to the 'people' aspects as well as to tasks.

The systems approach can provide a useful framework for the manager concerned with an objective consideration of the future.

The horizontal dimension is concerned with the problem of system complexity. In analysing any management proposal it is possible to look at the likely effects at a macro level, where all the social, cultural, psychological, technical and other impacts that can be identified are taken into account. This is the complex view. It is often helpful to restrict one's view to a micro level, concentrating on just a few of a impacts—perhaps those that are believed to be principally involved in the proposed change.

The systems approach reminds planners that, having analysed at the micro level, it is necessary to return to the macro level and check that what are considered workable at the micro level will also be workable at the level. This is greatly facilitated by first spending time in identifying those who have some interest in, or concern for, the service and considering the relationship between the service and the environment in which it has to operate. The horizontal dimension also reveals that a variety of different views and opinions may be held about the characteristics of a system and that these may be irreconcilable. What is good at the macro level of society may have a damaging effect on. the life and happiness of individuals; conversely, changes to make a small process more efficient have a deleterious effect on the complete system. This dimension, then, can be understood as emphasising the need for discussion and dialectic to establish what views are held.

The vertical dimension emphasises the need to consider planning at policy, strategic and operational level. The policy level is concerned with the achievement of objectives of the system, expressed in broad behavioural terms rather than as quantitative goals; it has sometimes been called the 'ought to' level of planning. Such objectives cannot be attained once and forever but serve as enduring guides for other levels of planning. For example, a company information services might state that its policy is: to serve is: 'to serve the needs of research staff and senior managers for information about the company's and its competitors' products and suitable markets and to furnish information associated with the development of new company products'. The objectives might also be ranked, perhaps in terms of how quickly they may be achieved, their perceived urgency, or their perceived importance to the system and the corporate environment.

The strategic level is concerned with the achievement of specific goals. At this level, the objective are taken as fixed, as the manager is concerned principally with translating them into outcomes, seeking the optimum strategy amongst several strategic options. In the previous example, information about markets might be gained from sources such as market reports and suitable statistical and demographic databases. Factors such as cost, time taken to supply information, convenience and confidentially would form part of the assessment leading to the choice of strategy. Taking these two levels of policy and strategy together, there is a recognition that there may be several ways of achieving policy objectives but the role of the manager is to select the best strategic path according to some quantitative criterion.

At the operational level, planning activity is concerned with attaining fixed strategic targets such as levels of growth or the development of new services. In particular, the focus is on the allocation and arrangement of resources, or inputs, to the system. This is the level at which 'ends and means', or tactics, are defined. The allocation is guided by the strategic plan, derived from the policy and strategy levels, but mediated by the need to use the resources committed to the project as efficiently as possible. Thus, to continue with the previous example, knowing that one searcher is more skilled than another in using particular databases would influence the manager in allocating project tasks to members to staff. Successful planning requires that there be a continuous interaction between these three levels. Policy objectives lead to the development of strategic goals which determine operational targets but resource availability and disposition may necessitate adjustment of strategies.

A large increase in price for using particular databases might, for example, encourage the manager in the example to select another route to the required information. Major price rises, coupled with uncertainty about staff availability, might persuade the manager to consult the parent company about a shift in policy for the information service, perhaps no longer seeking to supply information to all sectors of the company's research staff.

Planning is intrinsically concerned with the future. The time and causality dimension is concerned with reconciling two modes of forecasting. The first mode is simple extrapolation from the present state, sometimes called 'normative' forecasting because it assumes that the past is a good predictor of the future and that prevailing conditions will continue to apply. There will be an evident like between existing operations and planned operations; normative forecasting seeks to exploit this link by reviewing factors which influenced past performance and assessing the likely effect of these factors on such plans.

The second mode is concerned with exploratory forecasting, where a future beyond existing constraints is contemplated. It is characterised by the question: 'where are we now and where do we want to be?' Because the constraints are removed, if only in the imagination, the level of risk is greater. Less is known, more is unpredictable; the effect of conditions, previously thought significant, may be less clear. Depending on their attitudes to risk, managers may be more or less willing to indulge in exploratory forecasting. It is important to recognise that both views are necessary for an organisation to grow and to continue to serve the needs of its stockholders. The manager needs a 'rich picture' of both the predicted and the tenable futures to ensure that eventual plans are neither pedestrian nor unrealistic.

New ideas and novel approaches are risky: an overreliance on normative forecasting, which places emphasis on the past as a predictor of the future, may lead the manager to neglect opportunities for profitable and interesting development. Exploratory forecasting assumes great importance when developing a strategic approach to introducing new technology. One does not need to replicate past methods: something better may be achievable with the new technology. On the other hand, too much emphasis on exploratory forecasting may lead the manager to neglect the improvement of services based on well-known techniques.

The final dimension in Jantsch's model, that of 'action', refers to the interaction between planing and implementation. Planning should lead to action and the consequences of action should provide feedback for further strategic and operational considerations.

Traditional planning is often locked into dealing with symptoms. The approach is often, in jest, called 'fire-fighting' but the truth is that studies of managerial work demonstrate that many managers habitually spend their time in coping with day-do-day problems and rarely take the long view of where their part of the organisation is going. The systems approach to planning should lead the manager from dealing with symptoms to dealing with underlying and then on to opportunities, thus developing a pro-active rather than a solely reactive attitude. The approach may seem quite complex, especially when considered in the abstract, but its use should inculcate a set of attitudes in the manager which, to extend the metaphor, extends interests from day-to-day fire-fighting to the productive use of fuel and even to solar energy! The model is now complete combination of dimensions, can give a satisfactory view of the problem of planning which confronts the manager. Only when taken together, complete and entire, can the model begin to provide a suitable framework for thinking about planning. One should also be aware that model is an abstraction of reality: it can only ever reflect certain characteristics, thought to be important by its builder. It is not a substitute for reality. Jantsch's model will not cope with describing everything the manager has to do but it should not be regarded, either, as an ornate stairway to an 'ivory tower'. The astute manager discovers when such models are useful and to what extent they may be relied upon.

It is also important to recognise that the model depends on a conscious effort to design managerial structures which can gather the information needed and pass it back to components of the model. For example, the link in the action dimension between actions and operational decisions implies some means of detecting the effect of action on "the environment and of communicating that effect to those responsible for making operational decisions. When setting up new projects, an important part of the planner's job will be to decide what effects it is desirable, and possible, to measure and to consider how, when and to whom such effects shall be made known. Faced with this rather complicated task, some managers might remark that this is very well if one is faced with running a large service, with many departments, service points, many people and diverse responsibilities.

A very serious-minded approach to planning, with detailed attention to control methods and structure, would be absolutely necessary. But what if one is running a much smaller-seale service? Surely these techniques are unnecessary? Consider this: however large or small the enterprise, it is a professional responsibility to ensure that resources are used to create effective services. Because the environment tends to change, the type of services needed may also change. Only through some disciplined approach to planning can one ensure that opportunities are recognised. The small-scale enterprise may not need a complicated planning structure, with committees, formal reporting guidelines and so on but the discipline it enforces is needed. It is simply too easy, otherwise, to neglect the tasks of evaluation and planning.

As the speed of technical development increases it is important for us, as managers, to assess what is likely to be useful and then to manage its introduction. It is also important for managers to recognise that the use of technology will change jobs and will demand of people the use of different skills. It will not necessarily make life better, in any objective sense, but it will make life different and it is part of that managerial responsibility to prepare people for change. Only an approach to development which takes into account the people, the technology and the environment—an approach which encourages a strategic view—is likely to succeed: it is to his end that the systems approach was developed.

The word 'system' has become a common term, often applied to things which seem large or complex. It is so frequently encountered, that it can become quite difficult to decide what it means even within a defined context. When a manufacturer of washing powder, computer programmers, doctors, economists, astronomers and ecologists use the same word, 'system', in describing their interests, can anyone be sure what they mean? What is the connection between a computer system have anything in common? Can we sensibly compare the ecological system of our planet and the 'brand-new washing system' of the detergent manufacturer? What does this word 'system' mean if it can be used in so many and different contexts? Perhaps the word is in danger of becoming trivialised: should these disparate things all attract the name of system? Is it possible for users of the word to agree on a meaning such that it can legitimately be used to describe both the vast and the minute, the natural and the fabricated, the technical and the social, the concrete and the abstract? A comparison of various dictionary definitions of the word 'system' quickly reveals that compilers of dictionaries are no nearer agreement. In an interesting essay, Jordan recounts that at a meeting of experts from various disciplines the participants found it very difficult to define the word, but, despite this impediment, their meeting was quite successful.

Jordan argues that there is a 'core meaning' to the word 'system': the word can be used to described things which are seen, or thought of, as consisting of a set of parts connected in some distinguishable way. Whenever one person can indicate or describe a set of elements and how they are connected and can communicate this concept to another person can indjcate or describe a set of elements and how they are connected and can communicate this concept to another person, the use of the word 'system' would be an appropriate name for the thing under discussion. Jordan considers that much of the confusion arises because the word 'system' is often used in a specific context whereas its proper context is in describing abstract or general qualities. He concludes that the only things which need be common to all uses of the word are that each system, so described, should have a collection of identifiable entities and identifiable connections between them. The many uses outlined above can be considered to be correct but not necessarily useful unless the elements forming each 'system' are also identified and there is some purpose in viewing them as a collective unit. There is little point in using the word solely for effect or in a bid to add a scientific gloss to the ordinary. We can agree, then, that the word 'system' is difficult to define, but that it is possible to accept a general definition such as: a set of parts and functions, sometimes called 'components', which are connected by a network of relationships or actions. The pragmatist will probably wish to add that the set should have some defined purpose. Some writers underline this point by insisting that a system can be considered to be a collection of people, objects and activities about which it is meaningful to talk as if it has some unity.

Churchman also emphasises this by suggesting that, to be described as a 'system', the thing' under consideration must have objectives or purposes. Unfortunately, these may be quite difficult to discern: what for example, are the objectives of the solar system? The nervous system undoubtedly has a purpose but how easy is it to express? Wyllys notes that the difficulty has prompted the comment that 'system is a group of things that operates at a level of complexity higher than the highest level that we think we understand'. Within this seemingly facetious remark there is a core of truth because same discussions af systems verge an the metaphysical and have little practical value. The definitian outlined abave will encompass both formal and informal structures; clearly library and informatian services, like most organisations, have both structures in evidence.

The organisation chart, so often believed to represent the organisation, displays only one aspect: usually, the formal reporting and responsibility structure. The informal structure represents centres of pawer and influence, often based an people ar groups with some sort of comman interest. It is rare to find formal acknowledgment of the presence of an informal structure, although all are aware of it and use it. By acknowledging that the definition of 'system' can encompass both formal and informal structures the manager is reminded that changes will affect both and a strategy must be planned accordingly. The recognition may prampt the manager also to cansider whether other structures, such as a set of user groups, are present, The concept of 'system' thus drives us to a multi-dimensional view of an organisation, with many structures existing simultaneously. It is rarely possible to deal with them together, because of the complexity of the managerial problems, and the systems approach encourages us to concentrate on the structure or structures considered salient at a particular time, but not to forget the 'big picture'. The lack of a specific definition has another effect. It is vital to establish how the word is to be used within a particular context: for example, the library or information service manager's view af what set of peaple, objects and activities constitute the library system af a campany may well be different from that of, way, the director of finance.

Used properly, and with agreement, the word is useful and can serve to remind managers that organisations are complex and represent a subtle balance of abjectives, tasks, persanalities and events. Failure to define and agree on the constitution of the set of things comprising the particular system under discussian will lead only to confusion or, worse, resentment and defensiveness. In seeking to define a system in such a way that the definition can be used in discussion it is best to begin with trying to identify the systems companents; that is, the people, activities and events, and objects which together farm that system. In essence the process of definition sets the camponents apart from their surroundings and encloses them within a boundary. This process of grouping is quite familior. It forms part of the repertoire of responses which humans use far dealing with the camplexity of life: 'home' is recognised as comprising a different set of entities from 'work' or 'social life'. This can sametimes be demonstrated quite dramatically: it may be difficult to name or even recognise a person if we see them in a context with which we do not usually associate them.

System boundaries are also before further discussion can take place. The basis of the agreement will usually be shared view of a distinction between internal gools of the organisation or part of the organisation under discussion. An internal gool can be considered to reflect ideas about the strategy and tactics of the organisation, these being expressed in terms of how resources are contralled, whereas external gools reflect ideas about the effects of the work of the organisation upon the environment. The external gools are concerned with things outside the system boundary.

For an information service, for example, the user may be seen as outside the boundary because the availability of the service should affect the work methods of the user, but it is clear that those work methods are not under the control of the information service. The distinction between control and influence is a useful means of defining a system boundary. It is also capable of being used to separate parts of an organisation: the cataloguing department of a university library and the reader services department can influence each other, perhaps by suggesting improvements in the provision of access points to the catalogue, but it is unlikely that one will be in a formal position to control the other and enforce its view. The process of definition of system boundaries may be seen as a process of identifying and describing 'spheres of influence'. An additional aspect of the process of boundary identification is that it should aid the manager is preparing an organisation for change.

New targets can be set, new working methods can be tried and their effects assessed. Change in one part of the system can be monitored to detect its effect on the other parts of the system. The manager is able to view the system as a whole and communicate with it. This may not be easy, or possible, for components outside the boundary. For example, consider an information service manager seeking to change the production methods for a current awareness bulletin. The work of the present production team may be well understood and carefully costed. Senior management of the parent organisation responsible for the service may suggest the need for economics. The problem of high cost of production and changes likely to mitigate its effects may be discussed by the team, assessed and tested.

A climate in which change is acceptable or can, at least, be discussed has been created. To the senior managers outside the information system boundary the precise nature of the changes is unlikely to be important and may be incomprehensible without some knowledge of the present working methods: the principal concern of the senior managers is with the new costings for the information service and discussion with the information service manager will be in terms of those costings. The senior managers may also be users of the current awareness bulletin. As such, their use of the bulletin may be affected adversely or beneficially by the changes.

Bulletins are usually sent to many groups of staff within an organisation and the consideration of their value and use must include all groups. Just because one user group appears to be very powerful should not predispose the information service manager to consider only the views of that group. this example highlights another important idea implicit in the systems approach: the identification of roles played by individuals and groups within and outside. the system boundary.

In many cases, multiple roles will be discernible, often played by the same people. In facilitating change, the manager has to understand that a proposed changes is likely to affect each role differently: each individual or group playing a particular role will have different responses and will need to be treated distinctly by the managfir. Even so, where multiple roles are played, the cumulative effects of change on the differing roles may produce some complicated and highly individual responses. It is well said that all changes is a process of collective negotiation. The notion of system components can be explored further with the aid of a system model. This represents a simple systems model, one which shows the main flow of work and information about work around an organisation. It is an abstract view: no detail about any component is given but the components and their links are emphasised and the nature of the system is summarised.

This view regards the organisation as being an open system: the organisation is linked to its environment by the passage of inputs, outputs and control signals. This is a critical point: General System Theory, as developed by Ludwig von Bertalanffy, makes a distinction between closed and open systems. The closed system has no links to the environment and will become moribund because it lacks the capacity to respond to changes in the environment. This may take a long time if the environment changes very slowly, but the lack of adaptation means that eventually the environment will become hostile to the closed system.

General System Theory has attempted to develop a series of theorems which link the behaviour of all systems-biological, organisational, mechanical and so on. for our purpose, the important point is that open systems must establish a means of monitoring the environment and assessing needs. In addition to libraries and information services, the community study and user represent a major means of achieving this. It must be remembered, however, that there are formal, rather highly structured means of gathering information and that less formal channels are also useful. All information about how the library or information service and its efforts are perceived by users represents valuable information and emphasises the link across the system boundary to the environment.

It is almost impossible to think of library or information service which would not be open to its environment in this way but the simple reception of information is not enough: for a system to be open, it must also respond to that information. Change can be profoundly threatening but the tendency to explain away responses from users and not to change is a sure sign of closure in a system. The simple systems model also illustrates the important feature of feedback of both effectiveness and efficiency. It is now a familiar notion to most managers that a regular review of efficiency and effectiveness are a necessary part of any manager's job. There is a growing need to be able to demonstrate efficiency and effectiveness to those who provide the resources. The type of feedback specified by the simple systems model is 'negative feedback'. By sampling the output from the organisation and comparing it with some criteria a decision can be made about whether to adjust the input in such a way as to make the output more satisfactory. The theory is that negative feedback leads to stability in a system because the system becomes selfcorrecting. This may be true of mechanical or biological systems, but one suspects that social systems may not respond quite so neatly: for example, how long might it take an information service to adjust its cataloguing practices, even supposing the manager could persuade the staff that users did not find them suitable? Nonetheless, the principle of frequent assessment of effectiveness and efficiency, coupled with the conviction that the results should be sued rather than ignored, is a major point to be drawn from General System Theory. For sensible management thinking, the sample systems model needs to be elaborated. In particular, it is useful to try to define the environment of the system more closely and to consider what constitutes the organisation.

The model displays three environmental levels. The internal environment, which is contained by the system boundary, constitutes all of those elements or entities that are within the official jurisdiction of the organisation. The internal environment is composed of sub-systems, which operate within the context of the organisation and which interact with each other. A change to one part of the system may affect the working of another, because of this linkage. Part of the work of an alysing a system is concerned with the investigation of these linkages so that the effects of change can be more easily predicted. The operating environment constitutes the group of suppliers, customers and interest groups which deal with, influence or are influenced directly by the work of the organisation. The general environment constitutes the social, economic and technological context within which any organisation operates. The organisation has the greatest degree of control over its own internal environment is capable of exerting a strong influence through the operatmg environment. Strategic management requires information principally about the operating and the general environments, whereas administration is principally concerned with the internal environment. The complex system., model we have looked at presents only one aspic of the systems view of an organisation. It is concerned principally with the formal task-oriented view of the organisation: what the organisation does, or thinks it does. It is as well to remember that models showing other aspects may be equally useful: a systems model showing the various groups and individuals who have some interest or commitment or who expect something from the organisation is a useful reminder of which groups ought to be consulted about change. These 'stake holders' may well have very different and incompatible views of the organisation and its purposes: the views that have been expressed during the recent discussions about direct charging for use of public libraries are a good illustration of this divergence of opinion about basic values. Unless this diversity is acknowledged it may be very difficult to maintain balanced and satisfactory services. Yet, it is often the case that managers suggests a change and are then surprised to have it attacked from a completely unexpected quarter.

In viewing the organisation within the system we noted that the internal environment was made of various entities or elements. These are often called 'sub-system'. It is quite possible to take each sub-system, consider it as a separate system and reveal sub-systems within it. This approach enables one to recognise why the definition of system has to be so elastic: the system can be considered to be the complete organisation, part of the organisation, a separate process or even one part of a process.

The definition of the boundary depends, in each case, on what it is sensible for the manager to study in relation to particular problem. The systems approach reminds us of the need to consider a system in its environment and helps us to reveal the linkages to that environment and to other sub-systems, but it does not enforce a particular standpoint. The task of investigation is implicit within systems thinking: it should, of course, be implicit in all management thinking, but there are many examples of decisions and, indeed, complete management strategies, which owe more to whim and 'flying by the seat of one's pants' than to any concerted effort at defining and analysing problems. Not that this is always wrong: there are plenty of occasions where the opportunity for careful analysis and considered decision-making is denied to the manager. It is not to be relied upon, however, as the major management style of an organisation, especially where many people are involved, the environment presents social, financial or technological challenges or the future of the organisation is rather uncertain.

❑

3

Information Alerting Service

Several people have attempted to define information and information science and to formulate theories of information science. These interpretations broadly indicate five trends associating information science with *(a)* librarianship and graphic records management; *(b)* information theory of communication engineering; *(c)* language and communication; *(d)* information processing by brain and cognition; and *(e)* computer processing of information. Each theory represents some aspect of information science but not the whole. A generally acceptable theory is yet to emerge. These theories consider information in different ways.

For instance a fundamental category such as matter; a property of matter; structure or organization; the probability of the occurrence of an event; reduction in the degree of uncertainty in a state of knowledge (or similar construct); an event which takes place when a recipient encounters a text; data of value in decision making; public, communicated scientific information; and the message itself. Some of the proposals have concentrated upon the question of the effect of information, a number of them equating information with effect on a recipient, to varying degrees; while others have attempted to deal with the question of an operational concept, which has often been taken to mean mathematically measurable. Since the discussion is in the context of management, the theories and aspects of information science likely to have an impact on library management or managers of information are considered here. These are Shannon's communication theory, the physical nature of information, information and knowledge, information and communi-cation, sociological base of information, characteristics of information service and discipline contextual information.

Of the several expositions of information theory proposed so far, the only theory that has a sound scientific basis on the lines of physical sciences and engineering is Shannon's theory of information. Shannon's information theory, also known as communication theory, explains information transmission in terms of *(a)* source of information, *(b)* channel of transmission, *(d)* transmitter, *(e)* receiver, *(f)* destination, and *(g)* noise.

The information or message to be transmitted originated at the source and is transmitted to the destination through a channel. The transmitter encodes the, message as signals suitable for transmission. The channel carries the signals to the receiver which decodes the signal as the original message or its near approximation. The decoded message is received at the destination.

In discussing information and information science, one is faced with the problem of identifying the state of existence of information in terms of time, space, matter and energy. This has practical significance as it affects several areas of management, such as quantification of information transfer in terms of loss or gain, level of absorption and evaluation. This will also help in the application of other disciplines, *e.g.* entropy, to the information field. Since information is expressed in professional literature as process, a phenomenon, an act, indicated the need for establishing clearly its state of existence in terms of the fundamental physical concepts. Information, according to one view, is a fundamental property of matter and of consciousness, acting to connect the two by means of its relationship with variety and reflection. However, the introduction of consciousness brings information nearer to energy than to matter.

The terms information and knowledge are often used synonymously. It is contended that the phrase "knowledge and information" is redundant and occasionally refers to certain kinds of knowledge as information, while another view is that there is a difference. One crucial difference between knowledge and information is that knowledge is cognitively structured.

Any bit of information in a knowledge structure is related cognitively through the structure to all other bits in the structure. These cognitive relationships are synthesized as a structure, which, in spatial terms, may have any number of dimensions. Information, on the other hand, is that which modifies a knowledge structure in any way. Some of the information comes to us by direct observation of our surroundings, some from what others tell us, and some from reading and, possibly, other sources of which we are not consciously aware. Information which modifies a knowledge structure is the result of an information process.

Information has also been defined as the act of informing, and knowledge as the contents of the message. This does not define what "informing" is. Shera contends that epistemology is the foundation of librarianship. If this is so, it should equally apply to information science, unless information is treated as a physical quantity or neural phenomenon devoid of social and cognitive context. An analysis of the nature of human khowledge has a significant place in information science as it leads directly to important implications for the development of systems for classifying, indexing, and, in general, for analyzing graphic records so that they may be retrieved and correlated.

Applying the criteria of use, knowledge can be classified into fiye types:

1. Practical knowledge (which includes professional knowledge, business knowledge, workman's knowledge, household knowledge, political khowledge and the like).
2. Intellectual khowledge.
3. Small talk or pastime khowledge.
4. Spiritual khowledge.
5. Unwanted knowledge.

To deal with each of these types of khowledge, it is necersary to have a different form of rigor and approach. The different ways of using knowledge and *(a)* the proto-scientific way (scientific attitude), *(b)* everyday casual way, *(c)* expert way, and *(d)* "political" way. The genesis of human knowledge can be traced to observing and correlating the various phenomena in nature, that is, understanding the surrounding world. From the need to correlate the necessity to communicated ar:ises. Communication, "by its very nature, comes to be closely associated with the symbolic representation of attributes of observed phenomena, and such representation is, as a consequence, also linked with the analysis of phenomenal and with their correlation". Information science is concerned with communicating and correlating human khowledge together with symbolism and its role in communication.

Language represents the largest use of symbolism in human communication. Information activities are inseparable from language. Language is the most important part of communication in human society. Aspects of semantics and syntax are fundamental to the study of information transfer and its interpretations which are linked to the state of technological, social and cultural development of a society.

Viewed in the organizational and social contexts, communication has four fundamental features: *1.*Communication is perception. *2.* Communication is expectation. *3.* Communication makes demands. *4.* Communication and information are different and, indeed, largely opposite yet interdependent. The relationship between communication and information has implications for information science. Communication is always interpersonal and is interlinked with emotions and values, expectations and perceptions. Information, on the contrary, is impersonal, purely formal and devoid of perception and emotions. This difference becomes apparent if we compare communication in a discipline like mathematics with that in religion or literature. In communication, we perceive a configuration, whereas in the information process we convey specific individual data.

But the effectiveness of information transfer depends on the pre-establishment of communication, as information in its pure form devoid of perception will not give meaning. The main problem in communication is how to convey the information one wants to convey and convey it quickly without distorting the message. A related problem is that of dissemination, that is, making information reach all who would benefit from it. Communication is complete, from the point of view of the conveyor, only when the information communicated elicits the desired response in the recipient. This necessitates the study of communication media, form of message, format in which the desired information is transmitted, understanding the needs of the recipient, and his or her information behaviour. Thus, it is necessary to study the relationship between information and communication.

Society depends, for its development, on the accumulation and application of kowledge, knowledge grows because of the curiosity of man to inquire. Inquiry leads to gathering of information. New knowledge is built upon the knowiedge already accumulated in society by previous generations. The invention of speech and writing led to the growth of knowledge. Knowledge flourishes in societies in which intellectual freedom, a liberal attitude, and an opportunity for cross-fertilization of cultures exist.

Invention of scientific methods accelerated the rate of growth of knowledge, as witnessed in ancient Greece and during the Renaissance in Europe. The second half of the twentieth century has witnessed the fastest growth of knowledge, leading to an abundance of information. This can be traced to the development of science, innovation and technology. Information technology is pushing further the rate of production of knowledge, thereby paving the way for an information society. How are we going to manage this rapid growth of knowledge? How do we put this information to use? What policy decisions and organizational back-up are needed? These are some of the questions that need careful consideration. Answers to these larger issues, in turn, are going to shape the management of individual information agencies and determine their future prospects. Information moulds individuals and society. In individuals it affects their mode of behaviour, means of livelihood, creative ability and utilization of their leisure time.

To society, information contributes in the form of social sphere, it acts as an agent of social change, a promoter of public welfare and peace; in the cultural field, it helps in the creation of beliefs and truth; in the economic area, it acts as an agent of production and profit; and in the political area, it leads to power derived from the control of information processing. This shows how information, individuals and society are interdependent.

Hence, the study of information has to rely on a sociological foundation. Any theory of information science based solely on the lines characteristic of the natural sciences leads to the study of information as an objective phenomenon divorced, to a large extent, from information work as practised by information intermediaries and divorced also from the individual. Though such theories appear elegant and intellectually satisfying, they may not be of much practical utility. This is because the ultimate explanation of information actions resides in the motives and attitudes of individuals.

Organized information activities—generating, recording, distributing, processing and disseminating information—have become possible because of the characteristics of information. A characteristic is an indication of quality or special features. Characteristics of information comprise qualities inherent in it, qualities assigned to it, and qualities attributed by perception and social values.

An inherent quality of information is that it has none of the physical properties of colour, taste, mass and shape. Another inherent quality is that is perishable, unless it is stored in the memory of the brain. The same information, capable of being interpreted differently, is an example of attributive quality. Ownership of information and hence the right to receive a royalty by the owner, is an assigned characteristic of information. The study of the characteristics of information will be incomplete, at least in the context of organize; information activities made is isolation of the study of communication mode (codes, symbols, signals and sounds whose meaning is pre-established among its users) used for transmitting information and physical media by which information is represented through the use of communication mode (records). The most commonly used communication mode is language and the important physical forms of records are paper, magnetic tape, films and semiconductor chips.

Information service is concerned primarily with processing and servicing of records and their intellectual contents. To do this effectively, it is not sufficient if one has thorough knowledge of the characteristics of physical records; one also ought of know the characteristics and impact of communication media and those of information, as the three have a symbiotic relationship. Studies in information science, at present, mostly deal with processing and servicing of information in an organized set-up. Coverage of topics in information science literature amply proves this.

Content analysis of the Annual review of information science and technology for the years 1966 to 1983 shows the following composition: library and information services, including secondary publications service—38%; information processing, including information analysis and abstraction, storage and retrieval techniques, and evaluation—20%; computer and communication science—11%; information management—10%; user studies—5%; and information systems, reprography, information sciences and other topics—17%. Fundamentals of information science account for less than 3%. Source subjects such as linguistics, psychology, social science and epistemology hardly find any place.

Surely, this reflects a narrow approach to the subject. Moreover, it is situation where a part is made to represent the whole. The tendency to overemphasize the role of libraries and information services in the totality of information transfer could be one of the reason behind the narrow perception of information science. Information science, in its broader perspective, includes topics of cognitive science derived from the study of the functioning of brain, computer treatment of information (informatics), artificial intelligence, linguistics, library and information services, cybernetics, information theory, systems theory, epistemology, social sciences and economics.

Electronics, computer science and communication technology have brought about a sea change in the information field. Information technology is now able to create *(a)* new products, processes and machines that can be used independently, customized information packages, video cassettes, home information products, micro-processors, personal computes and reprographic equipment; *(b)* external dependent, database on-line information systems lime Chemical abstracts on-line services and Lockheed's DIALOG; *(c)* Cooperative library/information networks; *(d)* Videotex, *i.e.* broadcast or telephone-dependent mass communication systems like PRESTEL (UK); and *(e)* electronic information processing systems such as the electronic book. Information technology has been able to abridge time and space dimensions in communication. But it also creates problems. Introduction of technology affects a system in two ways: physical and psychological. The former is concerned with cost, location, movement and obsolescence. The latter affects the behaviour of individuals and groups involved in the operation and utilization of the products of information technology. Both bring about change and a need for managing change. The gap between advances in technology and the needed development of human skill with the requisite psychological, social and behavioural accomplishments is widening. Specific managerial problems created by technology involve the following activities:

1. Formulating policies on information at national and institutional levels.

2. International cooperation and control over information flow across transnational borders.

3. Defining the respective roles of private, public, government, profit and non-profit sectors in handling information.

4. Redefining the roles of information manager or mediator and ultimate user of the benefits of the new technology.

5. Defining (redefining where necessary) and legislating on intellectual property rights.

6. Allocation of and control over resources, including communication channels.

7. Assessment of the impact of information technology on individuals and society and initiating follow-up actions.

8. Development (including reallocation and training) or staff.

9. Study of user reaction to man-machine interface problems and developing programmes to meet them.

10. Development of requisite policies, strategies and organization for managing information at both national and institutional levels.

11. Validation and evaluation of different sources of information and technologies.

12. Selection of further areas of research and development in information technology and their applications.

Taking managerial decisions, especially those involving technology, is becoming progressively difficult, but choices have to be made. "All decisions involve risks: big decisions involve big, and highly visible risks that strike 'consuming terror' in the managerial heart". The problem is how to select the new technologies that will prove to be winners and avoid those that may turn out to be expensive losers. Information technology, at present, is in an experimental or first operative stage, while the management development in this regard is yet to evolve.

As each technological advance meets an existing need, it creates in its wake new needs, almost instantaneously. Unless information managers and users keep abreast of developments in the field, the gap between management and new technology will widen further. This will deprive information managers of the cushion period required for adjustment to the new technological environment. The managerial evolution will take an unnecessarily long time and thereby inhibit full exploitation of the information technology.

Library Automation. Beginning with the introduction of machine-readable databases, iriformation technology has increased the pace of mechanization and automation in libraries. Managerial issues in library automation broadly centre round: *(a)* factors responsible for greater application of technology, *(b)* changes likely to occur from such applications, and *(c)* impediments in the way of rapid introduction of technology.

Factors influencing application of technology:

1. The organization culture and the technological climate in the parent body of which the library is a part; the desire of the persons who matter in the organization; and the readiness of the users to accept the new technology.

2. The attitude and philosophy of library manager towards change.

2. Involvement of library staff. Inherent in technology application are elements that are detrimental to stable conditions. Motivated staff and their participation in decision-making process constitute a positive influence.

The changes that are likely to result from automation are:

1. Full automation is likely to blur the distinction between technical and public services. This calls for total restructuring of the work environment.

2. Large-scale access to information at remote places, made possible by new technology, makes existing organization structures unable to cope with the new library environment.

3. Need for more frequent communication among people working in different sections of the library.

4. Ergonomic and psychological effects of technology on users and staff.

5. Technology often brings in attendant desirable changes which otherwise would not be possible to introduce due to political, financial and administrative factors. These changes could be introduced for better library management.

Impediments in the way of rapid application of technology are:

1. Introducing new technology involves large capital investment and outflow of high charges in accessing on-line. This cost, partly passed on to users, forms an important factor that affects the pace of application of technology.

2. Hardware, software and databases coming in different standards make right selection of technology difficult.

3. Creating information on search media, *i.e.*, contents on disk, leads to certain formatting difficulties.

4. Graphics and colour texts are only now beginning to be widely available.

5. Library market is not perceived as a major segment by producers of new information products based-on new technology.

6. Uses still prefer printed media to that of electronic media. Electronic authenticity, and review standard of the text.

7. Copyright issues have not been fully settled. The situation is likely to aggravate further when full text transmission becomes more common.

Information usage exhibits traits influenced by the peculiarities of individual subject fields and by the approach to information generally followed by its practitioners. Information needs, its form of supply and mode of utilization, differ from field to field. Precedence in law and administration, citation in scientific and academic research and writing, structure in mathematics, ownership in economics, age and authenticity of sources in history, and expression of language in philosophy, law and literature are examples of differing traits of information usage. Approaches to information by scientific researchers vary from those of educators whose approach again varies from that of business and businessmen. Information usage by scientists and technologists has received adequate attention, but this is not so in other fields. A study of the features of information usage, unique or special to different disciplines will enhance our understanding of different traits of information, their structure, properties, sources and usage.

Economics Information

Recently, considerable interest has been generated in a field neglected so far-economics information. Some of the important aspects of economics information are now listed.

Information Asymmetry

This occurs when buyers and sellers of goods or services are not equally well informed about the commodity or service. It greatly affects the market performance of a given trade or businessman and thereby emphasizes the need for an in-depth study of the flow of information and information gaps affecting business, trade and industry, that is, the information gap between the buyer and the seller. Hence, there is a need for consumer protection.

Gross National Product (GNP)

When information is treated as a national, its generation and exploitation contribute to the GNP. Computation of the information component of the GNP is hampered by the lack of an agreed upon measure of the amount or value of information. The present method of computing the information component of the GNP involves taking that component of the GNP which is left out after according for the growth in GNP due to economic and industrial factors, such as capital, labour and production. In this, any assessment of the benefits accruing from information should include its indirect contribution to public good, besides the benefits derived by the individual recipient of information.

Agents of Information Transmission

In economics information, all marketing activities that affect a consumer's perception of a product, such as advertising, brand names and trademarks, act as conveyors of information and form a part of the information transfer process.

Information as Goods

Information as a commodity displays some peculiar properties, for example, a sale of information does not deprive the seller of the information sold, which is not the case with a sale of commodities.

Investing in Information

"The gains from investing in information are allocated to the investor by giving his control, not over the information, but, rather, over the economically valuable uses to which it is put. Presumably, this is the purpose of patents. An economic dilemma then arises. Without patents, benefits from investment in information are thought to be hard to appropriated, and hence investment in information is suboptimal.

Ownership of Information

Information generated through private or company research, development and inventions falls under the category of private ownership. Such information affects the worth of the company holding the information. When privately owned information becomes known, "some prices in the economy are likely to change, even if it is only the stock price of the firm that made the' discovery. Therefore, the holder of the information, with his superior knowledge, can speculate in the goods or assets whose prices will change. The result is a redistribution of income or wealth without any necessary concomitant social benefit. The point is that the private return to investing in information can exceed the social return, and at the very least these two quantities are likely to differ".

The development of a framework for information science can: *(a)* help the growth of the discipline; *(b)* assist the practitioners and managers of information by indicating different aspects of the subject and their effects; and *(c)* help in ordering the different approaches and viewpoints, as each of them forms a face of information science. Such a framework should account for the requirements of formulating fundamental laws, social context of information, and the requirements of practitioners.

The framework has two distinct parts: *(a)* theory and fundamentals, and *(b)* application and practice. The theoretical part represents the social, scientific, cultural, communication and behavioural science base of information science which goes to develop fundamental laws, theories and principles. Information study, to be relevant, must take into account five essential requirements:

1. Information in human, cognitive communication systems
2. Relationship between information and the generator
3. The idea of desired information
4. Relationship between information and the user
5. Effectiveness of information and that of information transfer.

The application branch covers the practical and professional side of information science. Applied information science includes the characteristics of information, the exploitation of which leads to practice.

❐

4

Technical Service in Library

Arrangement of books in a systematic way is necessary in order that readers could find them in a helpful manner. "There is no more important factor in the success or failure of a library than the classification of books and other material which form its stock. It brings the material together in subject groups on the shelves and in the catalogues and thus enables both librarian and reader to find books easily. In short, classification is the primary key to the assembling, finding, selecting and rejecting of books." Classification of objects by their real characteristics is so common a function of the mind of man in his everyday life that he is unconscious of the mental process that is taking place. Therefore, classification of books in a library is natural, real, and necessary to the organization of reading materials. Both the librarian and the reader must have the books classified, as it is the most sensible method for the arrangement of books on the shelves. An unclassified collection of books in a library is like a forest while a classified one, resembles a garden, well laid out, pruned and carefully tended, affording delight and satisfaction to the visitor. Every library, small or big must bring order out of disorder and facilitate quick access to the required books, by a systematic arrangement based on the objectives for which the library is established. The organization of books into coherent groups eliminates for the user of the library an extensive and useless search through a large number of volumes. It not only saves the time of the reader, but results in increasing and effective use of books which otherwise would remain unused.

Choosing a scheme classification is necessary to consider what system of bibliographic classification a library should adopt. A system of book classification which is based on subject characteristics, constructed in conformity with the accepted canons of classification, will be found satisfactory.

A classification system is a verbal chart of the whole of some part of knowledge arranged in a convenient order. The order of arrangement may be evolutionary, historical, utilitarian or arbitrary. A scheme is called general when it covers the entire field of knowledge, and special if it is restricted to a branch. Special classifications, in which the order of arrangement of its schedules is in direct relation to the needs of specialists, scientists, teachers, lawyers, etc., are the concern of the special librarian. But the librarian of a public library has to do with a general classification system, as the library is expected to cover all branches' of knowledge and the unlimited interests of the community.

In general classification schemes, the whole field of knowledge is divided into Genus (Main Classes), Species (Divisions), Sub-Species (Sub-divisions), Specific Species (Types) and Individuals (Members). The characteristics of division is the principle by which a class is divided. The characteristic may be natural or artificial according to the purpose of division. In applying the characteristics of division, minute and rigorous consistency is called for in order to avoid cross division. The classification must be flexible so as to permit incorporation of new terms without dislocating the existing order of the schedules as need arises with the growth of knowledge.

Book classification schemes must be provided with (1) a Notation, flexible, brief, mnemonic, pure or mixed, (2) a Generallia class, (3) a Form class and (4) Form 'divisions and (5) an Index.

A notation is a shorthand symbol used to represent the terms of a classification. It is a convenient means of reference to the order of subjects arranged in a classification scheme. It connects the index and the terms in the schedules. Its position on the catalogue entry directs the location of books on the shelves whose backs bear these. symbols, *e.g.* Dewey adopts pure notation of numbers 0-9 while Colon classification has a mixed notation of alphabets A-Z, a-z and numbers. In Dewey's Decimal Classification 954 represents History of India, where 9 is History, 5 is Asia, and 4 is India. This means that the position of books on Indian History gets fixed with this notation so that these come after 953 and before 955, which represent Histories of other Asiatic countries.

A Generalia class will indicate that it is not a specific class for a specific subject but a most general class. When a book covers multiple subjects, *e.g.* Enquire within upon everything or treats knowledge in general, *e.g.* Encyclopaedia Britannica; it will be appropriate to group them together in a separate class, for they will not go with books in other Classes, *e.g.* History. Science, etc.

A form class provides an appropriate place for books which are primarily read, used and appreciated for the form or manner in which they are written rather than for the subject-matter of the book itself. Examples of such books are found in the field of literature, poetry, drama, fiction, prose, letters, etc., as the forms by which books of literature are grouped, *e.g.* 820=English Literature (in D. C.) is divided into.

821 English poetry

822 English drama

823 English fiction

824 English essays

Milton's Paradise Lost and Shakespeare's Hamlet will not ordinarily be read for their importance in respectively.

Form divisions are provided in all standard schemes of book classification with a view to 'sharpen the focus' of the books in the subject fields. Books are written as histories, outlines, dictionaries, etc. of subjects, *e.g.* History of Chemistry, Outlines of Chemistry, Dictionary of Chemistry. In this example, the subject matter, Chemistry, is common to all the three books. The only method to keep Histories of Chemistry together and apart from Outlines of Chemistry is to add the form division to the subject, which will distinguish one book from another of the same subject. In order to apply these form divisions consistently, and memonically, Dewey has provided nine common form divisions and iixed their notation, *e.g.* :

01 philosophy, theory

02 compends, text-books, outlines

03 encyclopaedias, dictionaries, and so on.

These common subs-divisions can be used with any subject and should never be confused with 'form classes' peculiar to literature.

An index to the classification schedules is an alphabetical list of the terms used in the classification, with the appropriate notation mentioned against each one of them. The index will help quick reference to the schedules, but will often prove an undependable method of classification of books, especially when it is of a relative type as in the Dewey Decimal Classification. It can be consulted as a preliminary step but not as a final one in assigning notation to books.

These are called adjustments necessary, to fit in a knowledge classification of concepts or ideas, to a book classification. Excellent manuals and text-books setting forth the principles of subject classification can be found in W. C. Berwick Sayers' Introduction to Classification and Philip's Primer of Book Classification.

Among the existing schemes of book classification, the Decimal Classification of Melvil Dewey is the most popular, because of its simple notation, mnemonic features, relative index, limitless expansion of its schedules and a committee engaged in constant revision of the schedules, to suit the changing needs. Although later schemes like the Colon classification of Ranganathan and the Bibliographic classification of Bliss have come into existence, their use is very restricted, as they have still to be fully tried and perfected. As the Dewey Decimal Classification is most widely applied in libraries all over the world, it is appropriate for us to know more details about its nature, scope and use in modern libraries. The fundamental failings of the Decimal

Classification are that its main classes are set forth in no logical or convenient order and that its notation is fixed in an unsatisfactory manner resulting in overcrowding at certain places in the schedules. Indivisible specificity of subjects is sometimes not obtainable and at other times, if obtained, the notation assumes unwieldy length and complexity. Individual libraries find it necessary to make adaptations to suit their needs. Small and medium-sized libraries will find the Decimal Classification suitable whereas large and specialised collections require special classification schemes where minute classification will be necessary. Any such deviations from the printed schedules should be recorded for reference by staff at future occasions.

THE DEWEY DECIMAL CLASSIFICATION

Knowledge is divided into nine main classes numbered 1-9 and a tenth class numbered 0 is provided as a Generalia class, unlimited to any main class. The notation is pure and built up by Arabic numerals with a three-figure base, 000-900.

THE TEN MAIN CLASSES

000 General Works

100 Philosophy

200 Religion

300 Sociology

400 Philology

500 Natural Science

600 Applied Science (Useful Arts)

700 Fine Arts

800 Literature

900 History, including
Geography, Biography

Each one of these ten main classes is again divided into ten broad divisions:

000 General Works

010 Bibliography

020 Libray Economy

030 General Encyclopaedias

040 General Collected Essays

050 General Periodicals

060 General Societies

070 Journalism, Newspapers

080 Polygraphy, Special Collections

090 Book Rarities

It will be seen that the principle adopted is the same as the one followed in building the notation of the main classes by a third digit 0 to denote general works of each group. Similary, the other nine main classes are divided into ten component divisions. Each division in a main class is further sub-divided into the following ten sub-divisions:

510 Mathematics

511 Arithmetic

512 Algebra

513 Geometry

514 Trigonometry

515 Descripive Geometry and Projections

516 Analytic Geometry

517 Calculus

518 (Unassigned in the 19th edition)

519 Probabilities

The sub-divisions with three-figure base are further divided into ten sections by adding a decimal point to arrive at the specific sub-sections which are given below:

511 Arithmetic

.1 Systems of Arithmetic

.2 Notation and Numeration

.3 Prime Numbers

.4 Fractions

.5 Analysis, Permutation and Combination

.6 Proportion and Progression

.7 Involution and Evolution

.8 Mercantile Rules, Interest Allegation, Mensuration Gaging

.9 Problems and Tables

By adopting a similar process, every subject is provided with a place in the schedule. The notation is expanded in an unlimited manner, to reach the required degree of specificity. Fixing the norm of division into ten only has resulted. in overcrowding and illogical grouping of subjects at certain places and blank notation at certain places where the specific subjects have not been in existence or remain unidentified. So procrustean methods are adopted to find a place for a subject within a given notation whether it is logical or not. It has, therefore, rightly been criticized by special librarians and scholars who have stated that the scheme is unsuitable and illogical. "My own everyday experience of libraries of many types underlines for me the general point that the principal schemes of library classification in common use fail hopeessly to provide a suitable classification for geography books especially for the larger number of books now appearing in those important aspects of our subject, human and historical geography. The criticism appleis to both the Dewey-Decimal and the Library of Congress Systems. These systems divide the content of geography in a crude and unrealistic fashion, separating particularly of the physical aspects of the study of the earth's surface, which are included with the natural sciences, from the human aspects which appea under history economics and other subjects. Classes 910-919 in the Dewey Decimal Classification, for example, contain no provision at all for systematic aspects of the subject. Why should a geography book be dragged from its right and proper relationships with other books of the subject, to be fitted into a makeshift and quite unreal relationship with another subject? I insist that that the major systems of classification have lagged far behind the development of the subject, which is now one of sufficient standing and importance to demand a measure of reasonable treatment from the librarian.

Such criticisms are well founded and arise from a sense of futility over the use of classification schemes in libraries. Wholesale revision of the classification of books in a library from one scheme to another without fully studying and testing it will be a costly process. It will not justify the action, cost and the wisdom of change All that can be done to satisfy the user is to modify and alter the notation of such subjects, place them at more satisfactory places, follow the change consistently and stick to one scheme of classification.

It will not only be advisable, but vecessary, for the competnt classifier to study the main principles on which other important classification schemes are constructed.

The tree-figure notation and terms of the Decimal Classfication are reproduced to help small libraries in this country to get their collections broadly and readily classified.

000 General works

010 Bibliography

020	Libary Economy
030	General Encyclopaedias
040	General Collected Essays
050	General Periodicals
060	General Learned Societies
070	Journalism, Newspapers
080	Polygraphy, Special Libraries
090	Book Rarities
100	*Philosophy*
110	Metaphysics
120	Metaphysics: Special Topics
130	Mind and Body
140	Philosophical Systems
150	Mental Faculties, Psychology
160	Logic
170	Ethics
180	Ancient Philosophers
190	Modern Philosophers
200	*Religion*
210	Natural Theology
220	Bible
230	Doctrinal Theology
240	Devotional and Practical
250	Homeletic, Pastoral, etc.

260 Church Institutions

270 Religious History

280 Christian Churches and sects

290 Non-Christian Religions

300 Sociology

310 Statistics

320 Political Science

330 Political Economy

340 Law

350 Administration

360 Associations

370 Education

380 Commerce, etc.

390 Customs, Costumes, Folklore

400 Philology

410 Comparative

420 English

430 German

440 French

450 Italian

460 Spanish

470 Latin

480 Greek

490 Minor (other) Languages

500	*Natural Science*
510	Mathematics
520	Astronomy
530	Physics
540	Chemistry
550	Geology
560	Paleontology
570	Biology
580	Botany
590	Zoology
600	*Useful Arts*
610	Medicine
620	Engineering
630	Agriculture
640	Domestic Economy
650	Communications
660	Chemical Technology
670	Manufactures
680	Mechanic Trades
690	Building
700	*Fine Arts*
710	Landscape Gardening
720	Architecture
730	Sculpture
740	Drawing, Decoration

750	Painting
760	Enraving
770	Photography
780	Music
790	Amusements
800	*Literature*
810	American
820	English
830	German
840	French
850	Italian
860	Spanish
870	Latin
880	Greek
890	Minor (other) Literatures
900	*History*
910	Geography and Description
920	Biography
930	Ancient History
940	Europe
950	Asia } Modern
960	Africa } Modern
970	North America } Modern
980	South America } Modern
990	Oceania and Polar Regions

Dewey has adopted certain mnemonic devices so that by the addition of these numbers to the class notation, it is possible to bring out the form, language, and locality covered in a book.

The Common (Form) Sub-Divisions are:

.01 Philosophy Theory

.02 Compends, Outlines, Text-books

.03 Dictionaries, Encyclopaedias

.04 Addresses, Essays, Lectures

.05 Periodicals

.06 Societies, Proceedings and Transactions

.07 Study and Teaching

.08 Polygraphy Collections

.09 History

These Common Sub-Divisions can be used with any subject and are normally adopted with a 0 preceding the number, unless otherwise indicated, *e.g.*

Hinduism = 294.5

Dictionary of Hinduism = 294.503

Religion = 200

Dictionary of Religion = 203 and not 200.03

Another mnemonic device adopted in the Decimal Classification is the Geographical Divisions. These numbers are adopted from the country divisions under History 930-999. Instructions to divide a subject are given in the manner 'Divide. like 930 or 940-999'.

913 GeograPhy Travels Description

913 Antiquities, archaeology of special countries.

913.3 of ancient countries (sub-divided like 930-939)

913.4 modern countries (sub-divided like 940-999)

914	Geography of Europe	Divided like 940-999
915	Geography of Asia	
916	Geography of North America	
917	Geography of Africa	
918	Geography of South America	
919	Geography of Oceania and Geography of Polar Regions	

The third digit 4-9 stands for continents which can further be divided, *e.g.*

914.1 Geography of Scotland

.2 Geography of England

.3 Geography of Germany

915.1 Geography of China

.2 Geography of Japan

.3 Geography of Arabia

.4 Geography of India

and so on.

Examples of other subjects divided by country will amplify the mnemonic feature.

330 Economics

330.9 History of Economics

330.95 History of Economics of Asia

330.954 History of Economics of India

The third mnemonic feature is the language Divisions. It will be found that 400 Philology and 800 Literature adopt Language as the characteristic of division.

400	*Language*	*800*	*Literature*
420	English Language	820	English Literature
430	German Language	830	German Literature
440	French Language	840	French Literature
450	Italian Language	850	Italian Literature
460	Spanish Language	860	Spanish Literature
470	Latin Language	870	Latin Literature
480	Greek Language	880	Greek Literature
490	Other Language	890	Other Literature
491	Indo-European Language	891	Indo-Europeon Literature
492	Semetic Language	892	Semetic Literature

These language numbers can be used with other classes for obtaining further sub-divisions by languages.

HOW TO USE THE CLASSIFICATION SCHEME AND APPLY IT TO BOOK DISPLAY

The preliminary step in using a clasificcation scheme is to obtain a through knowledge of the principles adopted in its construction, the schedules, the exact meaning of the terms and the index to the schedules. Even someone who has worked with Dewey's Decimal Classification for several decades will still find fresh places for subjects, which new books bring in incessantly.

When a book is to be classified, the classifier should know what the main subject of the book is, its scope and aspect, so that its most appropriate class number in the scheme is determined. In the course of his decision, the prospective use of the book should be uppermost. Fixing a correct class number for a book justifying its utmost use, is a test of intelligence: It can be called the art of classification of books.

Practical classification, to the uninitiated, simply means referring to the index of a classification scheme where the notation is equated to the terms used in the schedules, which are arranged in alphabetical order, and providing a class number which happens to strike the classifier. However ideal the index may be, this procedure will not result in placing a book where it will be most used. The readymade numbers will not be apt, as a subject has more uses and aspects than one. A relative index, like the one provided by Dewey for his Decimal Classification, is highly suggestive and not determinative. The classifier's decision to fix a class number to the subject of a book is entirely a mental process. If the classifier makes an inappropriate decision, as he is likely to do by referring to the index only, the result is that the book is placed under a wrong number, far removed from books closely related to it, or at a place where it will be quite unexpected by readers. A striking example would be a book with 'Man' as its subject, say, Rabindranath Tagore's Lectures on Man, Andhra University, 1934. In the Decimal Classification there are several places for this subject, under Philosophy 128, Religion 218, Sociology 301, Biology 575, and Physiology 612.013. Classifying with the index alone may result in placing the book on 'Man' at a relatively unnatural place. A safer course and a more logical one would be to decide a place for the subject of the book and then refer to the index to check up the decision. If the decision is wrong, the index will disclose a variety of other possible places for the book. If the main class is wrongly determined, the error is of enormous magnitude and the purpose of classification gets totally defeated. It is, therefore, best to classify by reference to the schedule first and use the index as an auxiliary.

The responsibility of the final placing of a book at a place in the classification scheme must rest with the individual classifier. An experienced and conscientious classifier is always patient in checking his decisions in respect of a new book with the previous placing of similar books in the library's shelf list or the classified catalogue or specific subject headings in the dictionary catalogue to maintain consistency which is a virtue in practical classification. If, on occasions, it is found that a new book has been better placed and the previous placing of similar books is erroneous, steps should be taken to effect the change of class number of the previous books so as to bring them under the new number. "It is better to have six books on the same subject classified together at one wrong head than to have them all scattered in different places, according to individual views. At least the six books can be found together."

Dewey has provided rules in his introduction to the Decimal Classification. W. C. Berwick Sayers has clearly explained these rules in his Indroduction to Library Classification. Merrill in his Code for Classifiers has given a clear exposition of these rules by furnishing examples of difficult books.

In practical classification, it would be safe to follow these directions:

(1) Classify a book first by its main subject, and then by form, except in Generalia and Form Classes. The subject of the book should determine its class number and the number for its form or aspect can be added to it, to arrive at a specific number for it, *e.g.* Dictionary of Chemistry. Here the main subject being chemistry, its class number by the Decimal Classification would be 540. As the subject of chemistry is presented in the form of a Dictionary, the Common Form Division number for dectionaries .03 is added to it. The resulting class number for Dictionary of Chemistry will be 540.3.

In literature, the form or manner is more important than matter. An English historical novel is, therefore, classed in 823 and not in History of England 942.

(2) Classify a book at the most specific number where it will be appropriate. Background to Hinduism should certainly go in the main class, Religion 200, but as it deals with not more than one religion,

i.e. Hinduism, its class number would be not 200 but 294.5. Sometimes the class number may be lengthy, but the classifier need not worry on this account, for specific class numbers will eliminate overlapping places for books different in nature. Sometimes it is suggested that small collections can limit the class number to three figures only, but as the library grows, the need for specific numbers for books dealing with specific subjects or topics will arise, in order to distinguish the specific from the general.

(3) If a book treats two subjects, classify under the one that is more fundamental and fuller in coverage; if the two are of the same significance, classify under the first dealt with and refer to the second, *e.g.* Banking and Business. If business is of primary importance classify under it, and make an added entry in the catalogue for banking.

(4) If a book deals with three or more subjects related to one another classify under the one that is more fully treated or under the specific class that contains all of them, *e.g.* Text-book of Heat, Light and Sound, put under Physics or under one of the subjects, if fuller in treatment than the rest.

(5) When you have made a decision likely to affect future placing, make a note of it in your schedules and index for future guidance and to ensure consistency.

(6) Classify a book where it will be most useful and where the largest number of users are likely to look for it, *e.g.* Life of Mahatma Gandhi. This book would be of great use in the section dealing with India's political strnggle for freedom and people are likely to look for it under this head. It would, therefore, be more appropriate to classify it under 323 and not under Biography 920, nor under Hisiory of India, 954.

(7) If a subject is treated geographically, classify first by subject and then by locality, *e.g.* History of Hindu Mathematics, main class is Mathematics 510 and then India number 954 is added in the manner 510.954 to arrive at the specific treatment by locality.

(8) When one subject influences another, classify under the one that is influenced, *e.g.* The Impact of British Political Traditions on the Indian Political Movement-classify under Indian political movement.

In addition to the primary rules stated, it may be helpful to observe the procedure in practical classsification.

(1) Do not classify by the title only.

(2) Go through the preface of the book to know the author's views.

(3) Make use of the appreciation on the dust jackets.

(4) Glance through the contents to find out the development of the scope of the subject dealt with.

(5) Wherever the subject is difficult or doubtful, read through the text at random.

(6) If still uncertain about the exact subject, refer the books to specialists.

(7) Never depend upon the relative index alone for the class number of a subject.

(8) Maintain consistent placing by referring to previous placing of similar books, in the catalogue or in the shelf list, where no classified arrangement of the catalogue entries is adopted.

(9) Write the class number in pencil on the verso of the title page legibly at uniform position.

(10) As a daily routine, group the books roughly by the major classes and separate the books which contain fiction.

PROVISION OF A CATALOGUE OF BOOKS

A sure and successful method of guaranteeing efficient service to the reader is to provide a simple, workable catalogue of books and other reading material in a library. A library without a good catalogue of its books is unlikely to reveal to readers the entire range of its resources, however close the classification might be and despite open access to the shelves. A catalogue is primary and indispensable to both librarian and reader for a knowledge of the books, the subjects represented, and detailed information on specific and general subjects. No library can, therefore, be an exception to the making and provision of a catalogue of its books.

Recently, from 1970 onwards libraries in the West, specially national and big city libraries, have been exploring the possibilities of replacing the traditional library catalogues by machine readable catalogues, computerised catalogues, and other varieties operated by electronic controls. No one has till now stated that these new varieties of catalogues have proved foolproof and more economical than the simple manual catalogues. Although, the quickness with which information retrieved is spectacular, the investment in capital outlay and maintenance of these automated catalogues are quite high and beyond the available resources for a vast number of libraries in Asia. Perhaps in another five to ten decades, these possibilities might be considered worthwhile. For the present, the card catalogue seems to be the best choice for most of them, as it is capable of satisfying the readers in their approach for books or information.

Cataloguing is an art and based on rules. Specially trained personnel should be put in charge of the work of cataloguing. It is of utmost importance that a decision is taken on the form, structure and code of rules to be adopted and the fullness of details to be incorporated in a catalogue entry. When these preliminaries are settled, every book is catalogued under all possible headings, authors, titles, subjects etc., under which it is likely to be asked for by readers. The internal form of a catalogue may be alphabetical or classified. Irrespective of the form of catalogue adopted, it should answer fully and precisely the following questions which readers usually ask:

(1) Where can a particular work be located?

(2) What works are there in the library *(a)* by a given author *(b)* on a given subject and *(c)* by a given title? Sometimes

readers make enquiries in respect of series, editors, translators, etc. of books. The catalogue should, therefore, be made with a view to furnishing the answers to all possible enquiries of readers.

This decision will need consideration of the kinds of entries to be made, how to make them, and with what fullness and effect.

Entries in a catalogue are of two kinds: *(1)* Main entry and *(2)* Seconday entry or added entry.

The main entry is made for books, following a particular code of catalogue rules, generally under the name of its author, individual or corporate. But when the name of the author remains unknown, as in anonymous works, it is made under the best-known from of title of the book to be catalogued. Besides, there are serial publications, annuals, periodicals, weeklies, fortnightlies, monthlies, and quarterlies, whose main entry according to the rules will be made under their titles. The arrangement of the entries in an alphabetical order or classified order does not affect the style and fullness of author headings. The term 'author' is used broadly to indicate the person or body responsible for a work. To distinguish between individual authors and bodies which act in a responsible capacity as authors (Governments, associations, societies, and institutions) the term 'author' is used for the former and 'Corporate author' for the latter. In comparison with other fadors about a book, *e.g.*, the subject and title, the fact of author ship is more definite. The author's name is generally found on the title pages of books by their authors' names. For this reason, not only library catalogues but publishers' trade catalogues and bibliographies make the main entry for books under the authors' names. Variant forms of an author's name, when met, can be reduced to one consistent form for adoption in the catalogue, by adherence to rules in a catalogue code governing the entries of personal authors and other, collaborators.

The parts of a main entry are: *(1)* The Heading for the Author; *(2)* the Title or its extract; *(3)* the Imprint; *(4)* the Collation; *(5)* the

Series Note; *(6)* the Contents and *(7)* the Notes or Annotation. The tracings of added entries—indicated on the main entry are not considered as its parts, as they are meant for the use of the staff and do not affect the readers' use of the catalogue entry. Further, they are given on the catalogue entry either at the bottom of the card or on its reverse.

The following illustration of main entries *(1)* for personal author, *(2)* for corporate author, *(3)* for a classic under title, and *(4)* a periodical under title will clearly indicate the particulars and their style of presentation,

McColvin, L.R.

The Chance to read; public
libraries in the world today.
London, Phoenix, 1956.
284 p., front., illus., 22cm
(Personal author-Main entry)

The Library Association, London

Annual Report.
Library has
1956
(Corporate author-Main entry)

Mahabharata

The Great Indian epic or
the story of Pandavas and Kaura vas.
(Title as Main entry)

The Indian Geographical Journal

Madras, Indian Geographical
Society
Qly.
(Title of a periodical as Main entry)

Secondary entries are added entries of the book, besides the main entry. The value of the catalogue to the readers is as much dependent on these entries as on the main entry. Without the provision of the added entries for titles of books, collaborators joint authors, translator, editor, compiler, and the name of subject or subjects dealt with in the book, the catalogue will only be partiaHy helpful to the users in so far as it can yield information on the authors and their works. When the authors' names are not exactly known or unknown to the user, he will find the catalogue useless for locating a desired book or others biblographic information.

In the provision and maintenance of a catalogue service to the readers, the added entries create a problem, because of their number and growth. When one main entry is made for an author of the book, two or more added entries will have to be made for the same book, if full coverage of the readers' approach to the book is to be guaranteed. There will be little used added entries. These added entries are mainly responsible for increasing the cost of cataloguing. The card stock, the duplication machinery, and the clerical services involved in the making of added entries are factors in assessment of cataloguing costs. It is, therefore, necessary to judge with reasonable imagination the need and number of these added entries. Unwanted added entries are a luxury and waste and tend to make the catalogue irritatingly complex. It will be necessary to take into account the character and scope of each book in determining the number and kinds of added entries. Fiction will generally need title .entries and no subject entries; but for some non-fiction books, the title entries can safely be omitted when the subject heading chosen and the title of the book have a common terminology. It is, therefore, advisable to conclude that subject entries are necessary for almost all non-fiction books.

There are other added entries of names of persons as translators, editors, compilers, joint authors and the name of the series of which the book may be a volume and these entries are common to works of both fiction and non-fiction. Added entries under the names of these persons are to be made, when they are well known, as authors of their own works, and when entries under their names already are made and filed in the library's catalogue. It is advisable to omit entries for them, when no reader is likely to call for the books under their names. In short, the decision to make some or all added entries will depend on the standards adopted and the convenience of the public, for whom the catalogue is mainly intended.

Illustrations of these added entries provided below show their fullness and style.

Kaplan, Abraham. jt. auth.

Lasswell, H.D. and Kaplan, Abraham.
Power and Society, London,
Routledge and Paul, 1952.
3v.
(Jt. author—Added entry for two authors.)

Durden, J. V. jt. auth.

Field, Mary and others.
See how they grow: botany
through the cinema by Mary Field,
J.V. Durden and F. Percy Smith
Harmandsworth, Pengain books, 1952
(Jt. author—Added entry for three authors.)

White, P. D. jt. auth.

Graybiel, Ashton and others
Electrocardiography in practice; 3rd ed.
Philadelphia, Saunders, 1952.
(Jt. author—Added entry for more than three authors.)

Hurlbutt CC.S. ed.

Dana, J.D.
Manual of mineralogy; 16th ed.
N.Y., Whiley, 1952.
(Editor Added entry)

Redman, Alvin. Comp.

Wilde, Oscar.
The Epigrams, an anthology.
Lond.,
(Complier Added entry.)

Hackforth, R. tr.

Plato
Phaedrus. Cambridge University
Press, 1952
(Translator Added entry.)

Phaedrus. 1952.

Plato
(Title added entry)

Newnaturalist series.

599.0942 21 Matthews, L.H. British mammals, 1952.
M 43
551.5 22 Manley, Gordon. Climate and the British Scene.
M 27 1952.
(Series added entry)

ETHICS

Broad, C.D.
Ethics and the history of philosophy.
London, Routledge, 1952.
(Subject added entry)

MORAL PHILOSOPHY, See

ETHICS
(Reference entry)

The reference entry is made for synonymous subject headings in which the heading referred from is not used as a subject heading for books on that subject, but the heading referred to is consistently adopted in the catalogue. As readers are likely to look for books under the unused synonym, a reference to the heading used is necessary. The reference entries may be made from name to name and title to title, if alternative forms are met with.

Descriptive cataloguing is the term used for description of books and their identification by means of catalogue entries which contain relevant particulars about the books, with a view to making them easily accessible to the users. "The objectives of descriptive cataloguing are: *(1)* to state the significant features of an item with the purpose of distinguishing it from other items and describing its scope, contents and bibliographic relations to other items, *(2)* to present these data in an entry which can be integrated with the entries for other items in the catalogue and which will respond best to the interest of most users of the catalogue." The degree of minuteness of detail on a book in the catalogue entry will depend on the size of the library, its resources and its nature, general or special. Two dependable guides to descriptive cataloguing are the AACR and the L.C. Rules for Descriptive Cataloguing.

"*Subject Cataloguing,* on the other hand, involves analysis of the subject content of the book and the expression of that content in terms of appropriate classification numbers for arrangement and shelving purposes, and of suitable subject headings to provide for an alphabetic or Other approach through the library's catalogue."

Although the description of a book on the catalogue entry can indicate the subject content of the book as well as its classification number to some extent, a complete and full revelation of the contents of books cannot be achieved in several cases until one or more subject entries with appropriate subject headings are provided for them, *e.g.*

332.43 Lutz, F. A.

L 97 International monetary mechanisms, the Keynes and White proposals. Princeton University, 1943,

1. Coinage, International. *2.* Money. *3.* Currency Question.

It will be seen that in the above example, two more subject entries, under 332.42 and 332.5, will be necessary in order to provide effective accessibility to the subject content of the book as its location under 332.43 alone fails to achieve full coverage of the subjects.

Controversy over the provision and performance of subject headings is a long-standing one. Eminent librarians like Bliss and Ranganathan are divided in their views. Bliss holds the view that "Subject headings are more complete, more inclusive more expressive for many general concepts, more capable of minute and meaningful sub-division in many cases, and more plastic in showing inter-relationships than are any of the classification systems presently known." Classification and subject headings are complementary to each other.

On the other hand, Ranganathan advocates with strong conviction that the subject headings used in the alphabetic subject catalogues, or in the dictionary catalogues as well, have proved so completely ineffective and illogical that there is little justification for continuing the subject heading operations in cataloguing. A well-developed and synthetic scheme of classification can offer as many class numbers as the subjects contained in the book, in addition to the specific class number which may well replace the subject headings in alphabetic order. A unit catalogue card, with the class number of the subsidiary subjects, and a brief description of the book and a reference to the specific class in which the book is actually located can not only replace the alphabetic subject entries, which are filed only in the order of the alphabet, but can provide a convenient, compact and orderly grouping of the subject materials.

Subject cataloguing requires sufficient knowledge of the subject of the book, if it is to be adequately and appropriately analysed and placed under specific terms used as subject headings. As it is almost impossible to obtain the advice of experts and specialists in the subject field by all libraries and at all times, cataloguers themselves, who have a background study of the humanities and sciences, generally perform this function, which is, by and large, acceptable to expert opinion.

The choice of subject headings and the rules governing them have been discussed by C. A. Cutter and others. One common conclusion arrived at is the necessity of adopting specific subject headings and liberal references to them. In order to maintain consistency in the style and terminology of the subject headings, standard lists of subject headings. the A. L. A. List, the L. C. List, and Sears' List may be used. It should be noted that on some occasions appropriate terms and forms for new concepts are not found in them. Libraries will, therefore, have to make their own headings consistently and specifically and record them in authority files or in the official copy of the list of headings for future guidance and adoption. Another consideration in the making of these headings is whether popular or scientific terminology should be adopted for expressing the subjects. A decision on this point will be influenced by the currency of the term used. Obsolete terms should be avoided in the headings.

In order to establish the link between related and subordinate subjects, a network of 'See' and 'See' also' cross references will be necessary in the list of subject headings and in the subject catalogues. This is the only way to achieve the syndetic quality in the alphabetic subject catalogues. But too lavish provision of these cross references tends to become irksome to users and detrimental to the effectiveness of the catalogue. It is likely to add to the cost of cataloguing, which is considered too high by many library administrators and disproportionate to the catalogues' utility to readers.

All groups, scholars and specialists, cataloguers and documentalists, have been closely watching and investigating the new techniques in the production of the subject catalogues. Classification schemes recently adopted for coding subjects or terms in the punched card systems have led to vigorous thinking as to what are the essentials for subject catalogues. It will, therefore, be some time before definite decisions on the changing techniques and patterns of the subject catalogues can be arrived at. But it must be admitted that a total withdrawal of the subject catalogue from library operations will leave a gap which can at best be only partially covered by comprehensive classification schemes, mechanical devices, open access and classified catalogues.

KINDS OF CATALOGUES

There are a vairiety of catalogues in use in libraries: *(1)* the Author Catalogue, *(2)* the Name Catalogue, *(3)* the Alphabetic Subject Catalogue, *(4)* the Title Catalogue, *(5)* the Classed or Classified Catalogue, *(6)* the Alphabetic Classed Catalogue and *(7)* the Dictionary Catalogue.

(1) The Author Catalogue is the simplest and perhaps the oldest form of catalogue, which is fundamental to all other forms. It contains the main entries under the names of the authors of books, arranged alphabetically. The body of the author entry normally indicates the title of the book, its imprint and collation. The title in this context will include the names of other collaborators with the author, illustrator, commentator, compiler, etc. Entries under the name of these collaborators are made as added entries and filed in one alphabetical sequence. This kind of catalogue has a supreme value because it can bring together all the works of a person under his name irrespective of his being an original writer or a collaborator. When readers do not remember the exact titles of books or the specific subject dealt in it and remember the names of authors, this form of catalogue alone can yield the required information, as all the works of the writer in the library can be found at one place in the catalogue, although each one of them may be on different subjects and with distinct titles. Voluminous authors, like Bertrand Russell or H. G. Wells, are appropriate examples. In fiction catalogues, author entries are specially helpful, as otherwise the individual titles would

have to be looked for under various letters of the alphabet, *e.g.* Oliver Twist, A Tale of Two Cities, The Pickwick Papers and David Copper field of Charles Dickens. In the author entry system all these works could be found under Dickens, Charles. It will be demonstrated subsequently that an Author Catalogue or Author Index is indispensable to the effective use of a Classified Catalogue.

The uses of the Author Catalogue are of course, limited. Such a catalogue cannot yield information on title or subjects. This limitation can be reduced by providing a subject index, which can refer to authors and class numbers.

(2) The Name Catalogue is an extended form of the author catalogue, in which the names of persons as subjects of books, chiefly in autobiographies, biographies, criticisms, diaries, memoirs, etc., are also provided as entries. When these entries of personal names as subjects are arranged with the author entries, it is called a name catalogue. "The combination of author and subject limited to the person is of certain value as under one alphabet and under one style of heading, information about a person as author and as subject could be found. It is convenient to have in sequential array the works by, and about or on, an author. This form of catalogue is specially valuable for collections of literature, personal memoirs and autobiographies. The distinction between the person as author heading and the same person as subject is maintained by adopting different typographic disposition of the heading or using different coloured ink."

Person as author	Dickens, Charles. David Copperfield. Dickens, Charles. Oliver Twist. Dickens, Charles. The Pickwick Papers. Dickens, Charles. A Tale of Two Cities.
Person as subject	DICKENS, CHARLES. *A Critical Study* by G. R. Gissing. DICKENS, CHARLES. *The Soul of Dickens* by W. W. Crotch.

(3) The Alphabetic Subject Catalogue contains alphabetical entries of books in a collection under the name of the specific subject of a book as the heading. The body of the subject entry contains the complete record of a book in the same form and fullness as in its main entry. Several books on the same subject having a common form and style of subject heading will come together under one alphabet and will, therefore, come together in the catalogue. It gives the quickest service to users if they want to find material on a specific subject. If the users require related material, they are directed by cross references, "See also", to other headings which will be found under their own alphabets. The provision of "See also" references is not only incomplete but is exasperating to readers who have to search for books from place to place in the catalogue. This kind of catalogue will be adapted to general (Public) libraries, where the readers do not ordinarily pursue course of research of systematic, study. But when the liblary has a classified catalogue, this alphabetic subject catalogue will be an excellent and indispensable auxiliary.

(4) The Title Catalogue contains the entries of books under their titles which are arranged in alphabetical order. The body of the entry will indicate the name of the author, in the same fullness as in the author entry. The titles of books by the same author get separated under different alphabets, *e.g.*

David Copperfield, 1914
Dickens, Charles.
Hamlet, the Tragedy of, 1920
Shakespeare, William.
A Tale of Two Cities, 1928
Dickens, Charles.

This form of catalogue is intended to provide information on specific titles. In the field of fiction, this kind of catalogue is specially valuable, as more often the approach of the reader is by specific titles of books. Sometimes the title entries are not made for the classed books, because the titles are not catching and they are not likely to be asked for by titles by the readers. It will not, therefore, represent a complete record of all books in the library. Economics in cataloguing suggest the omission of entries for titles of books, which begin with words like Introduction to, Theory of, Manual of, Text book of, as it is very unlikely that these terms will be chosen by the readers in their search for subject books which will be looked for under their specific subjects as headings.

(5) The Classed or Classified Catalogue, as its name suggests, consists of entries of books in a collection, which are classified according to a given scheme of classification of books. Just as the class number determines the position of the books on the shelves, the same class number fixes the place of the entry in the classified catalogue. As improved and satisfactory schemes of book classification came to be adopted in libraries, together with open access to books, the classified catalogue gained popularity over other forms. The order of subjects in the classification scheme followed in a library governs the sequence of entries. Little attention is given to the alphabetical order of the headings of main entries. The striking superiority of the classified catalogue is that the entries closely related are brought together in a logical manner. The degree of soundness of this form of catalogue depends on the effectiveness of the process and on the characteristics chosen for division of subjects in the classification scheme. The display of entries in the classified catalogue offers to the user a complete range of material in a convenient order,. in which every specific subject is preceded by a more general one and followed by a more specific subject; the order is from the general to the specific subject, *e.g.*

Classified order of entries based on
Dewey's Decimal Classification:

500 SCIENCES

502 Hogben, Lancelot,
Science, for the Citizen 1938.

509 Dampier, W. C.
A History of Science, 1949.

510 MATHEMATICS

510.9 Bell, E.T.
Men of Mathematics 1937

510.9 Jeans, James,
The Growth of Physical Sciences 1947.
Book at 530.9

530 PHYSICS

530.1 Einstein, Albert and Leopold, Infeld,
The Evolution of Physics, 1938.

530.9 Jeans, James
The Growth of Physical Science. 1947.

It will be seen that in addition to the main entries under the specific (subject) class number of a book, there are added entries for subsidiary subjects dealt within the book under their own appropriate class numbers, *e.g.* Jeans, James. The Growth of the Physical Science is placed under 530.9 as main entry and under 510.9 as subsidiary entry, as the book also deals with the history of mathematics from Babylon to nuclear fission. The direction to find the book under its main entry under 530.9 is provided on the subsidiary entry. The purpose of such added class (subject) entries is to achieve full coverage of representation of every important subject treated in a book. As many added (subject) class entries as there are subjects in a book can be made. The problem of selection of subject headings, which is indispensable in a dictionary catalogue, or alphabetic subject catalogue is totally absent in this procedure.

The classified catalogue fails to answer the questions: *(1)* What books are there by a given author in the collection? *(2)* is there particular title of an author in the holdings? and *(3)* is there a book on a given subject? Unless the specific class number under which the book is placed and the entry is made is known, the users will find this form of a catalogue useless and unworkable, In order to get over this shortcoming, a subject index (an alphabetical list of subjects and synonyms covered by the books in the library, giving the notation against each), should be provided. It takes the form of a relative index, the terms limited to the subjects of books in the library. When once a subject index entry is made it will not be necessary to repeat it with the addition of new books on the same subject, *e.g.*

Electricity	537
Heat	536
Magnetism	538
Mathematics	510
History	510.9
Physics	530
Science	500
History	509

Another index, the Author Index, is equally necessary in order to enable readers to get at the work or works of an author. The author catalogue and the name catalogue may be used for this purpose. An author index entry will include the author's name, followed by the brief title of his work and date and lastly the notation, *e.g.*

Bell, E. T., Men of Mathematics, 1937	510.9
Dampier, W. C., History of Science, 1949	509
Emstein, Albert, Evolution of Physics, 1938	530.1
Hogben, Lancelot, Science for the Citizen, 1938	502
Jeans, James, Growth of the Physical Science, 1947	530.9

Unless these index entries are properly alphabetised and kept up to date the effective use of the main classified catalogue cannot be guaranteed. Sometimes it is alleged that the classified catalogue is too technical to be easily understood by the public. It is not as simple as the alphabetic types. This contention is more imaginary than real. Many readers, specially informed and with definite ideas of that reading material would suit them go straight to the open shelves where books are arranged by the classification scheme and find their way. The guides provided speed up the location of the desired books. When they could be at ease with a classified arrangement of books after a system of classification, there is no reason to suppose that they will fail to follow a similar arrangement of entries in the catalogue. When certain readers, express some difficulty in handling the classified catalologue, alphabetical author and subject indexes will certainly come to their rescue. Simple methods of educating the public on the classification system adopted in a library for the arrangement of the books and their entries in the classified catalogue will help in proper understanding and appreciation of the classified structure of the catalogue.

The library staff find the classified catalogue, of more help to readers when requests for books on subjects are handled. A select bibliography of books in a library on a subject, *e.g.* differential equations, can be prepared almost immediately by this form of catalogue, while in a dictionary catalogue it is not possible to be exhaustive. Periodical subject lists issued by libraries depend on the classified arrangement of the entries. The stock position of a given subject can also be revealed by this form of catalogue, as the entries are grouped by class number, both under major and specific classes.

The American libraries have displayed less liking for this classified type of catalogue. This may be due to lack of good systems of classification and deep-rooted tradition of the dictionary catalogue rendered firm in library practice by Cutter's Rules for a Dictionary Catalogue and the A.L.A. Catalogue Rules, which paid little attention to subject cataloguing. "In few American libraries where classified catalogues are maintained, the actual catalog is more complex, since multiple entries for the same title are made to provide for as thorough subject coverage as is necessary and feasible. Typically, the arrangement is by classification number, not by a subject designation, so that instead of having many titles listed under a few broad subjects, relatively few titles are found listed under the minute class number. In such a catalog the alphabetic subject index becomes of first importance, and in itself resembles a list, of subject headings similar to those found in a typical alphabetical subject catalogue as descrided below."

(6) The Alphabetic Classed Catalogue, which has recently been introduced in some American libraries as an altenative form of the classified catalogue and an improvement over the alphabetic subject catalogue, follows an alphabetical order of arrangement of large classes and systematic or classified order for sub-classes and specific subjects under them. Instead of adopting a few main classes as in the classification scheme, a larger number of main classes are employed as a convenient expedient. These are arranged in alphabetical order, while subjects following under each one of these extended main classes follow the order of the classification scheme. For example, Physics can be split up into and will have in addition the following large classes arranged in alphabetical order: Dynamics, Electricity, Fluids, Gases, Heat, Light, Magnetism, Mechanics, Molecular Physics and Static. The topics under each one will be arranged as in the scheme of classification *e.g.*

Heat	536
Theory, Nature	.1
Communication	.2
Action of bodies on heat	.3
Effects Action of heat on bodies	.4
Temperature	.5
Calorimetry	.6
Thermodynamics	.7
Applications	.8
Tables Problems Questions	.9

It is presumed to combine the advantages of the classified and alphabetical order. But, in actual performance, it stands in need of an alphabetical subject index as much as the classified catalogue. Users, when they do not know under what major class a specific subject and material on that subject can be found, cannot get at the information, except through the subject index. This form of catalogue has failed to gain currency in British and Indian library practice.

(7) The Dictionary Catalogue consists of entries of authors, titles and subjects, other added entries, and cross references, arranged in one single alphabetical sequence, *e.g.*

COINAGE, INTERNATIONAL.

CURRENCY QUESTION.

Dickens, Charles.

DREAMS.

ECONOMICS.

Enders, J. F. jt. auth.

FREEMASONS-RITUALS.

GOLD.

Lutz, F. A.

POLITICAL ECONOMY, see ECONOMICS.

Scott, Walter.

SULPHUR.

Tale of Two Cities.

In libraries, where the classified catalogue is in use, entries for fiction, both author and title, are usually separated from it and maintained as a separate catalogue, because fiction will not influence the strength or weakness of the non-fiction books. A similar consideration can prevail in case of the dictionary catalogue so that by separating entries for fiction, the load on the dictionary catalogue can be reduced without seriously affecting its usefulness. The only argument against the separation of fiction entries from the dictionary catalogue is that authors of both fiction and non-fiction works will have to be referred to in both catalogues.

This form of catalogue has been named the dictionary catalogue, because it follows the alphabetical order of the dictionary in arranging its entries. It is also claimed that it is as simple as a dictionary and can be used by anyone who knows the alphabet. The claim to simplicity must be qualified, for the entries in a dictionary catalogue are not homogeneous as the vocabulary of a language. There are entries for authors, titles, subjects, other added entries, and reference entries, each one set up in different style and typographic disposition. A good many of the readers have been found to remark that there is no order and logic in the dictionary catalogue on account of this mixture of different types of entries. But its popularity in the public libraries, specially in the United States, is unrivalled even to this day. The average reader using the dictionary catalogue can get the information on an author or title or specific subject in a direct manner. The rule of adopting the specific subject headings for subject entries of books can be called both its strength and weakness. For example, if one desires to know what material is available in the libraries on 'HORSES', he should look for the term under its alphabet. All the books in the library's holdings will be found under the heading 'HORSES'. It will not be necessary for the reader to possess the knowledge that 'HORSES' is a part of 'ZOOLOGY' or of 'DOMESTIC ANIMALS' or of 'LIVESTOCK' or of 'FARM ANIMALS'. But it does not mean that 'HORSES' as a subject is left unrelated to the other subjects of which it forms an integral part. The specific subject is linked up with the general and co-ordinate subjects by providing 'See also' references, *e.g.* DOMESTIC ANIMALS, see also HORSES; HORSES, see also ARABIAN HORSES, ENGLISH HORSES, etc. The disadvantage of scattering away the specific subjects under different alphabets is reduced by a provision of liberal cross references.

This method of specific entry is best adapted for finding specific information, while the entire material available in the library on a subject can be had only after continued and patient search from place to place as directed by the 'See also' references. As the books are arranged in the order of the classification scheme, it is considered an advantage if the catalogue entries for books are filed in an alphabetic order, which will supprement the classified order. Besides, this form of catalogue will not depend on the classification scheme for its success or otherwise in its working and usefulness. It is independent of the classification system, but dependent on the exhaustive qualities of the list of subject headings used for the choice of the headings themselves.

EXTERNAL FORMS OF CATALOGUES

Library catalogues may be handwritten, typewritten or printed. Early forms were bound registers with entries for books written on their pages, which gave place to printed, page catalogus, which remained quite popular till recent times. Because the page catalogue lacks flexibility in incorporating more entries appropriately for books added to a library from time to time, librarians have come to a common conclusion that unit cards 5" × 3" for catalogue entries, filed in drawers and housed in cabinets are better suited to keep pace with the growth in book stock of libraries, although certain minor defects are obvious in the card catalogue system. The modern practice is to maintain the library catalogue in card form. In order to fulfil the ordinary and day-to-day use of a catalogue, which is to help readers in finding the location of desired books on the shelves, the catalogue cards are provided with call numbers of books at a specified place on them. The description of books helps the readers to identify and choose the material. When the cards are made, they are compared, reviewed and filed in the drawers, according to rules for filing which may be alphabetical or classified.

The catalogue cards stand upright in the drawer, which has usually a capacity to hold 1,500 to 1:800 cards. These drawers are fitted with a simple mechanism, a self-locking metal rod with a groove cut at the fore end in which the sliding metal plate falls of its own weight through the slit and catches the rod from being pulled out. The rod passes through the punched holes at the bottom of the cards and holds them securely and in order. The drawer is secured in the cabinet by a gravity catch fixed to the side of the drawer hole in the cabinet, which falls into a groove cut on the side panel o£ the drawer at the end. The cabinet can be made of wood or steel. It is placed on a base at a convenient height 3' or 3'6" above the floor. Cabinets of different sizes and shapes can be had according to the needs.

The card catalogue displayed in this manner, although not portable, will be up to date, capable of endless expansion, and provide for easy withdrawal of entries.

It is essential that instructions to readers on its use accompany the catalogue.

GUIDE TO READERS IN THE USE OF THE CATALOGUE DICTIONARY CATALOGUE

The card catalogue is provided for the use of the readers in quickly finding books or information on books.

(1) The catalogue is modelled after the dictionary principle. All the entries are arranged in one alphabetical sequence.

(2) Every book in the library is entered under the name of its author, as well as under its subject or subjects.

(3) If persons other than the author have collaborated with the author in the capacity of joint authors, translators, editors, commentators, etc., additional entries are made under their names.

(4). If a book belongs to a well-known series, entry is made under the name of the series which will show other books in the series in the library stock.

(5) In case of fiction, title entries are usually made, but for non-fiction, title entries are made for striking titles only.

(6) In choosing subject headings, attention is paid to all possible forms of synonyms and one which is best known is chosen, while references from other alternatives are provided in order that the readers do not miss the book in whatever form of subject they may look up.

A reader knowing the name of an author of a work will look for the book under the surname of the author, as Milton, John, as author heading. The next line of the author entry contains the name of the work with its imprint and collation, *e.g.*

821.47		Milton, John
p		Paradise Lost. Lond., Mascmillan, 1908 183 p.

Another person who expects the book under the title will look up under the title heading, *e.g.*

821.47		Paradise Lost. 1908
P		Milton, John.

As this is a book of poetry, no subject entry is made, but a book like Discovery of India by Jawaharlal Nehru will need a subject entry, in addition to author and title entries. It is entered under its specific subject INDIA-HISTORY, MODERN and will be found under the appropriate alphabet. Readers should look for histories of countries, or localities under name of country and sub-division History, after it.

CLASSIFIED CATALOGUE

This catalogue is essentially a subject catalogue, in which entries are arranged in systematic order. The system is the same as for the arrangement of books on the shelves. Here it is the Decimal classification scheme by which the cards are arranged.

Every book is provided a main entry under the specific class (notation) representing the subject of the book. In addition, subsidiary subject entries are provided for secondary subjects of the book, *e.g.* Handbook of Electricity and Magnetism will be found under 537 and 538. As the book can be shelved at only one place, 537, a subsidiary entry for the other subject under 538 is provided in order to fully bring out the subject matter to the readers' notice. The direction to the exact location of the book is given on all subsidiary entries, *e.g.* 538 Handbook of Electricity and Magnetism Book at 537. This method brings together all related material in a logical and compact group.

In order to provide quick and direct reference to authors, and subjects, alphabetical index entries are provided, *e.g.*

Author Index	Starling:	*Electricity.*	537
	Strong :	*Magnetism.*	538
	Thilly :	*Philosophy.*	199
Subject Index	Electricity	537	
	Heat	536	
	Magnetism	538	
	Philosophy	100	

A brief synopsis of the book classification scheme showing the layout and order of the Main classes, Common Form divisions and Geographical divisions and other features of the scheme, to serve as a readymade explanation of the classified catalogue, can be displayed near the catalogue.

Maintenance of the Catalogue

The catalogue of a library influences to some extent the choice of a book by the reader, helps its location, enables the staff to perform their services to the public quickly and efficiently, serves as a guide and a first aid to the reference assistant and provides the acquisitions and order department with information on the library's resources. All the functions in a library are partly dependent on the catalogue for their successful performance. If is, therefore, very essential that the catalogue is maintained up to date and carefully revised from time to time to rectify any errors or inconsistent entries, headings, etc.

The activities connected with the catalogue maintenance are: "*(1)* the final preparation of cards for the catalogue, including minor revisions to printed catalogue cards, and the addition of call number and added entry headings to both printed and locally produced unit catalogue cards; *(2)* the reproduction of unit catalogue cards in sufficient quantity to meet the requirement$ of the library's catalog system; *(3)* filing; *(4)* routine cataloguing of materials as necessary; *(5)* editorial work on the catalogue to correct filing errors, reconcile differences in headings, correct or augment the reference structure, replace worn or soiled cards, and introduce new guide cards and labels as needed; *(6)* catalogue expansion and shifting as required; and *(7)* subject heading control and revision."

Economics in Cataloguing

Adoption of a common code of catalogue rules, the standard unit card 5" × 3" and agreed specification for descriptive cataloguing, has produced some measure of co-operation among libraries. Centralised cataloguing, in which a single agency catalogues for a group of libraries which may belong to the library system of a locality or to libraries in an extensive area following identical rules and procedures of cataloguing, has been tried with a view to bringing down cataloguing costs. A well-organised centralised cataloguing agency, such as the L.C. Card Division and the B.N.B. Card Distribution service, provides *(1)* a strong collection of expensive cataloguing reference materials at one place, *(2)* expert cataloguers, and *(3)* uniformity of catalogue entries for similar books. It saves the time of the cataloguing staff and repetitive functions in individual libraries. It may ultimately lead to the formation of Union Catalogues. These assumptions on economies in cataloguing have always appeared theoretical, for they have not provided full satisfaction to the readers using the library. The administrator and, in the background, the inquiring reader and the taxpayer wants the job done in the shortest possible time. . .. Until "Cataloguing-in-source" has become a reality most libraries, which serve over 15,000 population and which have a trained cataloguer, can handle their own cataloguing *(a)* economically, *(b)* with new books reaching reader shelves within a few days of publishers' release dates, *(c)* with sufficient detail, accuracy and good judgment as to author, class number and subject headings to produce an efficient catalogue. There is nothing magical about a printed card. The elaborate detail on L. C. Cards is of value in only a few large scholarly libraries where bibliographical completeness is looked for. A neatly typed card, produced in the library, without the paperwork of sending for, receiving, filing and finding printed cards may be the solution for many libraries which are now in the 1960's withholding books from prospective readers for weeks or months just to assure more perfect or more beautifully turned out cards than are essential.

Besides the foregoing steps, meaures like simplified and selective cataloguing are also open for adoption. Simplified cataloguing aims at reducing details in the entry to the minimum, while selective cataloguing aims at preventing secondary or less-used reading material from being catalogued at all. Both aim at a reduction of cataloguing expenses.

❐

5

Librarianship and Information Centre

Managers in public libraries and libraries attached to tertiary institutions are faced with the ethical issues and problems of providing free information services with dwindling resources where greater emphasis is being placed by government upon self-supporting or 'user pays' principles. Added to this is government pressure for greater financial accountability and for stakeholders to become increasingly more active in the operations of libraries and information centres.

Demands for lower personal taxation and increased privatization of many services influence how libraries and information centres are funded, structured and managed. Some types of library services will certainly be charged for in the future and methods of evaluating these and their relationships to the remaining 'free' services will need to be determined. In an effect to curtail expenditure it may not be easy to abandon services or levy charges. There may be enormous exit barriers to some services both on a social and economic scale. Library and information centre managers may find themselves locked into many more programmes than they can afford. They will therefore need skills in polities lobbying and negotiating in order to secure the necessary resources in a competitive environment. Strategic planning and marketing skills will be aimed.

A low coverage of too large a client market is inferior to a good quality service for a focussed market; and no library should be in the business of duplicating the services of other agencies.

Changes are occurring in the way in which libraries are evaluated. In the past, libraries have often been evaluated solely from a financial or economic perspective; that is, whether or not they have met their budgetary targets. Today there is increased emphasis on measuring performance; that usually means efficiency and effectiveness. Meeting efficiency critem involves the manager in value analysis; that is, ensuring that the optimum level of service is provided for the lowest possible cost something that all managers should be able to do. However, the ability to meet the effectiveness criteria is not always as easy to demonstrate, since invariably the interests of stakeholder groups are not stable. Indeed, many have individual needs which they wish to be met, and which often defeat the concepts of economies. of scale and efficiency.

Like most other organizations, libraries and information centres should have a corporate social responsibility, which involves satisfying the needs of the employees, public and community. This leads to the need for managers to integrate social objectives with the 'business' objectives in order to meet self-actualization and environmental demands. One of the methods by which this can be achieved is by worker participation in management.

Employees are increasingly becoming involved in corporate governance, and this involvement places greater emphasis on communication within the organization and the information-disseminating role of the manager so that employees are fully informed of the issues at stake. Increased importance is being placed upon the quality of life. For libraries and information is being placed manifested in the quality of working life for the organization's employees and a higher standard of living reflected in changed consumer demand patterns for library services. New values and structures are evident in society, which will not only be reflected in the demand for new resources but also in the work attitudes of staff and the corporate culture of the organization to which the library belongs. Stakeholders are those persons who take an interest in the library, or who have the capacity to influence its ability to achieve its objectives. Examples of stakeholders for a special library operating in the private sector are unions, activities such as environmental, health and safety groups, shareholders or owners, political, groups, suppliers, other libraries or information centres, employees .and associations for librarians of information personnel.

Any of these stakeholders can have an effect upon the organization's direction by impeding or facilitating the accomplishment of the library's goals. Some have more effect than others, but the library or information centre manager cannot afford to ignore any of them, and all need to be managed. This requires the library or information centre manager to identify who they are, their levels of influence and how each may politically, socially or economically affect the library's operations functions and future plans. These actions form part of an environmental analysis or situation audit. It is also important that the library or information centre manager ensures that sufficient resources are allocated to deal with them. Good public relations with all stakeholders is a necessary part of marketing the library.

Over the past 10 years, libraries and information centres have been greatly affected changes in information technology, and the rate of change is still accelerating in this area. The introduction of the various changes in work patterns, demands for new skills, job retraining schemes and in some cases, a reclassification of positions. Networking facilities have already caused managers to make new policies on interlibrary lending and reciprocal borrowing arrangements whilst it is anticipated that aspects of service delivery will change in the near future. Library and information centre managers need to be aware of the penetration levels and rates of the new technologies in order to measure their effect on the delivery of services and operations of the library or information centre. Such environments require the library or information centre manager to have the ability to think quickly with an holistic Crientation and perspective; to be politically sensitive yet entrepreneurial and risk-taking and to focus upon the process of planning and decision making.

Strategic management provides a comprehensive approach to managing the impact of a dynamic environment upon the psychological sociological political and other subsystems which can be found in a complex organization. In so doing it considers the organization's functional and managerial ability to position itself to cope with a changing environment. The strategic approach recognizes that an organization's long-term performance is affected by its strategic culture, managerial capability logistic capability and capacity, its technological thrust and its financial resources. These five features are critical to the organization's success. It losses any of these or they fall below a certain level or capacity the organization will cease to operate efficiently. As a result it may lose its strategic position in the external environment and eventually disappear. Strategic management uses a planning approach, and as such requires the sanction and involvement of top management. Top management is also required to provide the knowledge and foresight to determine both the activities of the external environment, and the organization. However, the planning process should also be a democratic people-interactive process. Whilst not everyone can be the planner, everyone should be involved to some extent in the top-down process. In planning for survival and success in a dynamic environment everything must be considered. The internal and external environment of the organization is studied, the results being used to provide input into the situation audit which evaluates the present situation.

It may comprise of a strategic four-factor analysis, critical success factors, a SWOT (Strengths, weaknesses, opportunities threats) analysis or an organization capability profile. The internal nature of the organization (Strategic culture, structure leadership style, technological thrust, and so on) should be evaluated with the external environment in mind.

Using these strategic management can focus on long-term strategic goals and environmental changes, with the result that they are better able to manage and control change and make their services more appropriate to user needs. Strategic management provides a comprehensive and effective management technique which can be used in dealing with complex and changing environments.

Librarianship

Let us now turn to a historical analysis of the emergence of a group of related but, at least initially self-consciously separate disciplinary and professional trends. Librarianship, an ancient occupation, clearly should be the first of these to be dealt with. Its origins lie close to the origins of writing could be inscribed, and above all to the social and economic pressures that led to the preparation, preservation, and retrieval of permanent written records. These were necessary to processes of stable government and commerce, to organized religions with commonly accepted rituals and beliefs, and to the cumulation and transmission of the knowledge of the times. Thus, we may speak of librarianship in the ancient world as well as in the modern world. Nevertheless, it was not until the last quarter of the nineteenth century that modern librarianship began to emerge as a professional occupation. As such, it was characterized by the invention of tools, techniques, and organizational structures that were widely adopted in the then rapidly multiplying university, college, public, school and special institutional libraries.

Strong formal associations of librarians were created at this time. Indeed, we may date the beginning of the professionalization of modern librarianship as an occupation in the English-speaking world from the foundation of the American Library Association in 1876 and the Library Association (of the United Kingdom) in 1877. Among the responsibilities of these associations were the oversight and continuing modification of commonly held beliefs about the goals and functions of various kinds of libraries. These associations helped provide a context for the emergence of an apparatus of systematic professional communication, regular conferences, journals, a small monographic literature in which knowledge in the field was codified disseminated for use, and made available for public discussion. Processes of formal professional education were created, institutionalized and gradually standardized.

Documentation in Europe

A different view of bibliography, one that resembles our notion of bibliographic control, was held at the turn of the century by Paul Otlet and his colleagues in Brussels. They had founded the International Institute of Bibliography in 1895 to create a universal bibliographical catalogue organized on new lines. Eventually Otlet developed his idea of bibliography in a series of now neglected but seminal papers into what the called "documentation" His concern was not to limit bibliographical control to cataloguing books in local institutions, but to find a way of creating a universal index of all documents that constituted records of knowledge books but also parts of books journal articles brochures, industrial catalogues patents, certain kinds of administrative records of governments the archives of municipalities, photographs, post cards, newspapers.

The problem was to find out what each contributed to the sum of knowledge, what each contained of potentially useful information and to express and connect this flexibly creatively to what already existed. Otlet had a clear idea of what he wanted from libraries in the new bibliographical order he was attempting to create. He believed that if the bibliographical apparatus or equipment of individual libraries actively contribute to the advancement of knowledge. Otlet wanted libraries to cease being mere depositories and to become vital institutes of documentation providing special information services on all matters of interest to all members of the public who might wish to use them. He wanted to see all libraries transformed into what he called offices of documentation and these to be jointed together in a national and international system of communication for sharing all existing resources, an international documentary network. He envisaged an important role for microfilm in this.

In the view of Otlet and his colleagues, through general bibliographic organization and control what they tended to designate as the new field of documentation encompassed traditional librarianship it went far beyond it. Traditionally, libraries were concerned with only a portion of the documentary record, for documentalists, the whole of the record lay within their scope. The methods to be used to exploit the record, and the institutional settings in which this work could take place, they believed could be more various and innovative than conventional libraries. Librarians reacted to the apparent competition and threat of assimilation by what was much touted as a new discipline essentially by denial. In continental Europe, just after the first World War, social relations between librarians and documentalists broke down; they have never been fully repaired. In England there was some mild general interest by librarians before the war in continental European documentalists and their work. This became stronger after the war, with the foundation in 1927 of an English member-organization of the international institute of Bibliography: the British Society for International bibliography. The English special library movement, which culminated in the foundation of the Association of Special libraries and information Bureaus (ASLIB) in 1924, shared many interests with British documentalists, and in 1937, the British Society for international Bibliography was absorbed by ASLIB. Thus, in England, the documentation and operated quite independently of the more, traditional interests and activities of the Library Association.

Library Science

In the United States, the situation was, a little more complex. Here, dissatisfaction with traditional practices of librarianship led merely to what might be called academic bibliographic scholarship, on the special information the special-library movement with its interest in the special information needs of business and industry. Appalled by the absence of rigorous research useful to libraries C.C. Williamson in 1930 asked "Can it be that there are no problems in library service that call for scientific research? Nothing more to learn? No unsolved problems?" And he quoted and slightly modified John Dewey in describing how a library science might emerge. There is no subject intrinsically marked off, earmarked so to say, as the content of library science. Any methods and facts and principles from any subject whatsoever that enable the problems of administration and service to be dealt with in a bettered way are pertinent... It may be doubted with reference to some aspect or other of Hbrary service there is any organized body of knowledge that may not need to be drawn upon to become a source of library science... In effect, the idea of a library science dates from the late 1920s and specifically from the founding of the Graduate Library School at the University of Chicago. This is school was established in order to bring the best standards of higher education to bear on the education of librarians and through the introduction of the Ph.D degree and the work of the school's faculty to promote research in the field. In a statement of policy for the school, Douglas Waples listed what the faculty considered to be the distinctive functions of the school:

1. The most important single responsibility of the school is to meet the standards of scholarship and research maintained by other graduate departments of the university both in the character of work undertaken by the staff and by the research interests of its graduates. 2. The major aim is research, defined as extending the existing body of factual knowledge concerning the values and procedures of libraries and their many aspects, and including the development of methods of investigation whereby significant data are obtained, tested and applied.... 6. Not all of the studies undertaken by the school need be confined to research in its restricted meaning of "search for abstract principles." In many instances, they may more properly be called service studies intended to increase the effectiveness of library service.... 9. An important function of the schools is the preparation collection and publication of monographs whereby the results of significant studies are made available to the library professions. It is only chance, either, that a minor classic of librarianship was written by an early member of the faculty of the Graduate Library School-Pierce Bulter's Introduction to Library Science. Certainly there was an attempt at the Graduate Library School to find new perspectives from which to study libraries and their problems. These perspectives were social sciences and historical scholarship. These methods were introduced to challenge the existing reliance on shared practical experience as the basis for the field's professional knowledge, with all that this reliance implied of a stultifying orthodoxy of dogma and belief. The importance in the United States of the Graduate Library Schools for the professionalization of and the appropriate institutionalization of an educational apparatus in the nation's universities for-librarianship has been widely acknowledged.

The Graduate Library School embodied what was for a time a unique and controversial approach to professional education its professors and students steadily produced a formidably body of research where before practically none existed. The school issued the first scholarly journal in the field. The Library Quarterly; and graduated those who became influential librarians or faculty members in other library schools. It we not until the late 1940s that two other library schools introduced doctoral studies in librarianship the Universities of Illionois and Michigan.

The 1950s saw a fairly rapid increase in doctoral programmes. These programmes by definition emphasized the importance of research, as opposed to training practitioners, and increased the volume and quality of the fields literature by reporting this research. Thus, the idea of a library science is hardly more than fifty years old, and any great volume or research in the field is relatively recent. It should be noted that the approach to creating a library science outlined by Williamson some fifty years ago still obtains. It is still to take the substantive problems of libraries and librarianship and apply to them research in the field has employed and continues to employ, the methods of the social science or is historical in nature. Latterly techniques of systems engineering and mathematical modeling or analysis (such as the techniques of operations research and the related and sometimes overlapping area of bibliometrics) have proved invaluable in conceptualizing library problems in a new way and providing powerful new techniques for analyzing research data. While the idea of a library science is now widely accepted within the library profession as desirable, it is only a little exaggerated to say that we do not yet have an extensive, distinctive, coherent well-integrated or systematized and scientifically derived body of theoretical and practical knowledge in librarianship. This leads to criticism of library science as a science and to suspicion of librarianship as a profession. That it is, however, exaggerated should be acknowledged because of the existence of cumulatively important subjects of library literature in the areas, for example, of systems engineering operations research, use and user studies classification and indexing management and measuring effectiveness among others. Nevertheless, it seems clear to me, despite the research that exists and the academic location of professional education that the empiricism of nineteenth-century librarianship-which the new library science was to test and perhaps ultimately supersede remains strongly present in the library profession today. That is to say, much of the librarian knowledge continues to be arrived at, and quite generally accepted in a pragmatic way through library practice and the shared experience of librarians.

Our cataloging codes and major classitication systems, for example are of this nature. It is probably true that the central core of knowledge underlying librarianship is still of this empirical kind and that consequently library science has failed to lead to an extensive and solid corpus of objectively derived, systematically examined and accumulated knowledge. Whatever knowledge of this kind exists, it may be thought of as peripheral or incidental to the central business of librarians-continuing to try, against increasing odds, to keep their organizations running reasonably effectively.

Documentation and Information Science

In 1933, Watson Davis proposed that a scientific information institute be set up to help foster communication among scientists and improve existing methods of bibliographical control of scientific literature would, toward these goals especially exploit the developing technology of microphotography. His proposal elicited widespread comment at home and from the European documentalists.

As nothing came of his proposals, he created in 1935 a Documentation Institute within Science Service, an agency for the popularization of science of which he was the director. He used the word documentation to include "all phases of issuance, use and interchange of recorded information." The word attracted him as a term because it had a wide circulation in Europe as a result of the work of Outlet and his documentalist colleagues while having no particular meanings associated with it in the United States.

The American Documentation Institute was created in 1937 as a kind of club to involve-through their directors or other senior officers—a wide range of libraries, learned societies, and government agencies in microfilm and other projects at first insufficiently supported and then more or less repudiated by Science Service. Though founded in 1937, the American Documentation Institute became a professional and scholarly force only with the publication of its journal American Documentation in 1950 and with the institute's transformation into a general membership organization in 1953.

Nevertheless, the early emphasis on technology, scientific communication and publication and new services offered through new kinds of institutions anticipated later developments within the institute. Here essentially, was an attempt, stimulated by technology innovation, to place library and library-related problems in the context of scientific communication. Vernon Tate's editorial description of the scope of *American Documentation* makes it clear that he, like Davis saw the European documentation movement as at last crossing the Atlantic to the United States and from his point of view finding in the journal a vehicle that would ensure its subsequent development. The journal was to deal with "The totality of documentation," and the definition of documentation given was that which had been accepted, Tata noted by the International Federation for Documentation, for witch the American Documentation refers to the creation, transmission, collection classification, and use of documents may be broadly defined as recorded knowledge in any format. Tate also went on to observe of the new work being done by documentalists: "Traditional methods of communicating and recording knowledge are being studied, reorganized and supplanted and in some cases revolutionized. In the following decades, it became clear that the documentalists considered them selves a breed quite apart from librarians. Unlike librarians, they were not documentation from a wide variety of scientific and technical fields. They were responding exuberantly to powerful social forces. As a Jesse Shera has said of this period: "First of all interest in the problem of information on the part of the scientific world and the federal government reached an unprecedented level.

Coupled with this was a period of accelerated technological development." The exploding world of scientific literature; new communications and information processing technology; mammoth programmes of governmental research calling fro new systems of information organization storage, and retrieval-these were the winds and waves of these new mariners the documentalists and the information scientists they formally became in 1968, when the American Documentation Institute became the American Society for Information Science. They invented a new language in which to discuss their work. They became increasingly involved with the computer and mathematics.

Machine-stored, manipulated and transmitted data inevitably involved a reassessment of what constituted a document and what documentation was. The computer raised the possibility of a wide range of indexing and retrieval experiments hardly possible before. And, indeed, it may well be that retrieval experiments in the 1960s constitute a first flowering of information science as a science. Certainly, information science as a discipline nourishing certain professional activities developed rapidly in the 1960s. In 1965, the first Annual Review of information Science and Technology appeared. It is of particular interest because it represents a relatively early survey of the literature of the field and its segmentation into what appeared at that time to be the accepted major disciplinary components. These components vividly exemplified the importance of the computer in giving shape and direction to both discussion and research in the field. The change of the name of the American Documentation Institute to the American Society for Information Science was intended to reflect the changing orientation of the society's members. The absorption of the slippery term information led to many theoretical and frequently tortuous attempts at definitions.

During the decaldes of the 1960s and the 1970s, there was also much discussion about what an ideal curriculum for information science might look like as opposed to those already in existence for librarianship. Many of the developments of the late 19605 may be interpreted as the latest culmination of ongoing attempts to create a more general understanding of how to facilitate access .to recorded knowledge than was possible in librarianship, which was perceived as being limited to creating collections of books and related library materials and to managing libraries, or to documentation, which focused on a more abstract notion of records of knowledge or documents.

In its turn, information science represented an approach to an even more abstract level of analysis; it included books and documents while not being limited to them. Information science has permitted the development of research that is more generally cumulative and generalizable, more readily enriched by importations from other disciplines. It has led to the' development of new options, procedures, and organizational arrangements for facilitating access to information recorded, or manipulated, in new ways.

Let us say that by 1970 this was the situation. On the one hand was a vigorous librarianship, its practitioners still blissful in their relatively undisturbed pragmatism despite the existence of an important scholarly apparatus for the profession involving in part the nation's graduate library schools and despite increasingly lip service to the importance of research for the development of their field. Their journal and monographic literature has become voluminous though fragmented. They aware organized into a number of large well-established professional associations with a wide range of competing sometimes conflicting; professional functions. On the other hand was the new, equally vigorous discipline of information science, with a strong research orientation underlying its professional and service components, its own small fairly homogeneous learned society, a generalized field of study (whose precise boundaries, however, were in constant dispute), and a recently established bibliographical and educational apparatus.

It is too simple to say that library schools aware of the limitations of library science and recognizing that information science might provide a more respectable disciplinary base for the profession of librarianship enticed or co-opted information scientists as faculty. Or that it was hoped that if a little information science were added to their library studies, library-school graduates might find the job market opening up. Or that information scientists could not really find a more congenial academic home (or parking lot) in engineering or computer science or mathematics department than in library schools. There may be some truth in all of these statements. We attribute a disciplinary convergence, insofar as it has occurred to essentially two factors. The first was the thoughtful recognition by leaders in the finding solutions to the same general problems, despite differences in terminology and orientation.

The fields of information science, information technology, information retrieval and documentation will not be treated as separate topics but rather as an integral part of library science thus we shall not be concerned with whether information science is part of library science or *vice versa*, but rather we shall assume that the educational process in a graduate library school must adequately take both into account. Swanson then went on to outline a group of substantive questions that might affect the immediate future of library education and research and that encompassed much of what information dealt with at the time. These two instances and we should stress that many more could be adduced, are of leaders in the field alive to new possibilities. They were indifferent to, or at least undisturbed by, jurisdictional disputes between certain librarians of the time who were fearful of computers and scientific method and some information scientists who were disdainful of the pragmatism and apparent parochialism of librarians. These leaders had a broad generalized perspective that allowed them to discern the general but common problems that underlay librarianship and the new developments in information processing that were sparked by the computer revolution. The computer eventually gave arguments overwhelming force in two ways. Its exploitation in individual libraries led to an almost universal interest of librarians in systems analysis that required identifying and recording library operations at a level of detail appropriate for possible computerization. And this inevitably called into question much of the conventional wisdom underlying library organization and administration.

The development of the Online Computer Library Center and later of other bibliographic utilities and networks and online indexing search services required librarians to move beyond the confines of their own libraries using a sophisticated electronic technology. Moreover, it become clear that problems involved in creating and exploiting these systems both locally and centrally were of a complexity and magnitude and yet of a solvability previously unparalleled in librarianship. Of course, the computer in and of itself was not responsible for these developments. The exploitation of the computer in developing new institutional relations between libraries and in improving local library processes and procedures was encouraged by the growing volume and complexity of materials that had to be dealt with and by a fiscal plight that has increasingly severe.

Nowadays computer-based systems that have been created as a response to these pressures have become one of the major foci of developments in librarianship. Technical requirements, operational refinement, and improvement of various systems have brought professional librarians and professionally active information scientists together in a way that makes them virtually indistinguishable. Librarianship as librarianship in this context typically concerns itself with the organizational, political, jurisdictional and economic aspects of the problems that these systems create and to which, in part they attempt to respond.

Employment Trends

The changes in the names of library schools reflect, in part another contemporary trend. The graduates of our library schools as well as becoming librarians now frequently go into information processing or information management, and they are called information specialists, analysis, or constants. This is the second development we wish to mention. To conventional library jobs, librarians now sometimes add aspects of records management, special indexing services, media management, and research analysis, and they often work in what is called an information center. It has become fairly generally accepted that there is a wide range of professional library and library like work that library-school graduates can perform successfully out side conventional library settings.

Journal Proliferation

The next change going to mention is the enormous proliferation of journals in the library and information science fields. Some of these journals have gone through interesting name changes: Information Storage and Retrieval has become Information Processing and Management; American Documentation and become the journal of the American Society for Information Science; UNESCO Bulletin for Libraries has become the UNESCO Journal of Information Science, Librarianship and Archives Administration. One group of new journals is clearly library related; Collection Management. The Serials Librarian, The Behavioural and social Sciences Librarian, Public Library Quarterly, Library Research, and the Journal of Academic Librarianship. Other journaJs, of no less interest to librarians have in their titles the new language of information work: On-line Review, Programme, and Data-Base. This phenomenon of a rapidly growing number of journals, insofar as it does not represent some from of collective madness, given the economic conditions of the times, must mean something. We can argue that the phenomenon is, in part the result of the commercial exploration of institutional pressure on librarians and library-school faculty to increase their publishing activities in order to achieve academic and professional respectability. But we may also argue that this literature suggests that a closely related range of subspecializations has developed and, in librarianship especially, achieved a certain-maturity-a range that progresses from matters of quite conventional librarianship through key areas in information science. Journals that tend to draw the boundaries of the fields as a whole, such as the library Quarterly or the Tournal of the American Society for information Science, include articles, over the whole range of issues and problems dealt with by separate journals, though we assume that there are different frequently distributions of papers across the subspecializations included in the general journals. Neither the field of librarianship nor information science, given this variety and overlapping of journals, can be perceived as unitary and strictly exclusive of the other. Rather, each is an agglomeration of parts, many of which may be regarded as common to both.

Terminology

The new language of librarianship is important because it is a terminological reflection of all the changes that have been occurring. It is this body of relatively new terminology that constitutes the fourth change that we wish to identify. Fifteen years ago, when we spoke of a catalogue, we meant sometimes a book but usually a card catalogue. We looked to the Library of Congress to supply catalogue copy in the form of cards or proof sheets. Now we speak, in addition of COM (Computer output Microform) and online public-access catalogue, of MARC (Machine Readable Cataloguing) data disseminated on magnetic tapes. In the mid-1960s new technology consisted of keypunch machines, sorters, printers, and a monstrous engine called a computer, to which indirect access was had in batch mode. Nowadays, there is an increasingly large group of librariahships who can speak with some familiarity of CPUs (Central Processing Units) and peripherals; mainframe, mini-and microcomputers; Baud rates and memory capacity; hard discs and floppy disks; and bubble memory. Reference librarians sensitive to the importance of understanding database structures and search strategies because of new kinds of cost considerations, are expected routinely to conduct what is variously called online or machine-assisted searching of bibliographic and nonbibliographic databases, access to which is purchased from database vendors in dial-up mode using the Tyronet communications systems. Other librarians buy software and hardware and turnkey systems from commercial censors who are part of something we now designate as the information industry. Once, cooperative schemes led to and reasonably complete only with enormous difficulty and at a prohibitive cost. Now, we have bibliographic utilities and networks for which the Union Catalogue function is but one, and that more or less incidental, of a great range of capabilities. The new language is essentially derived from computer applications in libraries and, as a consequence, is frequently the same as, or at least similar to, that used by information scientists, for whom, historically it can be argued, the computer provided a major disciplinary impetus. The shared language has helped identify shared technical and professional problems.

Structure of Associations

The final development to which we wish to refer is the structural recognition within the formal professional association in both librarianship and information science of major areas of both common and divergent interests. As early as 1951, the Special Libraries Association established a Documentation Division; this division is now the Information Technology Division. The Special Libraries Associations has a wide range of specific subject divisions and a Publishing Division as well. In 1962 the American Library Association created an Interdivisional Science and automation Division, now the Library and Information Technology Division. For most of its life, the Resources and Technical Services Division has had a Section for Classification.

In 1968, when the American Society for Information Science set up Special Interest Groups (SIGs), one of the first was for Library Automation and Networks and another for Classification Research. Some of the Special Interest Groups, Particularly in scientific and technical subject areas that are the object of Special Interest Groups have changed, the Library Automation and Network Group and the Classification Research Group have been maintained.

Among new groups are those for Community information Services. Computerized Retrievely Services, Non-print Media and Reprographics, and information Generation and Publishing. These all have counterparts within Library associations. The Public Library Association of the American Library Association, for example has a Community Information Section; the Reference and Adult Services Division has a Section for Machine Assisted Reference (also called computerized Search Services), the Resources and Technical Services Division has a Reproduction of Library Materials Section; the Library Information Technology Division has sections for information Science and Automation (the old name of the division), audio visual Materials, and Video and Cable Communications. These all reflected developing areas of mutual interest between librarians as an occupational group and information scientists.

The formal associations also reveal areas that do not overlap in so direct or important a way. The differences are clearest where library associations focus on quite specific matters. These are represented structurally within the American Library Association for example, by the type-of-library divisions. On the other hand, the information science association seems most different when it focuses on information and information processing in a most general way; represented structurally within the American Society for Information Science, for example, by special interest groups on numeric databases, the foundations of information science, and information analysis or evaluation. But librarians increasingly consider that they must be able to use effectively non-bibliographic databases; that the foundations of information science must inevitably encompass recorded information and its "potentiation" for society in organization such as libraries. Information analysis or evaluation may well deal in a generalized way with issues that a large literate in evaluating library and information services has already attempted to deal with.

A Disciplinary Continuum

We discussed first the emergence of four major disciplinary trends represent, that represent, in the case of documentation and information science especially attempts to find an increasingly general perspective from which to conceptualize, investigate, and find new and improved operational responses to problems that underlie libraries and librarianship. Next, we described certain contemporary phenomena that suggest a convergence of librarianship towards what has become known as information science. In the third section of the chapter, we want to take a more speculative approach to the relation between the definition of librarianship and information science. As a point of departure it is useful to examine the question posed by Swanson: What are the problems libraries are intended to solve? An immediate implication of this question is that, despite their antiquity, libraries may not be the only, the best, or even a lasting solution to these problems. Furthermore, if there are other solutions imaginable, it is important to be able to assess their relative effectiveness in the endless search for an optimal configuration of solutions. Libraries may be regarded as a major institutionalized response to the problems of providing generalized access to the record of what is known. They are a complex organization of access mechanisms. A collection of books and other traditional library materials organized according to the conventions of librarianship by a specially trained and deployed staff for the use of a defined clientele—this is a typical way in which libraries provide access to a portion of the record of knowledge. The explicit or implicit definition of a clientele provides boundaries as to what will be collected and how what is collected will be organized and made available. In addition, an individual library usually provides a range of staff, a variety of bibliographic and other tools, and creates formalized procedures for gaining both bibliographic access and sometimes physical access to that portion and form of the documentary record that is not directly incorporated into the library. As time has gone by, the ways in which what is known has been recorded, on the one hand, and what constitutes effective access to this record, on the other, have changed. As well as the variety of forms of printed record there are now other formats in which knowledge or information is recorded; perhaps the latest of these are electronic.

Access is required not merely to conventional library materials or to other formats of the record, but to what they contain as well, to their components or elemental parts that can be described as facts, ideas data, information. In some circumstances, access is provided not merely on demand but in anticipation of demand through selective dissemination of information (SDI) services. Furthermore, access is also seen as increasingly desirable in a limited number of areas of knowledge to the structured content of what has been recorded in these areas. The need to provide this kind of access has led to setting up information analysis centers and social-science data archives for example, and employing research analysis. This kind of access has, as a rule, required the participation of kinds of personnel different from those traditionally employed professionally in libraries; special training in the disciplines involved and in computer based statistical procedures have been thought to be necessary. Schools of library-and-information science nowadays, however, can and do provide some of this training.

As the volume complexity, and of formats of the record of knowledge or recorded information have increased and the number of users and the range of potential requirements of access to this record have expanded a variety of responses to these circumstances has occurred. Some of the responses have been made commercially by what we now call the information industry, which creates and sells bibliographic services and products to libraries, which constitute a major segment of their market, and also independently into an enormously various range of configurations of systems networks, and consortia.

Developments in telecommunications capabilities have been seized on as facilitating new kinds of institutional arrangements for providing different levels of access both through libraries and outside of them, as in the experimental home-based VIEWDATA or PRESTEL systems. New kinds of organizations have been created to provide new kinds of access, such as information centers and data archives.

A narrow and conventional definition of a library expresses a limited view of the format of the records involved and modes of access provided to them. But if these limitations are abandoned, libraries may be thought to embrace not only the arrangements and services of traditional libraries but of information centers and data archives as well. Traditional libraries fall into place on a historical continuum that has arisen as institutionalized responses to the need to provide access to information in recorded form have been developed, examined and modified. Such an approach to a definition may seem to be useful. It includes bookstores and office-filing and records-management systems. It may be argued that it extends to genetics and incorporates museums. While bookstores, office-filing and records—management systems involve what may be described as library like documents, they have in the past tended to fall outside the scope of librarianship. In none of these cases were the systems for, and modes of access is consummated only on a basis that librarians have tended to repudiate (except in the case of the rental collections some public libraries still maintain the payment of a fee.

Nevertheless, as book jobbers, for example, have developed extensive library like systems essentially for the use of libraries, book jobbers have become less hospitals, law firms and other institutional settings, filing and records systems have grown in a scope and complexity and in the sophistication of the technology through which they are maintained, they have began to attract the interest of librarians and information scientists. It is not implausible either to think of a museum as a library of artifacts Suzanne Briet, writing from the point of view of the European documentalists, espouses a definition of documentation almost as broad as this. "An antelope that has been 'cataloged' [in a zoo] is a primary document and other documents are secondary and derivative." It seems more dearly figurative to speak of chromosomes as libraries of genetic information: Certainly neither man or nature promises generalized access to the information they contain, despite the advances that have been made in genetic engineering. But it at this point of seeking appropriate definitions for libraries, documentation and information science and of exploring their ramifications that we may suggest the continued relevance of the historical development explored earlier by asking the question: What are the phenomena that information science studies?

When, however, the focus becomes not library and information work, but information science, the clarity, such as it is lost. Information becomes a phenomenon for scientific investigation, and the contexts within which it is examined and the investigative techniques to be employed depend very largely on how information is defined. Information as electrical impulses in the brain or as represented by certain biochemical phenomena or as the content of disciplines—this set of different meanings raises a serious problem of disciplinary encroachment. When is information science information science and not epistemology, psychology, biopsychology. Physiology or physics or journalism or the sociology of groups or anthropology? Thus, an ultimate consequence of the process of seeking an ever more general perspective for information science, for the problems of access to recorded and potentially comsultable or public information underlying the certain and development of libraries, may be the loss of all sense of disciplinary coherence in the field. We might argue from the point of view of the continue we described earlier that at one end is the librarian constructing a catalogue of books; at the other, because of the way in which information can now be conceived is the genetic engineer consulting the information recorded in and then restructuring DNA. Perhaps, however, there is a discontinuity between the two involving notions of symbolic representation and public consolation that more careful analysis and definition would reveal.

The point here is not so much the difficulty of definition or the slipperiness of terminology as the implication that the generalizing grocess described early in this paper may still be at work. It is a source of innovation and strength but it blurs traditional distinctions and can unsettle professional convictions. Librarianship, as Boyd Rayward says, is an ancient profession, as old as Babylon. But the government of society and its commerce has depended on the collection and use of information for just as long-from Babylon through the Domesday Book to the United States Census and beyond. Is not then information science equally ancient? We known about the Babylonian libraries by their catalog; we know about the use of information in government and commerce from the existence of inventories.

The principal characterizing principle of the organization of information seems to be list-making that is, we might say that the kind of list-making characterizes the kind of general information activity. Rayward quite rightly described the recent convergence of hitherto disparate disciplines or practices, but in referring to library and information science and bibliographers and documentalists, he seems to present a picture that does not always do justice to the complexity of the nature of the component forces. Further, his historical backdrop, with 1876 as the beginning of formal librarianship and the founding of the Graduate Library School in Chicago as the beginning of research in library science, does not really allow a large enough stage to accommodate the true range of significant characters.

In short, while we agree with Rayward's general thesis, we would like to extend it, with reference to some earlier history and other phenomena in the last century. We would like to begin by making a few formal points. Scientists in the late nineteenth century quite outside either bibliographic or library traditions were already coupling indexes and catalogs of scientific materials, because neither librarians nor bibliographers provided them. These were the protodocumentalists—they were not bibliographers.

From the eighteenth century onward, new libraries and new library practices veered between the bibliographic and documentalist traditions, as they tried, on the one hand, to be, scholarly in their catalogue descriptions and, on the other, to provide easily used "finding-tools" for their patrons. Rayward is quite right when he says that "[librarianship's] origins lie close to the origins of writing." However, we should remember that the earliest writings were inventories of property, goods and laws in Babylon, Mycenae, and so forth. Early library catalogue of Callimachus.

Similarly, in the Middle Ages, Monasteries kept inventories of their collections and sometimes used them as catalogues. Even as late as the end of the eighteenth century, libraries kept an internal inventory and perhaps an internal slip catalogue arranged by author/title and occasionally published a meager author/title entry catalogue for the library patrons. For example, between 1667 and 1840, even Harward college produced a public catalogue only three times. The library catalogue as we know it was really the product of the book trade: Aldus Manutius and his contemporaries in the late fifteenth century for bibliographic description: Andrew Maunsell and the English booksellers of the early seventeenth century for the subject catalogue and the early eighteenth century Paris booksellers like Marchand and Brunet, for the idea of a general bibliographic classification. We should not assume, however, that booksellers gave rise to the bibliographic tradition. Their aim was to sell books which they did successfully by grouping similar books and subjects together in their catalogue and describing them explicitly and practically to their customers.

On the other hand the classical bibliographer's delight is to record the diversity and differences of books in order to identity individual copies. Indeed, Rayward says, "These several bibliographical societies were interested in bibliography as an intrinsically regarding area of study that had:.... broad consequences for scholarship quite apart from libraries." Of course they were interested the eighteenth century had been a century of gentleman's individual scholarship. Now there was a hope of institutionalism—perhaps even a society like the Royal Society. Rayward asserts that "we may date the beginning of.... modern librarianship.... in the English speaking world from the foundation of the American Library Association (ALA) in 1876 and the Library Association (of the United Kingdom) in 1877.... But within a generation it become dear that neither libraries nor the existing organizations of librarians were able to initiate or even contribute usefully to the study of solutions to certain general bibliographic problems that lay outside the walls of these individual libraries. This was as true in the United Kingdom as in the United States. This is an almost Hegelian" interpretation of library history. For the American Library Association to be formed in 1876 meant the coming together of a large number of like-mined professionals. What had Charles Jewett, Charles Cutter, Justin Winsor, and Melcil Dewey been doing in the years before 1876? What had Edwards. Antonio Panizzi, and Andrea Crestadoro been doing in England before 187? Britain had passed a Public Libraries Act nearly thirty years before. The years 1876/1877 do not mark the beginning of librarianship they mark its formalizational conference of 1877 was a declaration of the existence of a solid body of knowledge and experience. Jewett had already laid out in the 1840s the three factors essential for solving the problem of universal bibliography: access to material, reproduction technology, and consistent descriptive practice. Jewett, and later, Dewey and Cutter, tried to solve the problem from within the library world, Rayward ignores the very real efforts made towards the standardization of bibliographic description by librarians like Panizzi: Jewett. Cutter, and others. It is true that conventional libraries did not produce a solution to general bibliographic problems in the last quarter of the nineteenth century-nor did bibliographers. The reason was not a failure due to anyone part of our general profession but the effect of historical development Jewett's three problems were never all solved satisfactorily at the same time.

Actually the problem had been that librarians, influenced by classical bibliographers, wanted to include a kind of formalized record in the manner of the bibliographers. This had begun under the influence of Panizzi's cry for "a full and accurate catalogue" and, by 1908, with the joint Anglo-American code, was somewhat divorced from the indexing tradition of Pool's Index, and so forth. Early documentalists wanted comprehensive coverage, sufficient (*i.e.*, perhaps minimum) record, and precise location. Unfortunately, in his discussion of library science, Rayward neglects special libraries, the true inheritors of the documentalists tradition. In the United Kingdom at least, in the 1930s/1930s (precisely the period Rayward addresses), there were strong forces binding together the disparate elements of scientific and technological information and formal (mostly public and special) libraries. Regional networks like Sheffield Interchange Organization (SINTO), Liverpool and District Scientific, Industrial, and Research Libraries Advisory Council (LADSIRLAC), and so forth, were based in public libraries (with the public library seen as kind of honest broker) and linked all kinds of library and information units for the exchange of nonbibliographic as well as bibliographic information.

To understand the true significance of these networks, and the position of the public library within them, the reader should realize that for at least the first half of this century, public libraries profession. It was not unusual to find city reference libraries richer in their collections and more active in their reference service than university libraries in the same cities. Rayward's suggestion that the formation of a theory of librarianship and library research began with the founding of the Graduate Library School in Chicago seems less cause and effect than a post hoc ergo propeter hoc argument. There had been many scholars, thinkers, and workers concerned with many aspects of library science between 1840 and 1940 most of whom owed no debt to the Graduate Library School.

It is true Jewett, Cutter, Bliss Sayers, and Ranganathan addressed individual aspects (although Cutter and Rangnanthan came close to addressing the whole field). It is probably true to say that, they did not develop a theory of librarianship but we wonder if one has ever been enunciated. It is frue also that much of the work in the late nineteenth century addressed practical aspects of library science but there are many fields in which research customarily addresses practical aspects of the discipline. We have mixed feelings about attitudes towards or definitions of research especially in library and information science. Library and information science is in an uncomfortable position vis-a-vis research fro two reasons: The discipline is structural rather than substantive and (partly for this reason and partly for historical reasons), it never amassed, or had time to amass, a solid quantitative base of empirical observations in a period of its development early enough to avoid doubts being cast on that kind of research or observation.

Librarians and information scientists very soon found themselves alongside researchers in other disciplines who had that quantitative base and who were now exploring theoretical implications. The profession may do itself a disservice if it seeks to emphasize only "respectable" research. Rayward alludes somewhat disparagingly to the empiricism of the nineteenth century yet, like medicine and law, we are profession with a job to do. We hope to improve by learning from research, but we can also improve through carefully considered practice. The best hope we have is precisely the tenor of Rayward's paper: That we are now seeing the convergence of closely related of knowledge and practice that for long, like siblings with territorial problems, have viewed each other at best with suspicion and at worst with outright paranoia. Information has already become the late twentieth century's biggest industry.

With a clear view of the nature, origin and potential of the components (that may thclude ourselves), we may see our way to the best resolution. We believe that this curiosity accounted for the unexpected popularity of Wienet:'s highly technical Cybernetics and the enthusiastic reception of the mathematical theory of communication. Programme-steered electronic computers, which made their appearance as practical device about that time also. Were enormous potential as logical, symbol processing information engines. Their enormous potential or revolutionizing our conceptions of problem solving and information-processing also stimulated a great deal of speculation research.

It is fruitless to engage in semantic disputes over when a discipline of information is not epistemology, psychology, biopsychology, and so forth. What matters is that investigators who identity with the information disciplines formulate researchable problems and make discovers, and contribute insights that clarify the nature and dynamic of information and knowledge. Their identification with a scientific community that calls itself information science may, presumably, provide them with ideas, methods, paradigms, and interactions. It may lead to success in ways that have not succeeded in other communities of inquiry.

To suggest that the primary focus of information science should be library and information work is stifling and unproductively restrictive. It is not likely to attract scientists in other areas. The conceptualization of information as the reduction of uncertainly by a receiver about which message, from an ensemble of messages, was transmitted over a noisy transformation of uncertainty with entrbpy, and claude shannon's theorem about the existence of codes that make it possible to transmit information at rates that come arbitrarily close to a specified upper limit with arbitrarily low probabilities of undetected error, rooted what others called information theory firmly as an engineering discipline. It placed information, in its technical sense, it was definitely divorced from meaning and the less precise interpretations that could connect it to uses such as information in books or documents. Shortly after largescale computers began to challenge the talents of engineers, mathematicians, and others those who later called themselves computer scientists to explore and realize their potential, information retrieval become one of the first application areas. It was a solution in search of a problem, motivated by the urge to explore all possible uses of computers.

It required a broadening of the information concept to include its semantic, pragmatic, and syntactic aspects. Very few of these precomputer scientists/engineers were affiliated with the American Documentation Institute (ADI) in the mid-1950s. Taffee T. Tanimoto and Hands Peter Luhn were the exceptions, and many of the early pioneers, such as Calvin C. Mooers, still are not active in the American Society for information Science (ASIS), the present name of ADI. It was during the discussion in 1960-1962 about these potential functions of an automated Library of Congress that the idea of a continually updated, on-line encyclopaedia like knowledge base occurred to me. Herbert Bohnert pointed me to H.G.Wells's 1936 world to vannevar Bush, Alvin Weinberg, Watson Davis, and charles Van then in force. These priorities had stressed improved general access to the record of knowledge by specialists.

The new priorities stressed a kind of system that primarily teaches, is a work of electronic art, espouses a human viewpoint, addresses and arouses the curious a average person, stimulates his or her curiosity, and aims to improve the world. Only secondarily does such a system seek to inform, perform a reference function, aim at the specialist, and accurately reflect the knowledge, opinions, prejudices of the time. The proposed system, now called WISDOM (Worldwide Information Service for the Development of Omniscience in Man), is still an idea though pilot versions have been implemented.

As a system, it is a social organ that is eventually to supplant the minds of individuals, a kind of community mind that may be the next stage in the evolution do mind. But WISDOM is also an emerging movement for the previously mentioned reversal of priorities, and several organizations have been created to further his movement. Paul Otlet may have a similar vision in 1895. Indeed, some documentalists and information scientists, such as Eugene Garfield, embraced variants of the idea underlying WISDOM in independent discovery. Which led to contributions of revolutionary impact, such as citation indexing and clusters based on coupling profiles (bibliographic coupling plus cocitation coupling). Such techniques apply not only to documents that comprise the written record but also to the individuals who use knowledge as well as to the fields of knowledge themselves that are only partially embodied in the records.

Librarianship, library science, documentation, bibliography, and information science in the narrow sense used by Rayward, have in common a focus on the written record and the physical documents-books, journals, manuscripts, musical sources, prints and so forth-that it comprises. Librarians are concerned with organizing collecting of such documents and facilitating their use by library patrons. As such, they need to cope with at least three tasks: *(1)* continually selecting from the growing record what to collect (possibly wedding little used items to make room if there are space limitations) *(2)* bibliographic control or organizing and maintaining the collections as well as maintaining the tools enabling them and their partons to determine at any time what is in the use of records in the library's collection. Information science, in the broader sense in which we interpret it is in contrast, concerned with information, knowledge, understanding, and wisdom. Here, information is used in its technical to remove a receiver's uncertainty about an ensemble. It is both a flow and a pattern that flows over a channel. This channel may have a memory that stores the encoded information pattern of bits as meaningless codes. The channel may contain a transducer and transformation that rearrange, encode, decode, or otherwise process patterns of bits, as in a computer. As a flow, information is a temporal change in a pattern. To be informed is to experience a change in some connective structure; to inform such an experience. Information becomes knowledge when it is given meaning, usually by a human mind. A person (or machine) may be said to know the answer to a previously unencountered question that is not merely a syntatic transformation of the statement troughs which that knowledge was acquired.

Knowing something requires the existences of a knowledge space containing niches for concepts, ideas, so forth, that are acquired. These niches are organized in to a web, and the way a niche is embedded into this structure, relating it directly to many other niches and indirectly to many more, is what gives it meaning at any time. Knowledge is stock; it may accumulate, but mere accumulation of knowledge is neither understanding nor wisdom. It is the latter that can help us to survive and learn to improve our lives. Knowledge becomes understanding when it contributes to change in a knowledge space, adding new connecting among niches and new niches, perhaps revising the entire or large parts of the structure. Certain new items of knowledge enable the knower to think of and questions never thought of before is needed.

Understanding leads to deeper answers to questions regarding how and why, while knowledge is mostly know what and know-how. Wisdom, in one sense the ultimate purpose of our intellect and the scientific enterprise, and therefore of central concern to information disciplines, means bringing knowledge and understanding to beat on shaping our world for human ends by human means.

Wisdom governs communications of information for purpose of control. It includes know-when, that is the choice of strategy times for action based on or justified by knowledge and understanding. Clearly, this emphasis is far from concern with access to the written records and even further from understanding is certainly necessary but it is far from sufficient as a profession and scientific foundation for the knowledge industries. The convergence hoped for by Rayward is certainly desirable, but it is not feasible so long as schools of library science take an attitude of the expressed in the following quotation from a resolution by the faculty of a schools of library science.

Librarianship and Information Science

Boyd Rayward has written an excellent general statement, well documented, of the historical development of Librarianship in relation to the emergence of the historical development of librarianship in relation to the emergence of document and the transformation of the latter in to information science. We shall not deal with stubborn problem of what constitute a disciplinary relation between librarianship and information science until a decision has been reached as to whether these areas of activity are in themselves, true discipline, we did so mainly because we did not know how else to classify what libertines do and the technologies by which they have striven to achieve their ends. Information science has yet to prove itself as a discipline.

Like librarianship, it is still largely an agglomeration of technologies drawn from other areas of study, particularly, in the case of information science, from mathematics and electrical engineering. In the final analysis, we are still compelled to say, that librarianship is what librarianship is a service and information science. is an area of accuracy that Librarianship is a service and information science is an area inquiry that seeks to measure and improve the efficiency of the librarian: but such as statement is inadequate because information science deals with only a part of what the librarian does. Viewed from the perspective of history, then, as admirably presented by Rayward, Paul Otlet and his associates who formed the Brussels Institute and subsequently the International Federation for Documentation (FID), were basically librarians. Librarianship has always been interdisciplinary in that its goal was to make the total record of the human adventure readily accessible to all. Otlet and his follows merely strove to expand the area of library activity to encompass a wider range of materials and improve access to those records by using a new technology. They adopted the classification scheme devise by Melvil Dewey to form the Universal Decimal Classification (UDC) and supplemented it by using certain sings and symbols of interdisciplinary relations.

Neither traditional librarians nor these innovators exemplified a new field of academic endeavour; both were essentially centripetal-drawing to themselves the products of scholarship and the accumulated recorded knowledge of many fields. Thus, they pioneers relied on librarianship for their basic principles and structures. They elaborated what had already been done. That they called themselves documentalists and their fields. Thus, these pioneers relied on Librarianship for their basic principles and structures. They elaborated what had already been done. That they called themselves documentalists and their field of activity documentation did not change their basic objectives.

When the documentation movement came to the united states, American librarians rejected the UDC even thought it was based on Dewey's system, because they believed it to be too complex; they turned, instead, to microphotography as a technology that would improve the accessibility and availability of graphic records as well as provide a substantial reduction in costs. Librarians even foresaw a time when microfilm would replace the conventional book. On this side of the Atlantic, documentalists were mainly librarian who had adopted a new technology; they was no alteration in the basic goals.

Because these American documentalists, most of whom were librarians, based their technology on the science of photography, they tended to regard themselves as scientists, tended to avoid the term librarian, and formed the American Documentation Institute (ADI). Thus began the fragmentation that has plagued librarianship ever since. By mid-century, microphotography had become firmly established as an important addition to the librarian's arsenal of technologies, and most of the members of the American Documentation Institute had turned to other interests. Those few who retained their concern for the further development of micro-photography seceded to form the National Microfilm Association, composed mainly of commercial interests organized for the promotion and manufacture of photographic equipment.

The remaining members of the ADI turned to new techniques for the organization of library materials which they characterized as information retrieval. These new interests were largely devoted to the application of electronic and mechanical systems for improving the accessibility of graphic records. Thus, there evolved such systems and mechanisms as Calvin Mooers's Zato coding, Mortimer Taube's coordinate indexing, Raplh Shaw's rapid selector and the searching selector fabricated by J.W. Perry and Allen Kent at Western Reserve University. The ADI was then largely composed of librarians, with the additions of a number of commercial organization, such as Eastman Kodak, Remington Rand and General Electric, which had research resources far beyond those of librarians.

The line of demarcation between documentalists and librarians was even then beginning to be drawn, and there were some suggestions that library schools should changes their names to schools of documentation. Librarianship was becoming a tarnished word, and may wanted to dissociates themselves from it as much as possible. This movement was intensified by the influence of Claude Shannon and warren Weaver and their work at the Bell Telephone Laboratories on the communication of information. The term information was misleading, but it was used by members of the American Documentation Institute as being descriptive of their major concern. Again, the influence of Shannon and Weaver became prominent in attracting mathematicians to their field, creating such technologies as bibliometrics and citation analysis. These phenomena had long been known to librarians, but their rebirth gave the phenomenon air of novelty and innovation. By the late 1960s, the term documentation had become old hat, and the ADI changed its name to the American Society for Information Science.

Today, even the special Libraries Association, founded in 1909 by John Cotton Dana (librarian of the Newark, New Jersey public Library) to serve the bibliographic needs of business and industry, is contemplating a change of name to something akin to an association of information managers. The flight from library goes on, leaving the old and respected name to typify, in the main, public litrary service. The trend would make an interesting science is rooted in attempts to extend the boundaries of libraries technology and give it revived respectability by endowing it with a unique name. The American Society for Information Science and its preceding organization, the American Documentation Institute, could provide an excellent subject for the study of that peculiar amalgam that is librarianship information science. Unfortunately, a thorough inquiry of this kind has not yet been made. However, in 1979, Donald W.King and two graduate students at the library school at Drexel University interrogated the entire membership of ASIS in an attempt to provide a profile of the membership of that organization. The study does provide some interesting insights. Of the 3894 regular members of the association, 52 per cent responded. Of the responded. Of the respondents, 24.2 per cent, the largest groups was 20.3 per cent, composed of managers, directors, or coordinations. Information technologists, analysts, and scientists came third, with 18.6 per cent, at which point the percentages drop off sharply. It is also interesting to not that in the survey of the primary employers of ASIS members, 35.6 per cent were from industry, 26.9 per cent were from colleges or universities, and 12.1 per cent were from the federal government. In the sample,

56 per cent were woman, while in the earlier ADI yeas, there was no more than a handful of woman. Whether or not these statistic reflect the actual situation is problematical in that women may be more responsive to questionnaires of interest to woman.

The enthusiasm with which many librarians, especially academic librarians, rushed to embrace new technology with only the most causal consideration of their appropriateness seemed to substantiate Kaplan's "Law of the Instrument" Simply stated, this so-called law holds that peoples tend to formulates their problems in such a way as to make as to make it seem that the solution to the problems demands precisely what they happen to have at hand. He illustrates this law by saying that a small boy given a hammer immediately concludes that everything needs pounding. A more sophisticated example might be that an executive who has acquired photocopying machine almost inevitably concludes that all of his or her immortal prose should be distributed throughout the organization in multiple copies. There are times when it seems that the goal of science is not to know or to understand but to use. In the American character, they has been a strong strain of utilitarianism, or, rather, pragmatism, and this is perhaps no more clearly evident than in Librarianship.

Librarians even went so far as to evolve a new discipline called informations science. They misinterpreted shannon and waver's specialized use of the noun information and assumed that it related to the communication of knowledge rather than the transmission of signals. Information theory, in contrast to the theory of librarianship, is severely limited in its communicative potential to the theory of librarianship, is severely limited in its communicative potential. It is objective is to provide the librarian with a system giving functional or operational access to the contents of documents, Information scientists give all of their attention to design, production, implementation and control of the system.

Thus, as H. Curtis Wright has so well pointed out. Our schools of library science are busily engaged in producting "control artists", technicians and mechanics who tinker with information systems but there are unable to solve problems of access and retrieval because they cannot control ideas. These control artists constantly mistake the symbol for reality and believe that continuing or figuring with these symbols solves the bibliographic access problems. This confusion between data and ideas lead to the confusion between data system and idea systems. Thus, wright is close to what Robert fair throne has called "making and parking" in document retrieval rather than information or knowledge retrieval. Librarians have becomes so concerned with process that they have confused substance with instrumentation. Processing data can performed by machine, but only the human mind can process knowledge or even information. Information science is based on data and their manipulation, not on ideas. Science deals with things, things that can be measured weighted, poured, fastened, or mixed together, whereas librarians are dealings only incidentally with things but primarily with ideas, concepts, and thoughts. Librarians are, or should be, characterized by their knowledge, not by their instrumentation.

We conventionally say that the computer is here to stay and we must learn to adapt to its powers and capabilities. We submit that the situation is quite the reverse. The computer is here to stay, therefore it must be made to adapt to the librarian's problems and needs. It must be kept in its proper place as a tool and a slave, or we will become sorcerer's apprentice, with data everywhere and not a thought to think. Librarians, ever sensitive to the somewhat meager social esteem accorded their activities, devised the term library science and eagerly seed information science as potential supports to their claims to professionalism. But science does not a profession make, and an overlay of scientific operations is not a sine qua non for professionalism. The term profession derives, of course, from the root verb to profess, to believe in, and etymological, a professor is one who acts according to his or her beliefs or convictions. Wright has recently reviewed the development of the concept from the Greek arete, which meant skill or proficiency in a particular job and a knowledge of the job in hand, to the well-known characteristics of a profession as enunciated by Abraham Flexner. Wright cites Socrates to the effect that if we wish to know what a good shoemaker, the first essential is to know what a good shoemaker is and what the purpose of the shoe are. Only then can we decide what materials are best for making shoes and what tools should be employed and the best techniques and methods for using these materials and tools. But such skill and techniques cannot be successful without an understanding of what is to be produced and what functions it is supposed to perform. Wright quite properly sees a direct connection between knowledge of a task and it is performance, citing the so-called Socratic Paradox that "Virtue is knowledge" Which was interpreted by his contemporaries to mean that we cannot be efficient unless we take the trouble to learn our job.

Librarians would do well to remember occasionally Moses or a pieta and think somewhat less frequently of shannon and Weaver. What, then, is the "shoe" that is the end product of the 'shoemaker" the professional librarian. We submit that there are three components in the concept of a library. First, there is acquisition, which involves knowing what to a acquire for a given clientele and how to acquire it.

Acquisition implies substantive knowledge of the materials and the uses to which that knowledge can and should be put. The second is organization, that is, ways in which the accumulated materials can be arranged and processed for maximum convenience. and efficiency of use. It is here, and only here, that information science makes its contribution to librarianship. The theirs is interpretation and service, which is the reason deter of the library, and it is here that information science reveals its greatest threat of dehumanizing the library's function.

To express the same idea in another way, the library can be seen as three interrelated spheres: the sphere of optimum content; the operational or mechanistic sphere; and the sphere of maximum context. If librarians parasites in sublimating librarianship to the lure. of the machine and the all importance of data retrieval their "shoes" will be very uncomfortable to the user, and they will leak at certain vital points. Jeans-like the library looks in two directories simultaneously. It looks towards the social science, because it is a creature of society, evolved to meet the needs of human beings working towards the solution of certain problems. Thus, the library qualifies as a social agency or instrumentality. But the library is also humanistic in that its characteristics, modes of access to its resources, uses, and values are humanistic. It is not, and never has been, a scientific enterprise. Except for some tinkering with its processes, scientific technology has made but little contribution to the development of the library.

A catalogue entry on the face of a cathode ray tube is essentially the same entry devised by Charles A. Cutter, and the fact that it has been transmitted across the continent in a fraction of a second may be a convenience to the user, but it does not alter the character of librarianship or transform it in to a science. Of the importance of the humanities to a world of science, a professor of history at the University of Machine has recently written: "Our society is a seamless web, and ultimately science and technology share the same values and are dependent upon the purpose which derive from the study of what it means to be human. The neglect of the humanities will bring in its train inevitably the decay of science." He goes on to characterizes an excessive dependence on science alone as "the higher barbarism, unless there is some human purpose that looks beyond the immediate technical and economic applications. The day will come when the hand will lose its cunning and life be found to be devoid of purpose. We are more dependent upon our poets than we realize." It is perhaps reassuring that all of us know successful scientists who enrich their profession reading with generous additions from the humanities; who are accomplished mature musicians; or who, like the distinguished astronomer Fred Hoyle, have made reputation in creative writing. Information theory is severely limited in its communicative potential. its only aim is to provide efficient access to knowledge, but the design of mechanisms, their production, and use of the system are its areas of concentration. We are, as Wright has emphasized, turning out control artists and data mechanics. This confusion of ideas with data can be dispelled only by distinguishing between data systems and idea systems. Thus, if follows that information science cannot qualify as a theoretical base for librarianship, and calling it bibliometrics or informatics does not alter the situation.

We librarians must constantly remained ourselves that our concern is with sociological and psychological phenomena, not physical objects and processes. Moreover, information science itself does not know what it is or where it is going. It cannot tell whether it belongs in a school of library science, engineering, management, operations research, or some loosely defined area of its own. There is already distinct evidence that the American Society are of Information Science is fragmenting itself in to variety of activities, some of which are mutually contradictory. The term symbolic interaction refers to the process by which people relate to their own minds and the mind of others; the process by which individuals take account of their own or other's needs, desires, means and ends, knowledge, and like motivations. Among sociologists this phenomenon is frequently known as social interaction.

In the definition of symbulic interaction, the word mind denotes instrumental activities that animals as well as human direct toward their environment. These instrumental activities, sometimes referred to as action or as psychological activities, are related to the organism's requirements and the conditions and resource in the environment that are relevant to meeting those requirements. The term symbolic includes the representation of those requirements through a system of commonly understood linguistic, or other representational activates, such as gestures, where by the content of the communicated message is transmitted to, and understood by, the intended recipient. Such a disripline of symbolic interaction reminds librarians that their area of concern is based on social phenomena and it provides for the contributions of philosophy, linguistics, and psycliology in the formulation of its unique purpose. That purpose is to make accessible the graphic records of human culture, so that people may understand the totality of the environment in which they find themselves and their own place in it. We who are librarians must constantly remind ourselves that information science is an area of inquiry, of research. It is not, as is librarianship, a service or a practice. Information science can provide the librarian with some important and useful tools to expedite library service, but the ability to communicate a message with incredible speed over long distance through the use of glass fiber bundles or laser beams or to strove vat quantities of recorder knowledge in computer like mechanism does not in any way alter the purpose of the library. That the internal-combustion engine can move vat quantities of the library remains unchanged to bring the human mind and the graphic record together in a fruitful relation for the growth of knowledge is still the goal.

Administration, management, architecture, and many other disciplines can contribute to the effectiveness of the library, but they are not librarianship. We who are engaged in library education must be aware that the librarian needs to attain certain specific skills in the uses of the tools that all these disciplines, including information science, have given us. But the hard core of librarianship remains basically as it has always been the mastery of the substantive content of graphic records. Librarians should be characterized by their knowledge and not by their instrumentation.

The most effective librarians enter the profession armed with broad generalized knowledge or with knowledge in a substantive content of graphic records. The idea, not the process, is our primary concern. The great danger with which information science threatens librarianship is the loss of control of the library profession to other and less competent hands. Of the dangers inherent in this threat, we do not now seem to be fully aware. The basic purpose of librarianship than is envisaged in the machine, and there is much more to librarianship than is envisaged in information science. If we permit ourselves to be mesmerized by the gadget. If we accept the flickering image of data on a fluorescent screen as knowledge, we will soon become like those mythical people of many centuries ago who mistook for the passing shadows reflected on the walls of a cave. So we conclude with the words of that distinguished librarian of Stanford and subsequently dean of the library school at Berkeley, Ray Swank: "The long experience and tested values of librarianship are still our most reliable and sophisticated resource for the solution of information-handing problems in most context whatever additional help may now be needed".

❐

6

Computer Based Information

This chapter provides information to help you install the network cards and cable connectors and ideas for running the library network cable. If librarian follow a few safety rules, librarian won't damage anything. The worst that can happen is the installation won't work. The best that can happen is the hardware works and librarian are ready to install the software. Time and energy spent preparing for the hob saves time and frustration while working on the job. There is nothing more discouraging than halting a project midway because librarian don't have the fight tools. Without the right tools, the result is sloppy, unreliable, and possibly dangerous. Preparing for the job includes knowing the basic rules of safety to protect yourself and the equipment, as well as making sure librarian have the proper tools. And don't imagine that librarian must complete the entire project in one day, regardless of how small or large your LAN.

Above all librarian must be aware of basic electrical safety rules when working with hardware. Electronic devices are sensitive to electricity, especially the nuisance of static electricity. For example, as librarians insert a card into the system, the static electricity in your body can travel through, and may damage, the card. Listed here are a few basic rules. Additional tips are included with each step of the hardware installation process.

(a) Always slow a system to become completely quiet after turning it off and before moving it. The hard disk is vulnerable to damage while it is still spinning.

(b) Always unplug any electrical device before removing any covers. Just turning of the power switch does not disconnect the system from the electrical current.

(c) Never consume liquids around and opened device. If, in the heat of the moment, librarians are sweating profusely, stop to wipe your brow. One drop of that salt water inside the computer could damage it.

(d) Always touch a grounded object before picking up a computer card or reaching inside the system.

(e) If librarian drop a screw inside the case, stop and immediately retrieve it. If librarian forget to get it and turn the system on later, you could seriously damage the computer.

(f) When working around electrical wire, be careful not to route network cable neat or over the wire.

(g) Leave the card in the protective antistatic plastic pouch until just before librarian need to use it. If librarian mist make changes to the switches or jumpers on the card, lay it on top of the plastic bag, which librarian have placed on a flat surface.

(h) Always use the right type and size tools. If librarian use a power screwdrive, be very careful not to overtighten screws:

(i) When cutting holes in wallboard, be very careful not to cut into electrical wire or plumbing.

Hardware installation can be very physically demanding. Librarians moving systems around and climbing ladders. Librarians will definitely be removing covers and bending over as librarians insert the cards. Remember to take it easy. The physical activity may increase your frustration level.

If librarian are doing the installation during non-working hours, librarians may want to talk someone into assisting, even if that person doesn't know the business end or a screwdriver. Sometimes it helps to have someone to talk with as librarian work through the problems they encounter.

The Necessary Tools for Librarians

Before librarians take the first step of the installation, prepare as they would for performing surgery-place all the instruments within reach. Then, when librarians need a specific tool, they can just reach for it. Don't use a flathead screwdriver to remove a screw just because they can't easily reach the Phillips screwdriver. Computer toolkits are widely available at computer stores.

Keep in mind that librarians will need different types of tools for installing cards and for installing cable. Here's a list of tools librarian might need to install a library network card:

(a) Four screwdrivers—a small and medium size of both flathead and phillips. Better yet, secure a series of hex head drivers if your systems have hex head screws.

(b) Find something to extract screws dropped inside the computer. A medical clamp called a hemostat is handy. A doubled-up piece of sticky tape on the eraser of a pencil will also do.

(c) A small mirror will help librarian see behind the system if librarian don't have the space to pull it out from the wall or can't bend over far enough to see the ports in back.

(d) A power screwdriver saves time when removing and replacing screws in the back of the system. Remember to keep a loose grip to prevent overtightening the screws. If librarian use the power screwdriver to remove and install the screws that keep the cards in, be very gentle.

(e) A small flashlight is useful as librarian peer down into the innards of the computer, especially if librarian are digging around for a dropped screw. A small, plastic flashlight is better than a large metal one in case librarian drop it into the computer.

(f) A small hair dryer is handy for blowing out dust in the system.

(g) Small needle-nose pliers help move card jumpers.

The tool list for installing cable is a bit more lengthy. Not only must librarian cut the cable, librarian must also strip off parts of insulation and then properly clamp the cable connector, such as a BNC or RJ-45, on the end of the cable.

Be sure librarian have the proper crimp for the connector librarian are using. The crimp looks like a strange set of pliers. Depending on the quality and tile specific tool. If librarian are making BNC connectors, this tool is essential, if librarian are using twisted-wire, there is a way to avoid making cable connectors.

(a) Get and use large, sharp wire clippers.

(b) Find a sharp knife to cut away insulation. Better yet, there are wire strippers that will cut the insulation to the exact measurements librarian need before attaching the BNC connectors. The Rs 5000 is well worth the savings of time and greater accuracy if librarian are making more than four or six cable ends.

(c) If librarian will be going through walls, find a drill with along 1/4-inch bit.

(d) Use wide masking tape or blank mailing labels to mark cable ends.

(e) Borrow two tall ladders if librarian are running cable across the suspended ceiling tiles.

(f) A small ball of string with a weight tied at one end is essential for pulling cable across suspended ceilings.

(g) Find a small keyhole saw if librarian need to make access holes in the wall.

(h) If the suspended ceiling has insulation, librarian and anyone working with librarian need gloves and a breathing filter.

With the exception of the cable crimp and wire stripper, the tools just described are readily available. The cable crimp and wire stripper should be available from the same source as your network cable and connectors. Make sure you get the proper crimp size for the BNC connectors and cable.

Selecting Test Systems

If librarian purchased a LAN starter system already have the software, two cards, and the proper type of cable with connectors. This cable may be from 15 to 25 feet long. Even if that is not long enough for one of their connections in the library network, it is exactly what librarian need for the first phase of their installation.

One of the most useful and time-saving steps librarian can take is to move two systems next to each other, as shown in Figure, for the first part of the library network installation. In most cases, bring another system as close as possible to the server. Librarian will use these two systems at the same time to test both the server installation and the workstation's ability to access the server. With the two systems side by side, install the first two cards, install the server, and then install the workstation. As librarian test and smooth out the process, you just shift from keyboard to keyboard to keyboard like a pianist playing a duet on two pianos. This beats running down the hall two dozen times to the nearest station to see if the server is working and if the workstation has made the connection.

As librarian would with any computer, make sure this temporary arrangement includes a sturdy table for the second system. Librarian may need another power strip if the receptacles are taken up by the server. Since librarian will have 15 to 25 feet of slack in the cable, avoid heavily traceled areas where coworkers could easily trip.

Installing Library Network Cards

Above all, before installing the library network cards, read the accompanying documentation. With luck, librarian won't have any surprises. Those surprises occure when librarian have two cards trying to use the same settings. In most cases, the default settings on the card will work. Try those settings. If they do not work, librarian will find out about if fairly quickly and can worry about those finer points later.

Make sure librarian have located and written down the technical support number. Find the page in the documentation that shows the specification, including the I/O base address and the IRQ. If all goes well, librarian won't need this information. If Librarian need to change some settings, it will be important.

Installation Steps for Librarian

Librarian should install any new computer part slowly and carefully. The smaller the changes, the less work librarian have to undo when problems arise. Here are the steps librarian should follow.

(a) Turn on the computer to make sure it works.

(b) Turn it off, unplug it, and remove the cover.

(c) Remove the mounting bracket from the back of the system.

(d) Touch grounded metal to discharge static electricity.

(e) Gently blow out any dust.

(f) Locate an empty slot in the motherboard.

(g) Remove the card from the antistatic plastic bag.

(h) Test the card.

(i) Test the system.

(j) Insert the card.

(k) Plug the system back in and turn it on.

(l) If librarian have problems, turn off the system and study the next section, "Network Card Problems".

(m) Install the LAN software,

(n) Turn off the system. Replace the slot screw.

(o) Replace the cover of the system.

Turn on the computer to make sure it works. Run through a few of the main programmes. Make sure the mouse works if librarian have one. If a printer is attached, make sure it prints. If there is a modem, check that as well. There is always the chance that something was not working correctly before your installed the library network card. It is maddening to try to fix a problem that librarian think was caused by the card but was actually present before the card was installed; checking the system beforehand eliminates that possibility Once librarian are satisfied that the system works as expected, turn it off, wait until it is completely quiet, and then unplug it. Librarian can disconnect it from the wall or from the back of the system. Remove the cover by unscrewing all the screws around the edge of the back. The cover may have to slide all the way forward before librarian can lift it off. Some covers just slider forward an inch or so and then lift off. Keep the cover screws together in a safe place.

If no maintenance has been performed on the system within the past six months to a year, Librarian will have an accumulation of dust. Use the hair dryer or other gentle; blower to push the dust out of the system. A vacuum is not recommended; nor is blowing with their moist breath. In the motherboard, locate the slot for the library network card, using their flashlight if necessary. Make sure the slot has sections if librarians are installing a 16-bit network card. If it doesn't must install an 8-bit card or, alternatively, move an 8-bit card from a 16-bit slot into this currently open 8-bit slot, thereby opening up a 16-bit slot.

Remove the mounting bracket, shown here, by unscrewing the small screw at the top of the back opening in the case: As librarian loosen the screw, hold it carefully so you don't have to fish it out of the system later. Keep the screw handy, but save the mounting bracket somewhere else. Touch grounded metal to discharge static electricity. Then stand very still while librarian reach for the library network card. Remove the card from the antistatic plastic bag. Lay the card on top of the bag if librarian need to make any adjustments to the jumpers or dip switches. The slots on the motherboard have small spring contact stirps that match the contact strips on the bottom of the card. As librarian insert the card, librarian may have to rock the card back and forth very gently to get it all the way into the slot. The mounting bracket on the card should be exactly at the top edge of the system back support. Do not use excessive force to insert the card. Librarian might damage the library network card or motherboard.

If librarian knew for sure the card would work, librarian could just put the cover back on. But there is a chance that the card will conflict with other cards in the system and librarian may need to make changes on the card. With the cover still off, turn the system back on, be very careful here. Librarian have an open system with power in it. Anything, librarian touch or drop into this open system could damage you, the system, or both. If there is a major problem, librarian might get extra beeps or the system may not boot up. The odds of this happening are slim, but possible. If this occurs, Refer to the next section of this chapter. If the system starts normally, librarian are ready to test the card. Most card manufacturers provide a disk with utility software, including a programme to test the card. Refer to your card's documentation for the name of that programme and then run it.

If the card test programme runs, then try using the, major software programmes installed on the system. This step is essential because if don't and librarian load the LAN software. Librarian won't know if the problem is with the card or the LAN software. Make sure you test the mouse, the printer, and the modem by running programmes that use these devices.

If librarian had problems with their library network card or application software test, turn off the system and unplug the card again. Then refer, to the next section of this chapter. If librarian did not find any problems, install the LAN software for the server or workstation. Librarian need not worry about setting up the entire directory tree. If no problems were noted, turn off the system and unplug the cord. The temptation may be to jest replace the system cover, leaving out the network card retaining screw while the power is on. Don't! The screw must be replaced in the network card, especially because the cable pulls on the card. Attempting to do this work with the power on is very hazardous. With the power still off, replace the cover of the system. If librarian use a power screwdriver, be sure librarian don't overtighten the screws in the back. Once librarian have installed one network card, don't assume that the installation will be the same for all the other systems. The only way this occurs is if all the systems are exactly the same brand, have the same cards, and use the same software. If librarian bought the computer systems one or two at a time, even from the same manufacturer, there may be different problems.

The only difference on the second system, temporarily sitting next to the server, is that the software librarian install will be for a workstation, not a server. Even if librarian plan to make each system a server in a peer-to-peer scheme, start out with the simplest configuration settings later. Also keep in mind that when librarian attempt to start the workstation software for the first time, it will not complete the process until the two systems are attached with the library network cable.

Network Card Problems in the Library

Library network card manufacturers try to create card settings that work in the majority of computers. If librarian have a system with one serial port, one parallel port, and no unusual cards, there is a good chance the default settings will work. On the other hand, if librarian have a CD-ROM drive, a second serial port, a music or some other special card, the network card may have the same settings already used by one of those devices.

Most network installation manuals provide suggestions to resolve conflict between the library network card and other cards in the system. Those recommendations include changing dip switches and moving jumpers Dip switches are small sets of usually eight switch, By setting these switches on and software to use as a reference. The manual should show the numbers used for these settings. Make sure librarian know the on and off positions on the block. Use any small pointed device to move the switches. Here is an illustration of dip switches on a library network card:

Librarian may also have to move jumpers on the cards. These jumpers are small plastic blocks that fit over two metal pins. The inside of the jumper contains metal. When the jumper covers two pins, it closes the circuit, creating another setting on the network card. In many cases, there will be two rows of pins with four of five pairs. A jumper is to cover only one pair of pins. Here is a set of pins with one jumper.

Most network cards have just one set of dip switches a although there may be many sets of jumper pins. The network manual will have a drawing of the card with the different pin locations and names. On some cards, the setting are also printed next to the pins. Use the needlenose pliers to gently pull the jumper off the current pair of pins: and then push the jumper back on the new set of pins with your finger. However, before making changes to these settings, sketch the original location of the jumpers and dip switches. If librarian continue to make changes, make a new sketch for each setting. Also write down the value for that setting.

When librarian make changes to the card. Librarian will also make changes to the library network software. The whole purpose of making these changes is to avoid conflicts with other cards in the system. Since the library network software must be told those new settings on the card, librarian will need to reinstall the software or make changes on the command lines contained in the CONFIG.SYS or batch file use to start the library network.

Making changes in the card settings to resolve conflicts can be a very tedious process. Librarian should make only one change at a time in the card. Two changes at the same time might cause additional problems. To make and test changes, follow these steps:

(a) Make sure the system is off and unplugged.

(b) Touch grounded metal to discharge static.

(c) Gently rock the card out of the slot.

(d) Sketch the current dip switch or jumper setting.

(e) Place the card on the antistatic bag.

(f) Make the change or the card.

(g) Plug in and power up.

(h) Reinstall the library network software or make the changes in the batch file to reflect the new card setting.

(i) Insert the card back into the system.

(j) Attempt to start the library network.

(k) If the library network appears to work, continue to test your applications. If not, return to step a.

Another effective but time-consuming approach to resolving conflicts is to remove all the non-essential cards in your system, leaving only the video, disk drive, and network cards. If the network card works, librarian then add cards one at a time until librarian locate the card causing the conflict. This information is very helpful for anyone providing technical support. The number of possible settings and conflicts may seem overwhelming. Your ability to solve the problem depends on your perserverance and technical support. There are many sources for help. Don't be reluctant to begin working down your list, starting with the library network card tech support phone number. As do all cards, the library network card uses a number of settings to work within computers. These settings include the I/O port address, the interrupt requests, the base memory address, and other settings, and they are a major reason why librarian might have problems with the network card installation. This is because no two cards in a computer can use the same IRQ, DMA, or I/O port address. While it is not essential that librarian know how these settings work, understanding the basics may help you try different values to get your network card to work. The methods used to change these settings may differ. Older cards use physical methods, described in detail in the next sections. Newer cards, though, may these changes with software. Librarian run the special software programme to make the changes once the card is plugged in those new settings are then saved on the card. Librarian can run the software again to make further changes.

The I/O Port Address

Each card in the system has unique I/O port address. Many of these are reserved for specific types of cards, such as the video card. For example, librarian can't have two VGA display cards in the same system. Other card addresses are not unique to the card type. Network cards, as well as other cards, fall within this category. This is why these cards have dip switches to change the I/O address.

Any "extra" cards in the system, such as a CD-ROM, music speech input or output, digitizer, or scanner card, may already be using the default setting on the network card. If librarian have one or more of these cards, librarian will need the documentation for these cards to determine that setting. If that card works correctly, librarian are better off making changes to the network card instead.

The possible addresses for network cards range from 2EOh to 380h. The dip switches can be set either ON or OFF. With eight positions, that number expresses a binary number from 0000 0000 to 1111 1111, or 0 to 255 decimal. The catch is that the numbers used to represent the I/O address are in hexadecimal. Therefore, the number 300h is represented as 0011 1111 on the switches. Librarian need not know hex to make the changes, but librarians must make sure their switch settings match those in the network card manual. Change the settings on the network card and software to aunique I/O address. If it still does not work, return the address to the original setting and consider changing the IRQ.

Interrupts

While the I/O address represents a unique ID to the computer, the interrupts are used to get the computer's attention. When the card needs to send something to, or through, the system, it "Interrupts" the current processing. The system then checks the card to process that task.

The IRQs range from IRQO to IRQ15. As with the unique I/O, the interrupts also need to be allocated, one per card or action. The standard interrupts include IRQ4 for COM1 and IRQ3 for COM2. If you have an LPT2 port in your system, the IRQ5 is also being used. In most cases, though, the IRQ5 is a good choice if you have both COM1 and COM2 in your system. Librarian can try the IRQ2, but this interrupt may not work well in 286 or faster systems. On most cards, librarian change the interrupt by moving a jumper. One row of pins on the card represents all the IRQ settings the card can use. Some network cards have just three settings, while newer cards may have five or more pairs of pins. As with the I/O address, will have to check the IRQs used by other cards for potential conflicts.

Base Memory Address for Library Network

The network card contains its own memory to buffer the transactions on the network cable. This must "fit" within the memory addresses that DOS can use. The network card memory fits in the reserved memory between 640K and 1024K, called high DOS memory. The common settings for network cards include COOh, DOOOh and D800h. Just like the I/O address and IRQs, this setting must be unique in the computer. For example, EGA and VGA display cards and some hard disk controller cards use the area starting at COOOh. Librarian will use another set of jumper pins to change the base address if librarian have conflicts here.

Other Settings

Network cards have even more settings. These include the DMA, the channel, the cable type, the node address, the remote boot PROM, and the reconfiguration timeout, and they rarely need to be changed. Make changes to these settings only if advised by tech support or with specific directions from the network card manual.

Making Cable Connectors

Once librarian have installed two network cards, are ready to connect them with a cable. If Librarian purchased a network kit, typically you get one cable section already made. Librarian can use this cable to test their network with one server and one workstation. Once librarian are satisfied that the beginnings of a network. Librarian can run the cables and make the permanent connections. Even before librarian begin tossing cables, he need to know what he must do to attach the cables. As mentioned, make sure you have the proper tools to make reliable connections.

Installing BNC Connectors for Library Network

Librarian use BNC connectors for network coax cable. Make sure librarian the specific BNC connector for the cable size. The connector is too large, the cable corne apart. If the connector is too small, the coax cannot slide inside the connector.

When purchasing the cable and connectors, get specifications for the amount of insulation to trim. These measurements are very important for proper contact between the cable and connector.

The actual BNC connector Kit contains three pieces. The smallest piece, the tip, covers the inner wire or the cable. The second and largest part is the actual twist connector. The third piece is the sleeve. This slips over the cable insulation and clamps the cable to the end to the twist connector. Making cable connector requires some practice. Cable connectors are not that expensive. Librarian may want to take a few feet of cable and few connectors and sit down to practice. This practice time helps later when librarian are in a rush to see if the whole LAN works. These are the steps for making a connector:

(a) Cut the cable, allowing several feet of a slack.

(b) Trim the insulation.

(c) Insert the sleeve on the cable.

(d) Attach the tip and crimp.

(e) Slide the connector on the cable.

(r) Bring the sleeve up and crimp.

(g) Tug on the connection to test its strength.

Make a clean cut of the cable with heavy duty wire cutters. If the end gets smasshed or hacked off with a knife, the connector is much harder to attach. Using the guise, trim the insulation to the exact measurements. If librarian want to make the cleanest and most accurate trims, purchase a cable-stripping pliers. Work over a piece of paper; the braided portion of the cable sheds tiny wires as you trim it.

Insert the sleeve on the cable and move it up the cable a foot or so. If librarian forget this step now, librarian will work to get the main connector on the cable and then have to take it off again to put on the sleeve.

Attach the tip and use the crimp to bottom end slightly. The crimper tool has a special area for this purpose. This assures good contact between the wire and the tip. Move the sleeve up and over the end of the connector. The sleeve should touch the bottom of the connector and cover part of the insulation. Use the crimping tool to squeeze the sleeve, insulation, and braid against the end of the connector. Some crimpers create a six-sided crimp; other produce two edges on the sleeve.

Tug on the connection to test its strength. If it wiggles, seems loose, or comes off in your hand, cut whole thing off and try again. Do not try to repair your first attempt. Weak connections in library network cable will eventually drive you to despire.

Making solid BNC connectors is a real skill. As long as librarian accept the fact that librarian will need practice and librarian will make a mess of the first few, he can do it.

Using Twisted-Pair Connectors for Library Network

With the RJ-45 twisted-pair cable connectors, librarian have eight wires to handle. Librarian must strip the insulation from the cable without cutting the inside wires. Each wire must then be inserted in the proper slot in the plastic connector and then crimped with the special tool. If one wire is crossed or is not crimped properly, librarian may spend hours tracking the problem to that source.

The better approach when working with twisted-pair cable is to purchase the cables with connectors already made from the computer to a vendor. Librarian then run the cable connector from the computer to a receptacle librarian have installed in the wall. The receptacles are easy to wire because they use screw-down connections.

Librarian strip the insulation, wrap the wire around the post, and screw it down.

Other Connection Methods for Library Network

The RJ-45 and BNC connectors are the most common for small library network. If librarian decide to have someone run the cable and make the connections, listen carefully to the method that person suggests. The cable and connector companies constantly improve their products and the ways to use. them. Do keep cable across an expanse of space is variously called tossing, pulling, stretching, stringing, or running cable. Each word describes the methods used to install cable. The most common ways to ceiling or pull it through the walls.

When librarian begin using space outside the normal working rooms, librarian are affecting the construction of that building. One of the best and most serious reasons to get help with your cabling project is to work with someone who knows the what building codes. An electrician experienced with network cable knows what kind of cable the building requires. Not only can the electricians do the hard physical labor, they make sure the cable is properly routed to avoid interference and potential breaks.

Before librarian hire electricians to do the cabling, make sure they have experience and understand the limitations of the medium. For example coiled up in the ceiling—"After all, librarian never know when librarian will need it". This potential vendor does not understand the limitations imposed by network cable.

In some situations, placing the cable will just be beyond the capabilities of a novice cable installer. These situations require special tools and expertise, and might include the following:

(a) Workstations on two or more floors in the building.

(b) Cable layouts exceed the rated length and require repeaters.

(c) Building code requires special installation.

(d) Your library has strict work rules.

(e) The cable must be installed through duct work.

(f) Librarian want network outlets in the walls.

(g) The cable must be pulled through cable conduits.

When looking for a contractor, remember that librarian can supply the cable and finish the connectors themselves; some LAN specialists mark up the cost of cable 200 percent or more. Librarian will want the contractor to tag the ends or each cable and test for continuity before he or she is finished.

If librarian install the cable themselves, He'll need at least one other person to help Someone needs to be on the receiving end as he pull the cable from one spot another. When working on ladders and around electrical equipment, it is also a good idea to have two people working together in the event of an accident.

Other Routes for Cable

Running cable throughout buildings is an important consideration in the building's construction. Designers also recognize the need to add cable later and provide conduits and access areas for telephone, power, security, fire alarms, and other types of cable. Depending on the age of your building, routing cable from floor to floor may not be too difficult. But because this requires a knowledge of all the other cables in the path, this kind of cable installation is usually beyound the abilities of a small LAN installer.

If you do need to cross floors, you building owner may have contractor who regularly works in the building. If the building's contractor does not know how to run network cable, you may have to pay the extra expense of teaming up the contractor with a network specialist.

Testing Connection

If you like to measure success in small pieces, you may want to run a section of cable, install the connectors, attach it to the network card in the workstation, and see if it works. With some Ethernet networks, remember to move the terminator cap to each successive station as you build your network section by section. This methods helps you locate a problem system or cable run immediately.

Other installers place all the cable, put on all the connectors, attach all the systems, and bring up the LAN, all at once. This approach is more dramatic and arguably more efficient for a professional installer. If you like this approach, you'll have to use a process of elimination to discover any problems you have.

In all cases, make sure there are no systems powered on and attached to the network when you work on cable or attach another station. If you use the "try each connection" approach, you must run turn of all the systems on the network before making further connections. You then need only turn on the server to test the latest connection.

Development of Modern Library

To a large extent the rise of Christianity during the Middle Ages was the salvation of much of the material that has survived, though Christianity itself must be help responsible for the destruction of much that was not in agreement with their doctrines.

In fact, the question is whether many of these so-called libraries would not be more correctly called small book-collections. Be that as it may, the medieval library was not only small but also extremely limited in its functions. it acted mainly as a depository of lithurgical works which were mostly used only at church services. It is true that these libraries contributed towards instruction but there was little sign of the large, learned, scientific library nor of public libraries until, towards the end of the Middle Ages, and particularly with the inception of the universities, the scientific library outside the church came to the fore.

The Renaissance, Reformation and Humanism

During the Renaissance, the Reformation and the period of Humanism the purpose of the library was mainly that of study and research, for which all types of material were preserved. The invention of printing stimulated the founding and expansion of libraries, and also the development of the collections into something approaching the accepted definition of a library. This was partly because the printed book and not the manuscript formed the basic stock, and partly because the collection and preservation aspects aimed more at its use for educational and study purposes. This, too, contributed to the increased size of collections and so resulted in the growing importance of proper organizations for the convenience of the user.

Of course this was not so in all libraries of that time, for very soon the size of library collections brought prestige to the owners and many of the collections can justifiably be called show libraries. Yet in them was found a revival of the classical library, the chief function of which was preservation and the chief aim education.

We find, however, the core of the modern conception of the library in the aftermath of this period, particularly in the Baroque period, when the social "show" aspects of the library had to make way for utilitarian aspects in the service of science. We cannot state that the Renaissance library was not already moving in this direction. The Renaissance library was in fact made available and accessible to students and researchers and in this respect served science, and judged by its aims and functions it must be regarded as a scientific rather than a public library. Its general accessibility, did not, as indicated, make of it a public library.

The Baroque period brought newer conceptions about education and these inevitably influenced the library as educational Instrument. It was mainly the aims and functions of the national and university library that underwent a marked change during this period, in that they were used to serve study and research. A shift of emphasis from preservation to education was consequently noticeable from the beginning of the Renaissance to the end of the 17th. century. In the meantime libraries were attached to various institutions even such as universities, but still the accent remained on preservation, education and research so that no new type of library became evident, although study and research began to receive increasing emphasis.

SOCIAL AND SCIENTIFIC LIBRARY

In the distinction between the social and the scientific library the former was said to have developed from the existing libraries owing to a change in the structure of social life. In the same way as this structural change is a product of modern times, so is the public library a product of our time. In considering the structure of the library in the RSA the social library was subdivided into the subscription public library (or subscription library) and the free public library or public library, while the scientific library was subdivided into a large number of types of which national, university and special libraries are the most important.

The review of the development of libraries made it clear that the subscription library had to make way for the public library to such an extent that it has survived in exceptional cases only. As a result, the terms, rate-or tax-supported public library, social library, free public library and public library, became more or less synonymous, so that we confined ourselves to the use of the term public library to typify the free public library, subscription library to distinguish the subscription public library and social library as the generic term.

From the review we deduced that the modern social and scientific library emanated from the original scientific library. The contemporary and the historic scientific library, however, exhibit differences, the most important of which are to be found in the retrieval of material and in the shift of emphasis in book-stock. Previously, work on the human sciences former the main part of most general collections, while the universal scientific library retained a balance between the human, social and natural sciences, and the technologies. A shift of emphasis in the contents of modern published records and in research was largely responsible for the subsequent change, in which the social library emphasized general educational and recreational literature and the scientific library the information transfer.

This trend must be linked with the clinetele of the two types of library. From the social library the broad masses demanded popular scientific library the student and researcher looked for specialised subject literature and information. In discussing the distinct types of library we said that in the long run the library is typified by the reader or user and his needs and that on this depend the aims, objectives and the functions of the particular type oflibrary. We also said that the task performance is directed at the attainment of the particular aims, from which we can deduce that library tasks are similar in all types of library, but that the degree to which they are executed is determined by the aim. Thus, a book will be indexed in all types of library; but since the social library is interested mainly in accessibility of the item, and the university library in its subject content, it is obvious that in the latter the indexing will probe more deeply.

The tasks or subsidiary functions performed in any library can be summarised as:

Acquisition. The processes or functions of acquisition indicate those activities in the library by means of which books are selected, bought, and added to the collection.

Processing. In this process the book is prepared for the reader's use. Here the following subsidiary functions are identifiable:

> ***Cataloguing.*** By means of this process material is described as a physical entity as well as indexed.
>
> ***Classification.*** By this we understand the process of analysis of material and systematization of the subjects contained in it in accordance with one or other classification scheme so that the material can easily by traced according to subject and so that the books on a given subject can be assembled without difficulty.

The functions of cataloguing and classification are usually summarized under the broad concept catalography.

Signaturing. This function embraces the activities by which the book is marked as the property of the library, codes are entered in it, usually on the spine, according to which the book can be arranged and located on the shelf, *i.e.* the position number, and the cards, date label, etc., which are essential for issue, use and identification purposes put into it.

Circulating. Some libraries, in particular public libraries, make their stock available for use at home. In fulfilling this function a record must be kept of the user, the book lent and the period for which it may be borrowed.

Information (Reference) Work. One of the most important tasks of a library is to provide information. To make this possible the staff has to look up and trace the necessary information to answer enquiries.

Management. For library service to be possible, book-stocks, personnel, buildings and finance are necessary. These items must be so organized that they can be used as profitably as possible and so that the most efficient service can be rendered. This calls for proper management in which the processes of planning, organization, administration (or directing) and control are distinguished.

While all library tasks and functions are carried out with a view to the final realization of the aims, such tasks and functions can be enumerated as follows:

— the selecting and collecting of books that will best succeed in providing education and information;

— logical and analytical organization of the bookstock by indexing (cataloguing), systematization (classification) and arrangement in accordance with subject, for quick retrieval of both items and information;

— the issue to readers of those books to readers that will offer the greatest benefit for their own enrichment;

— the provision of information on demand for the benefit of uses;

— instruction and guidance to groups and individuals in the use of books for purposes of education and information;

— publishing and interpreting bookstocks and library services to groups and individuals for their own and the development of society;

— economic management of the means for the efficient attainment of library aims.

Library tasks and functions therefore include all the activities that are necessary for the eventual realization of the aims of the library, each being carried out in accordance with the emphasis on the aims characteristic of the particular type of library. The social library will do the same with the emphasis on depth. Recreational literature, which forms a considerable part of the bookstock of the social library, requires mainly an author approach in indexing; in the scientific library a subject approach is more desirable. All indexing in the scientific library will consequently follow a subject rather than an author approach.

Since depth analysis varies in intensity in accordance with the type of scientific library, the special library will index its subject literature in far greater detail than, say, a university library in which case we may refer to micro-analysis as opposed to macro-analysis.

Various writers and organizations list functions and aims in their own particular ways. For instance, the American Library Association (ALS) states that aims of the public library include the following:

(a) self-education of all people in the community;

(b) enrichment and further development of the subjects in which individuals undertake formal education;

(c) support for the educational, social and cultural activities of groups and organizations;

(d) satisfying everybody's need for information; and

(e) encouragement of healthy recreation and constructive use of leisure time.

The Public Library Research Group of the British Library Association (London and Home Counties Branch) distinguishes between aims and objectives as follows in expressing the aspirations of the public library:

Aim

To contribute to sustaining the quality of life in all its aspects-educational, economic, industrial, scientific and cultural and promote the concept of a democratic society in which equal opportunity exists for all to develop into true citizens, with whole and balanced personalities leading to an increase in the sum total of man's happiness and awareness of himself, his fellow men and his environment. This contribution is effected through the public libraries as a multi-purpose information—education—culture agency. It should make freely available the records of man's experience in the form of books and related materials to all who may ask, and thus promote and foster the free flow of information and ideas.

Objectives

1. Education. To foster and provide means for self-development of the individual/group at whatever stage of education, closing the gap between the individual and recorded knowledge.

2. Information. To bring to the individual/group accurate information quickly and in depth, particularly on topics of current concern.

3. Culture. To be one of the principal centres of cultural life and promote a keener participation, enjoyment and appreciation of all the arts.

4. Leisure. To play a part in encouraging the positive use of leisure and providing material for change and relaxation.

The British statements make it clear that the reasons for the existence of the social library can be found in education, provision of information and recreation. We can furthermore deduce from the British exposition that we must differentiate between aims and objectives, the former being situated in the attainment of an improved and democratic way of life, and the latter in activities which make education, information and recreation possible.

Briefly, the British point of view is that the social library is an agency or means of propaganda for the improvement of a specific way of life. Although writers accept that this may not be so, yet here it is clearly inferred that the social library is an indispensable instrument in the socialization of the community. The Russians accept the social library as an agency for the realization of the communist ideal, and the Americans accept it as such for the American way of life. According to may authorities these views nullify the true educational purpose of the social library to such an extent that it is no longer a free means to education. Obviously, in any country the social library must of necessity adapt to and be integrated into the current conception of life and the system of government of the particular country. To strive deliberatively for this, as the British put it, immediately raises the question as to whether the social library as a free means to education is not thereby threatened.

We cannot agree with the British in their definition of objectives, for what they term objectives are in fact functional activities and should therefore be classified as functions; but we do subscribe fully to the reality of the distinction. In fact, the British are the only ones who have made this distinction.

In the light of previous statements, a distinction of this nature plays an extremely important part in management science insofar as the former justifies the organization's right to existence, while the latter entails the objectives to be pursued in order to reach the aims. For this reason the aims are immeasurable ideals seeking realization, although the ultimate is not clear. On the other hand, the objectives are measurable elements which can be altered or added to from time to time as they are realized. Education might be an aim of this kind, whereas the objective set could be the number of books read, the number of people served, etc., which must be realized within a certain time. Once the desired numbers have been realized, new objectives are set while the aims remain unchanged.

This method entails pursuit of both measurable and immeasurable objēctives. Quantification or measurement can be appliēd to amongst others, the number of books issued, the number of borrowers enrolled. However, this does not indicate the quality of the service, depth of answers given, etc. Quantification of quality is therefore extremely difficult to effect, although quantity is far easier to measure.

In the establishment of aims, quantification therefore has no role, whereas in the formulation of objectives it is decisive with regard to quantity and/or quality. If the *raison d'etre* of the social library is to be found mainly in education and recreation, as maintained by the Americans and the British, and that of the scientific library in the provision of information and preservation, we can say the following:

Education

The educational purpose is fundamental to all types of library, and for the social library it is its main reason for its existence. Everything the social library does can be traced to this aim.

The social library, as have been seen, owes its development to a need to offer the masses the opportunity for education, and so to act as an instrument of informal education for the community as a whole. In the USA in particular, but also in the .RSA and elsewhere, the social library is considered the best agency for the advancement and presentation of adult education. In spite of the existence of the many other educational means in modern community—travel, films, newspapers, radio, television—the social library takes its rightful place alongside tnem, for as long as it can hold this place it will remain one of the most powerful means for the informal education of both adults and children. In the USA the social library has become the official instrument for the presentation of adult education, but unfortunately this is not the case in the RSA. Possibly this is due to the fact that in the RSA the social library is generally accepted as a purely recreational facility.

In principle, the social library addresses itself to all social groups. The question is whether this principle is being realized, for it is apparently only the more literate who are using the social library. In Europe it would appear that the masses and not the learned groups use the public libraries. In communist countries where the social library serves the state as a means of propaganda it is orientated towards the broad strata of the population, while in Britain, the USA, Canada, Australia and various other Western countries the social libraries serve groups varying from the better-educated to the learned. There are probably many reasons for the current state of affairs in the RSA, the most important apparently being the absence of class differences and the lack of generally available and well-equipped scientific libraries. This last situation has rapidly changed since the 1960's, though the public libraries such as those of Johannesburg, Cape Town, East London, Durban and others still have to make large scale provision for these needs. The public library, as a well-known American writer has maintained is in fact the secret weapon of the educated man.

The education of the broad masses must be linked with the rise of democracy. Each community is based on certain fundamental suppositions which decide its spirit and form. These assumptions have a bearing on the value of the individual and the community in the society, the basis of human relations, the role of the state and conceptions affecting religious, cultural, education and economic affairs. Any culture reflects these fundamental conceptions and its vitality is very closely connected with their development and survival.

In a democracy these ideas must be respected and put into practice by the broad masses, which presupposes individual participation. Furthermore, in a democracy the people believe in opportunity for the individual and in his right to make decisions, and such individual decisions mean something only when they become the decisions of the masses and therefore the decisions of the government. Conversely, the government itself remains a democratic institution only as long as it respects the fundamental principle.

In such a social context the social library as an educational medium has an extremely important role to fulfil: firstly to ensure the freedom of the individual, secondly to retain the possibility of free access to all knowledge for individual decisions and thirdly, and with all responsibility towards the state, to help protect these freedoms in the interest of the individual and the state. This further presupposes a sense of responsibility, objectively and without prejudice orientated to the individual, the masses and the state, and can be realized only in an awareness of the responsibility which provides the best, most constructive and the progressively retentive.

The professional literature constantly emphasises that the public library should respect the absolute freedom of the individual and that in its pursuit of objectivity it should put no obstacle in the way of investigation. This premise can be fully supported and should be pursued in all respects. However, it can be compared to a knife, which is a marvellous instrument, but is also a tool in the perpetration of the worst crimes. For this reason the public library must never lose sight of its educational aim, but should provide only the best and by means of the healthy and objective selection policy allow guidance in the educational process to come into its own.

Accordingly, and in keeping with its objectivity, the public library may in no circumstances make itself available as an instrument for propaganda. This means that the library may adopt no specific point of view on religion, politics or any other controversial question.

A standard of this nature is in keeping with the objectivistic conception of libraries, although there is the possibility that absolute objectivity might result in apathy and neutrality. If, as a democratic institution, the public library has to take its rightful place in a democracy it cannot do otherwise than propagate a democratic way of life through the composition of its stock, service, and image. The social library in the USA has accepted this task, namely propagation of the American way of life, and has in this way become, in principle the same propaganda instrument for the USA as the social library in communist countries. Thorough comparison will reveal fundamental differences in individual freedom, which are relevant here. What is important, however, is that absolute objectivity is not possible, nor is it desirable. It is in the interests of the individuals that the state and the community respect his freedom, but only as long as the individual fully complies with his responsibility to them both. The social library must at the same time make all literature accessible, propagate the democratic way of life and promote responsible action towards the welfare and rights of the individual, the happiness and peace of the community as a whole and the security of the state. Here, then, is complete agreement with the British point of view insofar as they use the public library to propagate their aim of an improved and more democratic way of life.

Another aspect of the educational purpose that has been raised by the British and Americans to a separate aim deserves out attention. Side by side with education, the ALA sets cultural enrichment as aim of the social library, and the British speak of the public library as a focal point of cultural life, promoting more active participation in, and enjoyment and appreciation of the arts.

Although these statements are accepted they are seen only as part of the educational aim. Yet the purpose of education is to impart information and knowledge, mould individual and independent thought, as well as enrich man culturally and in this the appreciation of the arts forms an important part. If we accept this, when we need no further argument to prove that cultural enrichment is an integral part of the educational aim. Indeed, if this aspect is taken from the educational purpose the same can be done with the moulding of independent thought, intellectual enrichment, economic improvement, comprehension, etc. All these things are a result of education and cannot therefore be set beside education as a separate aim for libraries. Briefly this means that the social library is a powerful instrument in adult and continued education and in shaping the individual into a thinking, informed, happy and responsible citizen of his country—all in the interests of the individual, the community, and the state.

Scientific libraries play an equally important part in the education of the individual and the community, especially those libraries accessible to the general public, as are national libraries. However, the tendency here is for the reader to use the scientific library only when engaged in formal study or research. Universal scientific libraries which are concerned with formal education fulfil their educational purpose as an aid in the hands of educators, which is why university, college and school libraries serve formal education by means of their educational programmes. These libraries play a less active part in education than does the social library, although their indirect help is of paramount importance in the educational programme of the institution to which they are attached. As part of the educational programme of the uriiversity and college, research programmes are equally part of the educational aim of the library. In fact, without library facilities research is impossible, for it is through the library that not only the position of research can be traced in the field of any specialisation, but through it the researcher can obtain indispensible recorded information.

Even the special library plays an important part in the educational programme of a country by its continued support of research in and outside the institution to which it belongs.

Provision of Information

All libraries possess books and all books contain information—real or fictive. Our only concern here is the former. Some libraries use this information mainly to answer questions and others to attain an educational aim. For this reason the difference in the use of information differentiates the social from the scientific library. The former fulfils an educational aim by, among other things, the use of information while the latter fulfils its informational aim entirely with it.

We have identified the selection of books as a library function. By this all books are accessioned on the grounds of the real or fictive information they contain. Fictive information is normally found in the literary genres. Such books are used chiefly in the social library for purposes of recreation, but in the scientific library, if they are in fact included, for the study of literature. Special literature as the bearer of "real" information is chosen by the scientific library mainly for the information which it contains. Selection, acquisition, indexing or retrieval, dissemination and communication of information all work towards the realization of the informational aim. How this is executed depends on the type of library, the purpose for which it is used, the level on which the information is needed, as well as the circumstances under which the service takes place.

The informational aim is the reason for the existence of the scientific library, and hence it is accepted as a matter of course that the scientific library in all its activities is orientated towards finding and providing information. Factors that determine the range and level of information in the scientific library are chiefly the clientele served, the type of institution of which the library is a part, the research programmes supported and the financial resources.

The social library is fundamentally orientated to the fulfilment of a general educational aim. In the process, information is used, whereby the provision of information becomes part of the educational aim itself. Whether the provision of information is an end in itself in the social library depends mainly on the size of the library, the nature of the community, the proximity and/or presence of other sources of information such as scientific library and information services, and demand. It is clear that the central branch of the Johannesburg Public Library will offer an information service to its community while a demand for it exists. Even, as in this case, with the close proximity of two university libraries, the demand always justifies such a service. Furthermore, the fact that the university libraries are not generally accessibly to the public, as is the Johannesburg Public Library, contributes to the justification for an information service by the JPL. It possesses a bookstock and an information service which has won renown, and in this type of fact the outensible inconsistencies evident in libraries are often to be found.

Recreation

The ALA has stated that one of the aims of the public library is to encourage healthy recreation and the constructive use of leisure time, and the British are in agreement with this. However, is the social library justified in spending public income on recreation when so many other facilities for recreation exist? The answer to this is that the recreational facilities offered by the social library are among the few, that offer intellectual recreation which is freely accessible to all. We argued earlier that the recreational aim formed part of the educational aim, and at most could be defined as a subsidiary aim because mental relaxation in itself has little meaning. Only when the aim of intellectual recreation is improvement in reading-skills, language and style, stimulation of intellectual development, and individual thought, etc. is the social library justified in having intellectual recreation as one of its aims, which, as such, cannot do otherwise that form part of the educational aim. Scientific libraries have no recreational aim. Where they do possess reading matter for recreation this has been collected as part of the national book-production, as in the national library, or because the study of language and literature requires it, as in the libraries of universities, colleges and schools, or because there are no social library facilities in the vicinity, a fact which sometimes compels even special libraries to keep recreational reading matter.

Since readership involves the study of the value of reading, including the reading of recreational material, we can confine ourselves here to the comment that the social library is a powerful instrument in its offer of healthy mental relaxation as part of its educational aim.

Preservation

Throughout the ages the book, as manifested in its many forms in various times and places, has been collected and preserved for two reasons: firstly because of its contents and secondly for the value of its format.

It seems that in ancient times the former consideration was the main one, though in the absence of proper records we can hardly judge which was the main consideration. What we can say with certainty is that with the collection of documents in the great classical libraries of Nineveh and Alexandria, the contents were considered extremely important and that the collected documents were collected, retrieved and preserved for study purposes. Another important element of the classical period was that libraries were national possessions. Indeed, it was the desire for personal glorification that moved most rulers to fund large libraries, archives and museums. In spite of this there institutions can be accepted as national possession and not as the private property of kings en emperors. During the classical period little, if any, distinction was drawn between libraries, archives and museums. The chief task of all sections of these institutions was the collection and preservation of documents. The library departments looked after the collection of the written word, whether on clay tablets, as in the Babylonian Empire; or on papyrus rolls, as in Egypt. Ironically enough it was not the library of antiquity that preserved the written record for us, but the tombs and monuments of that time.

The division of the three sections of the classical institutions into separate institutions followed chiefly after the invention of printing, and after a definitive division has been made between the manuscript and the printed book although the unity of the three sections persisted in an institution such as the British Museum until very recently when the British Museum's Department of Printed Books, Manuscripts, Maps, etc. became part of the British Library set-up in England. Moulded on the classical example this institution closely resembled the Alexandrian Library in organization and in content whereby museum, library and archive was combined into one institution. Be this as it may the different nature of the artifacts in the museum collection of these classical institutions brought about a natural separation of library and museum. On the other hand it remains difficult even today to draw clear dividing-line between library and archive, for the archival function forms part of the work of both institutions. In the former it is done with regard to no-official manuscripts as well as printed books, whereas in the latter it is mainly a matter of official government documents in unpublished but also published forms. Throughout the middle ages and up to the present these fundamental characteristics of the classical library can be traced to a greater or lesser extent in the preservation activities of libraries. The early Middle Ages preserved books for their contents alone, but there is sufficient evidence that in the middle and later Middle Ages the aspects of format, such as decoration, calligraphy, binding or even the material on which the document was reproduced, often constituted adequate reasons for the preservation of an item.

The humanists were more or less exclusively interested in the content value of books, whereas the later baroque libraries can justifiably be called showlibraries where books were collected and preserved for their outer appearance rather than for their content. The invention of printing made books a part of daily life to such an extent that contents of necessity played a very important part in the collection, possession and preservation of books by both public and private bodies.

Today, especially with the establishment of various types of library, the preservation function is applied differently. In the national library where the main issue is the collection of the national book production such books are completely and permanently preserved for posterity, both for their content and their format. In the university library, books are preserved on a semi-permanent basis for as long as they are of importance for study and research, and the accent is on their content value since in this type of library it is particularly a question of the preservation and accessibility of information for study and research. The special library is principally interested in the most recent developments and remains only material of current importance. Here the interest is in only the content value of the book collection. In the social library the preservation function varies with the type of material. Works used for relaxation have a temporary and usually limited utilitarian value and after and period of use are often withdrawn and got rid of by means of donation, sale or even destruction. In contrast, books on special subjects used for the provision of information are normally preserved for far longer, often until new editions with more recent treatment of the subject replace them. Special collections however, permanently preserve books on a particular speciality. Thus a special collection on a writer such as C. J. Langenhoven or a general collection of africana will be assembled on the particular subject and permanently preserved.

Multi Media Catalogue and the Computer

A basic problem in special cataloguing, is whether or not to incorporate entries for various special material in a general catalogue of a library. This issue can be considered under three main headings: *(a)* the compilation of a separate catalogue for each individual form whether each is book or nonbook; *(b)* the compilation of a special multi-media catalogue incorporating all nonbook materials; and *(c)* the compilation of a single catalogue to include entries for all materials in library whether book or nonbook.

A precedent is set by various agencies which issue single-medium lists and catalogues. Some of these agencies are firms and other organisations which deal with specific medium and so of course these examples cannot be said to advocate separation in retrieval systems in libraries. A well known example is the British national film catalogue, recording the stock of one organisation. However, we should mention that the Library of Congress, which receives all materials under copyright deposit, issues separate catalogues for such forms as films and filmstrips; and phonorecords; and in the past it issued one for maps and atlases. We should also mention that BNB issues a separate publication of scores and works about music in the British catalogue of music, even repeating the entries for works about music as compared with BNB itself, although classified according to the BCM's own scheme.

Notwithstanding, we recommend the principle of integrating, as far as possible, entries for all forms. The chief reason for this is that information enquiries do not necessarily cite a particular form, and even if they do they may not cite yet other relevant physical forms. This may happen because of ignorance on the part of the enquirer, who may be, say, book-oriented, and may not know of other forms. Current awareness services might include, under certain subject headings, not only bookform materials but any form of presentation of a subject. Such a facility would, we suggest, be of direct value mainly in teaching institutions, at all levels. As will come up again later, it would be vital to emphasise clearly the physical form, since the use of a document, by a teacher for example, would depend on the availability of suitable apparatus for playing, screening, etc.

A further factor in favour of integrated catalogues is the increasing use of various forms in conjunction with each other. This situation is no novelty. The fact of accompanying material has been long known and catered for in codes. A very common example is that of a recording, which will perhaps be on disc, with accompanying letterpress material, such as one of Chaucet's Canterbury tales together with a copy of the printed text. In the past, the accompanying material has usually be regarded as subsidiary, even though in fact it may have been necessary for the full exploitation of a document, ego a film strip intended for instructional purposes with accompanying teacher's lecture notes, or records. Contrary to current emphasis on the audio-visual 'kit' as a new phenomenon, we suggest, then, that this form has been with us for it is difficult to decide which is the predominant medium, *e.g.* as to whether a sound recording 'accompanies' a text, or the 'text 'accompanies' a sound recording. For this reason, as-well as to ensure that all materials are exploited as fully as possible, we suggest that a so-called multi-media catalogue is needed. However, since accompanying materials is often in textual form, it seems reasonable to reach the logical 'the media' and conventional textual material in the same catalogue. For similar reasons it is theoretically justifiable to include any 'special' textual material such as serials in the integrated catalogue. As we have let alone the average library user, to decide what is, arid what is not, a library should be recorded in one integrated catalogue, with the usual author, title and subject approaches.

Nevertheless, there will still exist the need for a physical form approach, mainly, we feel, for the librarian's benefit for stock record and housekeeping purposes, but also in some cases for the immediate use of the library's clientele. The latter may happen, when, say, a teacher is making up a film or record programme for general use, or when a new piece of equipment has been acquired and the teacher particularly wishes to experiment with it. The librarian's need may arise from the need for a stock record for such purposes as stock-checking, statistics, accounting, and calling up of items not received. Strictly speaking, these last are not catalogue uses, the basic object of a catalogue being the exploitation of stock by users, whether directly or indirectly. However, as we know, much of the data, for housekeeping purposes is the same as that used for exploitation. Inevitably, with the use of a basic set of data for various purposes, there arises the concept of an integrated systems approach, with the use of a computer for selecting from a comprehensive store, and manipulating the data to specific ends. From the user's or librarian's housekeeping point of view, entries for documents in a particular form could be selected, manipulated and printed out in whatever order was required for the purpose. An essential need is to be able to list all materials in a particular form, eg filmstrip. In turn, this means that each physical form must not only be represented, as in standard, eg AACR, cataloguing practice, but also it must be a field on its own, and with a tag to facilitate its use as an access term.

Nowadays AACR is justifiably regarded as working basis for much full bibliographic cataloguing, and its structure is usually assumed in MARC formats, whether for book or for nonbook materials. AACR does include provision for spelling out some physical forms a potential tags.

Phonodisc could reasonably be made a field, with its own tag. Similar provisions apply for other physical forms starting with the stem 'phono...', such as phonotape and phonowire. It should be possible to enable a search to be made on the stem 'phono' to facilitate retrieval of all sound recordings, whatever their physical form. Incidentally, in the example given above, the full stop (period) has been omitted at the end of the author heading, and following 'Phonodisc', despite its being, inconsistently, included in the code.

However, by accident, the code may have provided a means whereby nonbook, as differentiated from book, forms of material might be retrieved by computer, the full stop acting as a searching and retrieval device for most 'special' materials as opposed to conventional materials. According to AACR, other special forms are not so conveniently indicated by a potential field attached to a uniform title.

A problem exists for music scores, which are not designated as such in headings or uniform titles, although in some instances the word 'score' occurs in the collation. Yet another problem occurs even when a potential field is suggested in MCR; this is when there is a possible difference of opinion over a term to be used. This would not pose much of a problem for locally generated data, but it could cause some degree of difficulty at least it locally generated entries using the 'British English' term had to be merged with, say, LC generated entries, which naturally would use 'American English'.

Similar types of problem are manifested by the many other forms of document, when it comes to computerised manipulation and retrieval of selected forms, as well as of subjects. And, as we feel we can assume, computerisation is the only feasible hope of achieving a multiple-access approach to both information as such and special forms of presentation.

We wish to sum up, at this point, that not only a multi-media catalogue may be needed, but also that a generously multi-approach catalogue is needed. There should be approaches along the lines of a principle which we feel Cutter would have approved. Potentially, in one sequence, one could approach or trace information according to, not only author-type and title headings, but also subject headings and physical form headings; subject headings could consistently be subdivided according to form of presentation. As we have said, such a complex manipulation of data arid approaches can be realised only through the use of the computer.

Some libraries are already computerising, or planning to computerise, their bibliographic data on special materials. In some cases, systems are being, or have been, introduced for certain individual forms, depending on local need, eg the Library of the Western Australian Institute of Technology has a multiple-approach computerprinted catalogue for slides. At the time of writing other media have not been planned for in this particular instance. Despite some academics' pipe dreams of an integrated systems approach, there is a lot to be said for experiment with a single medium. Problems relating to programming, computer storage, and access can be identified and solved comparatively inexpensively. However, we suggest that such achievements should be regarded as research and development projects rather than as ends in themselves. A most important aspect of such an experimental project is actual use of the resultant catalogue or index. In a comparatively 'closed' situation, as in the library of an educational institution, potential users of such a system can be canvassed and their comments recorded and analysed. Such a catalogue use study, if carefully planned and executed, could be extremely helpful as a pointer towards the potential exploitation of a comprehensive system.

When libraries reach the point of finally appreciating that so-called 'special' materials are not so special that they may be rejected as 'normal' stock, or if actually acquired hidden away and largely avoided, it should be possible for multi-library catalogue use studies to be made. From these could emerge an idea of what library clienteles really need in relation to special materials. Judging by one experiment, in Pearl River Public Library, New York, when a multi-media catalogue and even stock. integration policy is implemented, the users readily respond to such facilities: 'Users do like to find related materials on a given subject on one place'. Admittedly, as the article says, 'one situation does not connote a trend'; but we suggest that this situation is at least a symptom of the, as yet, unrealised potential of once-'especial' library materials.

The Gilbert Report is confined in scope to audio-visual materials used in education. However, education and modern teaching techniques are probably the main stimulant to the increase in use and acceptance of at least the large audio-visual sector of special materials likely-or even unlikely-to be encountered by most librarians. Further, the report interprets 'education' in a broad sense, and some documents which might formally be dubbed 'recreational' are likely to be embraced by its proposals. This interpretation does not affect the variety of physical forms, but it could affect the size of any central store established, and this in turn could mean that any local library's stock of nonbook materials may stand a reasonable chance of being as well comprehended by the central store as, say, a general library's book stock might be covered by MARC tapes.

The physical forms contemplated are listed as follows:

Sound or Audio Recording

Gramophone record: a recording of sound on disc.

Sound or audio tape: a recording of sound on magnetic tape carried on an open reel.

Audio cassette or cartridge: a sound tape contained in a cassette or cartridge. Visual images: still

Slide: a small unit of transparent material containing an image, mounted in rigid format, usually 2" x 2", and designed for use in a slide viewer or projector.

Filmstrip: a roll of film containing a succession of images designed to be viewed one at a time.

Transparency: a sheet, or combined set of sheets, of transparent material, carrying information, designed for use with an overhead projector.

Wallchart: a large sheet of information arranged in tabular or diagrammatic order, designed for public display.

Flipchart: an integrated graphic presentation on separate sheets hinged together in easel format.

Flash card: a card having words, numerals, or pictures, designed for rapid identification, with or without an integrated sound track.

Art Print: a printed reproduction of a work of art-eg painting, drawing, sculpture, etc.

Print: a picture with accompanying text which makes the print significant for study purposes.

Picture or Drawing: a two dimensional drawing, painting, portrait, photograph, or a print of any of these, produced on opaque backing.

Visual Images: moving

Film: film, bearing a sequence of images which create the illusion of motion when projected, and carried on an open reel.

Film cartridge: a length of motion picture film contained in a cartridge.

Film loop: an endless loop of motion picture film usually contained in a cassette.

Videotape: magnetic or other tape, carrying a series of TV images recorded magnetically, electronically or holographically. (Any of these may bear an integral sound track.)

Visual Images with Sound

A recording of moving visual images may carry an integral sound track (eg Sound Film).

A set of slides, or a filmstrip, may be accompanied by an associated sound recording on a gramophone record or, more usually; tape (commonly referred to as Tape-Slide).

Programmed Materials

Carried on transparent, opaque or magnetic substrates and designed for viewing directly or by projection, or for use with a computer; may have the physical form of a book.

Artefacts and Realia

Map: a flat representation of part or all of either the earth or the heavens.

Globe: a sphere with a representation or a map of the earth or of the heavens.

Chart: a sheet of geographic or other information arranged in tabular or diagrammatic order.

Relief model: a three-dimensional geographical map other than a globe.

Diorama: a scene reproduced in three dimension by placing objects, figures, etc. in front of a representational background.

Model: a three-dimensional representation of an object, either exact or to scale.

Realia: actual objects or specimens.

Microforms

(*Microreproduction:* a miniature reproduction of printed or other graphic matter which cannot be utilised without magnification.)

Microfiche: a microreproduction on a flat sheet of film.

Microfilm: a microreproduction on a roll of film.

Micro-opaque: a microreproduction on opaque material.

Aperture card: a card with an opening or openings within which micro-reproduction on film is mounted.

Combinations

Kit: a combination of items in two or more media designed to be used as a unit.

Game: a boxed set of materials designed for educational play.

It is envisaged that any records of documents would include commercial, 'semicommercial' (from, say, professional bodies), and even some locally produced items. Incorporated—in fact the core of such a data base would be entries from large national collections in Britain such as the National Film Archive and the British Institute of Recorded Sound.

We might note at this point that in 1972 a proposal was made from another source that there should be a 'British national discography' along the lines of the British catalogue of music and of course BNB itself; if such a work were realised its contribution to the type of data base contemplated could be substantial. Also here we might recall that the Library of Congress has a potential which has progressed beyond this stage: its catalogue coverage already embraced audiovisual materials thanks to US legal deposit, which appears to be automatically comprehensive of all physical forms of documents. We hope that the new British Library when it emerges will have copyright coverage at least equal to that of the Library of Congress.

To return to the Gilbert Report, with its attempts at cumulating such data as is at present available in Britain, we have to appreciate that, at the moment, a large variety and types of records would have to be drawn upon to realise the hope of a comprehensive collection of bibliographic data on nonbook materials. It is anticipated that such information could be reconciled, and incorporated consistently into a central store, without the central cataloguers having to sight the actual documents. This situation may, at first sight, seem to be analogous to that of compiling union catalogues of, say, books, or serials. However, in such cases, it is usually expected, or at least hoped, that entries have been compiled by professional cataloguers and, at least to some extent, according to a standard recognised code. We feel that Gilbert possibly minimises the technical difficulties in such a process. However, we feel that such a process. However, we feel that such a project is possible, and that bibliographic niceties so dear to some-dare we say, conservative-cataloguers must give way to the immediate need of producing data of use to many libraries. To digress, but with a purpose, we might recall that some BM cataloguers seem to have wanted to delay indefinitely the photo-printed BM catalogue while they indulged their penchant for bibliographic perfection on the bibliographic information needed all over the world. We had the privilege of meeting Sir Frank Francis, then BM's director, in the early 1960's and he commented that, in effect, he had to get his cataloguers to eschew academic bibliographic niceties and to get on with producing a catalogue for real live use. Librarians must have in mind not colleague-cataloguers' academic criticism, but the ultimate use of their product in document and information retrieval. In short, if any minor errors emerge-hard luck. The main concern should be use of the data to enable documents to be identified and exploited by users of libraries all over the country or even the world. In sum, then, we support the layman's proposition of integrating data from whatever source so that it can be drawn upon in real live situations. It is better to have some-however inconsistent-sort of information about nonbook materials, and soon, than wait for the millennium when all material is catalogued perfectly down to the last punctuation mark. We do not apologise for this apparent tirade: there are still far too many cataloguers who derive more satisfaction from the use of a square bracket than from the knowledge that they are serving users' needs for information today, not in three months' time when they finally have finished their games and pass on their toys to a vague depersonalised public whom through unfortunate library management they never meet.

So, then, we keenly recommend the concept of the centrally accumulated data base hoped for in GILBERT, and we further hope that people can be found to do the accumulating, assimilating, and production for use of such information.

However, to realise such a hope, two needs must be borne in mind: *(a)* an overall organisation; and *(b)* a detailed organisation for the manipulation and output of bibliographic data according to the needs of requesting centres, assumed to be libraries which receive and formulate enquiries.

(a) is worked towards by a system as reproduced from GILBERT. This includes four components: *(a)* the actual producers of documents; *(b)* central cataloguing agencies; *(c)* a computer store; and *(d)* printers for producing usable hard copy as required. It is technologically possible for *(c)* and *(d)* to be parts of the same apparatus: Ii lot depends on the physical type of product expected in reply to an enquiry, and the type of physical presentation acceptable by users. A single enquiry might be satisfied with a 'one off computer printout, but a resource centre's own complete catalogue may demand a more sophisticated physical presentation.

(a) is further enhanced by the system reproduced from GILBERT. The essential advances of this system on the previous diagram is that it introduces the real users of nonbook materials, and it shows how they are integrated into an information retrieval system ranging from producers, via a central store and enquiry-coordinating service, through catalogue agencies, and back to enquirers. A major component of this system is the Central Bibliographic Service, linking libraries and similar information service centres with a computer store and with cataloguing agencies, and, ultimately, with users of nonbook materials the final objective of the exercise.

So far, we could envisage the service as providing computer-printed lists for individual enquiries. However, this concept would, in effect, put the cart before the horse. Before individual searches are initiated, it is reasonable to expect general lists to be searched, in much the same way that index medicus may be searched manually before a MEDLARS search is initiated may computer. The report, then, envisages a printed bibliographic service, which corresponds to the records of normal books covered by BNB or in the film world-works covered by the British national film catalogue.

A noteworthy quotation from GILBERT is that 'no significant problems were encountered, and that there is every reason to suppose that the MARC system can be used for the cataloguing of NBM. The inference is that all nonbook materials could conveniently be catered for in the MARC format, and presumably entries for all forms could be integrated into once catalogue.

The sample catalogue entries would be part of a so-called HELPIS system: Higher Education learning Programmes Information Service, as an adjunct to LERMISTOR: Learning Materials Information Store. But, confirming what we said earlier, the range of types of materials and of actual documents prepared for the system make it some likely that the actual store of bibliographic data, and the spadework which would go into programming in the broadest sense, would encompass a lot of the work of all sorts needed to make the hole system operative.

It may be useful at this point to try to consolidate the main components of creating the type of integrated system envisaged in the report as a whole, and as demonstrated microeconomically by its sample Catalogue of materials available for exchange produced in March 1971 and including a variety of audiovisual materials.

First the documents have to be made, and, as with printed monographic media, they come from a great variety of organisations, and may range from commercial materials for national or even international distribution, to perhaps items locally produced for use in just on educational institution. An example of the latter-local products-which comes to mind, though in fact Australian, is a series of video-taped lectures made in the Princess Margaret Hospital, Perth, for the education of nurses. A decision must be made somehow and somewhere as to which documents are to be recorded in the central system. A sort of parallel situation in letterpress materials might be the locally printed or typewritten reports on research, eg higher degree these, produced by the thousand in colleges and universities. Such products may be merely academic exercises or they may transpire to embody an original contribution to their subject and therefore have value in a broader context.

We then come to the need for all such worthy documents to be catalogued, adequately and according to a generally accepted method. An obvious need is that documents on one subject but in varying physical forms and from a diversity of origins must finish up with a uniform subject J:leading, whether verbal or codified. This operation would call for the recognition of a uniform subject approach if it were to cater ultimately for a wholly consistent integrated record at the projected central store.

Then comes the need for items entries to be selected and to be notified to the central store. Approaches and description need to be either consistently expressed or given fully enough in whatever form for consistent records to be brought together accurately at the catalogue compilation centre. The problem of integrating dissimilar entries for similar documents is as old as the compilation of union catalogues, and goes back to at least medieval England when a union catalogue of the manuscripts in monastery libraries was compiled. The problem is vastly intensified nowadays because of the fantastic increase in the quantity of documents, and in the present context it is inevitably exacerbated by the variety of physical forms. A J Wells has stated. The largest single problem in system terms arises at this point since there is no unique identifier for each item which would provide a ready means of eliminating duplicate standard descriptor fields from the file. This is a major problem since the same item may be input into the data bank from any or all of the agencies. Inevitably here we must bring up the fact of standard book numbers, and further, international standard book numbers. There is an obvious need for some form of unique identifying tag for nonbook materials, just as there has developed a system for normal books in several countries, eg Britain and the USA. To plan and execute such a system would involve a lot of planning, and in fact we find it hard to envisage it being carried through. Presumably a prefix for each form would be required, as well as a unique number for each document. A unique identifying system does already exist for sound recordings in disc form, even though the notation used, assigned by manufacturers (*i.e.*, publishers), is often complex. It is conceivable that at least commercially produced documents could be subjected to the same type of routine to which publishers of books seem to have responded so well in those countries not using standard book numbers. It would appear that cooperating publishers of books have readily appreciated the value of such a system. All we can hope for at the moment is that publishers of nonbook materials would respond to the appeal and convenience of just such a system.

The next stage is the assembling and editing of bibliographic data at the relevant centre and its feeding into the store, say in computer disc form of facilitate the random access envisaged. This stage necessitates the allocation of tags and fields in a uniform way: this is why we have inferred that initial compilation of data should be made, if at all possible, according to an accepted code for author/title and description and according to a standard system for the subject approach. UDC is the most widely accepted system—whatever faults it may have at present. An advantage of UDC is that it has built-in symbols for various types of physical form, which can be represented either through the use of the colon for linking 'main' notations, or through the addition of symbols, to represent physical forms. We suggest that in a central store the use of 'main' notations would represent the type of flexibility required for access according to physical form, as well as the obvious requirement for access according to the subject of a document. Further, experiments have demonstrated that UDC—despite its occasionally awkward facet indicators can be computerised. The inputting of bibliographic data might, we feel, be the most difficult part of the operation-possibly even more difficult than locating information in the firsr-place. However, experiments with MARC—based formats seem to indicate that the project is viable. Input would embrace the functions of both bibliographic-oriented and retrieval-oriented catalogues, as we call them. This means that bibliographic detail in description and approaches would have to be as detailed, minute, and varied as might be needed by any user of such a system. If, for example, the system were to be completely acceptable and useful, it would have to embrace 'depth indexing' as well as the more conventionally expected approaches and detail.

We now come to the ultimate objective of the system: use. It is envisaged that the data base would be drawn upon in four main ways:

(a) Machine-readable data, in the form of magnetic tape, could be obtained as required by user-libraries and resource centres, preferably using 'Standard Nonbook Numbers' for access, but the system should cater for other approaches such as conventional author/title headings a s commonly cited and as arrived at by the application of, say, AACR. We reiterate here that work is in progress on a new comprehensive nonbook code in Britain, but at the time of writing this had not been produced. A decision would have to be made as to which code would be implemented, in the same way that users of MEDLARS must conform to the index language used as tags for medical subject terms. If a decision could not be reached, there would need to be additional fields to cater for tags according to the two or more codes used, either in the form of added entries or as references, at act as s sort of translation system between apparently rival headings. However the store would be structured, the resultant tapes would be used by local libraries and centres to construct catalogues for their own stocks, selecting whatever details and approaches were relevant to their needs.

(b) The central store could be used for printouts resulting from searches initiated by local libraries, etc. in response to requests for comprehensive information according to any approach: subject, physical form, author, collaborator and so on. Such a function would be similar to that performed by various data banks in selected subject fields at the moment. It is envisaged that such searches would be made mainly in subject areas, with physical forms as a further basis for selection depending upon the availability of apparatus for use of the various media. But it could also be used in support of, say, experiments, or programmes for entertainment or education, using a particular medium, an obvious example being the moving film, or 'motion picture', or 'cinema' depending on the approach term used in the system.

(a) and (b) could overlap in that a local centre may acquire magnetic tapes to use in local specific subject and/or form searches.

(c) A more sophisticated application approaches the limit of accessibility to data stores usually envisaged, in that a local centre could possibly be on line to the central store. We know that mainly, according to our observation, on-line systems seem to be operated by industrial and commercial organisations. So, it is technologically feasible that a similar system could be used for objective information retrieval via a local community-oriented service. This seems a logical next stage of development leading on from the, now common, linking of libraries and information at the local centre-screen display, facsimile printing, or normal printout would depend on local facilities.

(d) Finally, comes the vital factor of location of required documents. In this respect, the central store would serve as a union catalogue. A field in the store indicating local holdings would need to be established, but this could be a fairly routine matter. It could also serve as an approach for printing out of local holdings. A notation could be established to ensure that various degrees of 'local- ness' could be identified. As already mentioned in the context of subject and form approaches, UDC might be implemented here, using its 'place' numbers. Of conrse, union catalogues could be printed out as required.

Despite the lists produced in the US by NICEM (National Information Center for Educational Media), there is not in progress any system attempting to do all that needs to be done. We feel keenly that the time will come when either such a system has to be realised or we shall lose contact with nonbook-based information and its sources.

Electronic Service Library

Despite advances in technology and the hype of salespeople, library management systems still look and feel very much like their parents and grandparents which were sold as, 'housekeeping systems'. Designed to replace inefficient manual systems they were, and still are not essential components in the transfer of information from the library to the user. The OPAC is now a common front-line tool and in a few places community information is available at the OPAC terminal. We suppose on that basis they should then be called OPADs [online public access databases].

Library management systems are but a segment of a world of information technology and elsewhere there are a variety of systems which are designed primarily to present the customer with information which they can use directly, but in electronic form. While the age of the library management system has blossomed precisely because there are libraries, these other technologies are the product of a wider market. That we can exploit, systems which have a large consumer base gives security to what we do—if two or three library management system suppliers cease trading panic could ensue, whereas if two or three CD Rom database producers pull out, what do we care? there are plenty left. However, if we have some minimal 'clout' in the LMS market we have very little in this wider world. Before we get too euphoric about the future of these technologies within libraries we should remember that it will only look rosy so long as the products run in parallel with out business and we can prove our intermediary role in of value to the customer.

The clutch of technologies which cover electronic information delivery include CD Rom, online access to remote database hosts, videotex/teletext and automated community information. They are all well known applications some of which have been around for years-online access must soon be celebrating a quarter of a century of service. That does not mean that every library uses them or that in those that do the systems form a major part of the service. Public libraries are still very much about lending material for home use how often are you reference librarians asked whether it is possible to borrow a reference only item? However, information as a commodity has always been vital to our service and with the growing demands of students and others, it is unlikely to diminish in the near future. We should not, therefore, undervalue systems which can provide access to large, up-to-date databases which are user friendly in ways which old manual systems could never be.

If the face of public libraries is to change radically during the next ten years it is probably in the area of electronic information delivery that we will make it happen. These technologies have literally the potential to give the power of information searching to the customer rather than through the librarian to the customer. That does not mean we are an endangered species if such a situation comes about the systems will need to be managed, exploited and the customers trained. It does mean that our roles may change. That is the real challenge of electronic information delivery.

In the last survey hyperbole was necessary to describe the impact that the CD Rom had made on public libraries. Like the compact disc in the audio market, the CD Rom has been the high flier of the late 1980s and will continue to change the way that we operate as librarians (and listeners) well into the 90s. Just to remind you, before looking more closely at the data from the present survey, in 1987 two libraries indicated that they were considering using CD Rom while in 1989, 49 were actually in the thick of it. A variety of databases were being used, but all were using Bookbank which was the catalyst for most libraries.

In four years the number has gone up 50 times, since 1989 it has more than doubled. Any way you look at it, CD Rom is a popular delivery system for information and is likely to continue its sweep through public libraries. The data are pretty self evident, there are increases everywhere. Northern Ireland scores a full house while all other authorities show a rapid take-up. Only Scotland and the Non-Mets lag behind the 60% and over which is seen elsewhere. I commented last time that the size of these two exceptions might create barriers to buying the system and that still seems to be the case; although the relative cheapness of the hardware and the real savings and benefits of using Bookbank for example, continue to raise question marks about these discrepancies. There are in the end only two possibilities. Either the scale of operations in these two types of authority is such that resources cannot be found for what elsewhere is spreading like wild-fire or, the nature of demand means that other priorities must take precedence.

Looking closely it is not clear that all authorities are using Bookbank, although the vast majority are. Indeed it may well be that those who did not report its use felt that it was not worth mentioning! The data also show, however, that a wide range of databases are now in use, ranging from those of local relevance, such as the Northern Echo (affectionately known as Panda), to national newspapers, official publications, British Standards and the odd encyclopaedia. Selection tools remain a popular sue of the CD Rom equipment and alongside Bookbank we now find Bookfind (from Bookdata), American Books in Print, BNB and the British Library Catalogue.

Respondents were asked to indicate whether the systems were staff only or made available directly to the public, without staff intervention. Of the 101 total, 66 indicated that their systems were staff only while nine report direct use by the public. That leaves 26 who said nothing about access. From the databases the 26 'question marks' are using I am pretty sure that they are not providing public access, which means that only about one tenth of CD Romers are allowing customers to get their hands on the technology. Of the nine allowing public access, a fair smattering (five actually) are providing it to the Northern Echo, evidently a strong catalyst to encourage public access. This balance of 10% public access to 90% of authorities using staff as intermediaries is in marked constrast to the developments taking place in university and polytechnic libraries where CD Rom networks (clusters of terminals linked to a jukebox of CD Roms) are seen as an essential means of giving the customers what they want. For a whole variety of reasons we in public libraries are taking a different approach. The case for CD Roms as selection/bibliographic aids is won, the case for purchasing databases to support reference and information services looks set to be a victory, but, perhaps because of the diversity and differing levels of customer ability in public libraries, direct access is not yet seen as the highest priority. We certainly hope that we are not, since it is costly to provide one PC and CD rom drive per database and, if there are fewer PCs than databases, switching disks in and out all the time is a pain. The evidence from the academic sector is that the task is labour intensive and leads to disks 'disappearing'. With the jukebox well out of harm's way and a menu of databases to choose from at the terminal the process is much simplified. We are confident that the benefits of direct public access and the provision of networks will appear in the returns when this survey is undertaken again. The breakthrough will come when three criteria can be met. First, that jukeboxes can be readily connected to the big networks supported by library management systems so that the richness of CD Rom databases can be exploited at terminals far and wide. So far, experiments have hit a number of problems of software compatibility and lack of intelligence on the networks and these problems have kept the breakthrough from coming, but come it must. Second, search software can provide a standard query language which is applicable to all CD Rom databases so that the user once trained can sue any system, and finally, that reasonable pricing structures can be negotiated with CD Rom publishers for networking agreements.

Online access to remote database hosts has been around for a long time. It must have been in use outside esoteric research labs for twenty years and many public libraries have been providing online access for upwards of ten. In some ways the potential of online access is not unlike that of CD ROM-providing the ability to search very large stores of data with the added advantage that the information can be as up to date as today. The risks of incurring high costs through long searches has damped any enthusiasm for providing direct public access to hosts, but online access remains an important toro to those librarians involved in the provision of information services.

Pricing structures which do not discourage the occasional user and the wide availability of microcomputers have seen a steady increase in use over recent years. What used to be a hit-and-miss affair using dedicated terminals and devices called acoustic couplers has become a simple and reliable matter of hitting a few keys. However, we suspect that a continuing subjective feeling that searching online is expensive and complicated has created some barriers and the growing availability of databases on CD Rom which incur no cost at point of use has influenced decisions on whether or not to use online searching. There is no conclusive evidence that the two methods overlap significantly, however subjective evidence suggests that an important use of CD Rom is the formulation of search strategies which can then be used during an online search. Also, it would appear from a recent report on the 1991 International Online Information Meeting that demand for online hosts continues to grow despite the popularity of CD Rom databases.

Turning to the data from this current survey, there are now 107 authorities using online searching. That is a 10% increase over the figure in 1989, which was 97. Looking at the percentage changes since 1985, we can see that there has been a slowing down in the increase—the change between 1985 and 1987 was 30% up, and 1987 to 1989, 13%. This suggests that the majority of those libraries who see online searching as an asset to their services have already begun using the technique and that the increases seen in the past are tending to plateau. Whether the remaining 60 authorities suffer a financial barrier, a psychological one or simply do not believe that online searching is relevant to their services cannot be evinced from the data available. However, as we shall see below, the nature of the databases most used implies use by libraries who prioritise bibliographic and business information as important. Perhaps the non-users have set other priorities for their services.

The fact that only 25% of Scottish authorities use the technique influences significantly the overall total. Non-mets are also at 25% but they are only four in number, yet Scotland, with the largest number of authorities, lags far behind. We cannot claim an in-depth knowledge of Scottish library services, however elsewhere in this review we will see that they tend to plough a separate furrow in their use of IT. The other data show manly steady increases and no decreases, from which we may conclude that once adopted, online searching has lasting value to service delivery.

A trend which previously proved of interest is the method of access used to search online hosts. Trend is an important word in this context since, on occasion, the replies received from the questionnaire needed some interpretation. When compared with 1985, the data from the current survey reinforce patterns which were noted in 1989. The fairly even mix of dedicated terminal, Prestel and microcomputer which existed in 1985 has been routed by the micro which now stands head, shoulders and keyboard above all other access methods. Not really very surprising when you come to think about it since the micro has been widely adopted as the access medium for those who operate outside our world. Modem boards can be fitted into machines and there is bags of cheap software around to be played with. Insofar as online searching can be a suer-friendly business, the micro can facilitate it since it is possible to set up dialling and log-in codes for rapid access, and the micro can still be used for so many other things. The other signifieant feature of the data its the steady increase in the number of authorities using the circulation system as the medium of access. While five is a very small figure when compared with the micros, there are some interesting implications in the decision to use the library management system for online searching. First, most of the new systems allow you to do so, and have done for some time. There is nothing particularly fancy about it, but for very good reasons most libraries have shied away from doing so. While in principle it should be a good thing to provide online access in a variety of locations, where the information is really needed, it requires trained staff to use the systems effectively arid untrained staff can run up some hefty bills in no time at all. Use can be limited to defined terminals, but the strategy which has been to focus online searching to key locations where specialist staff, capable of knowing for certain when online should be used, are on hand. Without doubt, the use of the library management system as a delivery medium holds great potential and we will be very surprised if more libraries do not take the plunge (or the risk?). Certainly if the complexities which remain in host interfaces can be reduced so that infrequent users have a chance of getting in and out more quickly, there is every incentive to widen the network, and that is precisely the value of the library management system 0 it has a wide network of terminals.

The truth of these comments becomes more clear when the total terminal population is considered, rather than the use of the medium alone. What we have been looking at so far is the number of authorities using each method, rather than the number of terminals used by each.

	1989	1991
Dedicated terminal	45	68
Circulation system	35	61
Microcomputer	121	263
Prestel, etc.	4	2

The above table provides a comparison only between 1989 and 1991 since the information is not available for 1985 or 1987. Of course, there can be no certainty about the freedom which is allowed for all of the library management system terminals to be used for on line searching, but the potential is clear. Other points to note from these data are that although the number of dedicated terminal users has risen by only one in two years, there has been a 50% increase in the terminals in use; suggesting that while this route may not be the one chosen now by new entries, for those already using the method, it is of sufficient value to encourage wider availability. Finally on hardware, there are now a 'great many micros being used for online searching; the total more than doubling while the number of authorities has only increased by 14%.

Next we must look at the purposes for which online searching is being used—the hosts being accessed. Just as with the CD Rom world, we are facing more diversity all the time. While 'umbrella' hosts can give access to a wide range of databases, sometimes duplicating other hosts, there are also individual database providers who are being used by public libraries. The two obvroas examples are laser's Viscount interlending service and V olnet, which is a database of importance to the voluntary sector. In reality rather than this diversity being reflected in the data from libraries, the range reported is very similar to 1989. This tends to suggest that the markets being served by online searching are quite clearly defined and are common to most users.

If these data are considered in conjunction with the 'other' category, the trend in the use of online searching is quite apparent. Blaise is still an important source of bibliographic information, but with a growing range of CD rom-based products it may become less used. The major use for online searching is clearly business information. Added together these business-orientated databases dominate Blaise by a factor of more than three to one. The only joker to be found is Acompline, which is unique in providing current information on local authority affairs and which is still quite popular. The fact that access to this database, which is provided by the London Research Centre, is free may have something to do with this continuing popularity.

The last two aspects of online searching which can be considered here relate not to the technology or the range of services available, but how they are delivered to users. The first factor is the costs which are passed on to users and the second is the management of the service-staff skilled in the techniques and how it has changed traditional provision.

Charging policies ought to tell us a great deal about the priorities of libraries and their responses to changes especially those outside their control, whether from competition or from the comments of the Minister for the Arts! Back in 1989 made some observations about the reasons for the high level of certain replies. Discretion, for example, could be an excuse for saying one thing and doing another-telling everyone that certain categories of user are charged, or charges are levied when a search is requested, while not bothering because of the hassle of recovering the money. No comment, on the other hand could be an excuse for doing almost anything; anything that is except charge. The use of online searching has grown up in a tradition where it is the exception to levy a fee for a service at. point of use. The whole point of public goods is that they are funded from individual contributions (rates, taxes) which bear no relation to level of use made by that individual.

The management of the service includes the organisation of specialist staff and the changes which have resulted from the development of online searching. There is just as much need to have highly trained staff undertaking searches as there has ever been. Despite developments in the design of user-friendly interfaces, online searching remains a special skill, both in the knowledge of command languages and in the formulation of suitable search strategies. It is likely to be a long time before access is provided to customers without the need for a trained intermediary, since cost rises and effectiveness falls if the searcher is not properly trained. Libraries were asked to indicate numbers of locations of trained staff and 86 provided replies, as apposed to 78 in 1989. As with all questions demanding more than a yes or no reply, we must be cautious about making too many assumptions from the data. The evidence provided in the replies shows that all but a very few authorities focus their online services (and staff) in key locations-usually reference libraries, business information centres and the like. The average number of trained staff in each authority is something over four, a slight increase on 1989, but remains fairly stable. It seems that whatever changes may face public libraries in the next few years, this is at least one service which will continue to require 'gatekeepers' to make it fully effective.

Changes in the form of other services resulting from the use of online searching was the last question asked on this subject. Again, since the data re textual rather than precise responses, only general conclusions may be drawn. Despite that, the replies add some detail to the overall picture of online searching in public libraries. Fifty seven authorities commented, compared with the 39 who did so in 1989. Of those 28 implied in their reply that online searching had enriched the range of services available. Eight libraries reported that printed sources had been cancelled and ten that there had been no significant change; either because online had been used for so long that no-one could remember what life was like before, or online was such a new acquisition that there had not been time to see any impact: On the other hand, two authorities reported dramatic changes to the scope and method of service delivery.

While online searching involves only a few staff and demands small amounts of the budget, it is an important and emotive topic. The trend which has emerged over the past four or five years is for the databases to form part of services to business and now, for those services to be viewed in many places as 'suitable cases for charging'. The CD rom/online searching duopoly should be a key focus for our attention over the next few years and will, I am sure, be the subject of further research. Indeed, a recent report from the Centre for Communication and Information Studies at the Polytechnic of Central London reports research which looked in much more detail at the actual pattern of database use by analyzing bills from a range of authorities, and interviewing a sample of users in great detail. The general trends reported above are echoed in the research results and the report is well worth reading to gain a clearer picture of what the future may hold.

We cannot end this section without saying something about LANet since Email is just a special sort of online searching. We suggested that is most public libraries used LANet regularly, it might be used as a medium to distribute the results of this survey. There are now more on the network, but so far as I can ascertain, it has not become an important element in the pattern of our communications. What is puzzling is the fact that the academic network JANET is widely used by university and polytechnic libraries and librarians to talk to each other. Quite why this difference should exist is not easily explained, yet the result is that once again you are reading the results in hardcopy.

Videotext/Teletext

By and large, through this survey until now we have seen a mixture of steady growth in some applications, dramatic growth in others. Turning now to videotex and teletext we are in the realm of technologies which have been around for some years, have become well established, to the point where we are beginning to see them superseded. We can remember a time when there was much talk. about Prestel (videotex) as a major medium of information delivery. Organisations were clamouring to. be a part of a readily accessible and widely spread public network. Today Prestel is still around, but many new systems have arrived which are Prestel-like in their utility, but have much more power to exploit data resources. Such systems are now used in private viewdata networks, closed user group systems providing information using the format of Prestel, but managed by some local information provider. Teletext, an information system available on broadcast television networks such as Ceefax and Oracle has never been a critical element in publicly provided information services since the data cannot be manipulated locally and is usually of momentary interest—news, racing results, etc. Moreover, it is common for home use television sets to be sold with Ceefax and Oracle decoders as standard.

The trends for teletext and videotex show a situation which has matured to the point where use has levelled off and appears at present to be falling slightly. We have already indicated possible reasons for this above. Private viewdata, on the other hand, is growing steadily in popularity as a medium for the delivery of information tailored to the local community. In six years there has been an almost threefold increase in the systems in use and we may expect this to continue since often these systems are developed as corporate information systems, sometimes managed by the library service sometimes not and while libraries may find themselves low down on the corporate IT programme private viewdata systems may not.

Analysing use at the level of the authority provides only a general picture of developments and that to establish more clearly the impact made it is necessary to consider the penetration of systems within individual authorities. Respondents were asked to report the numbers of terminals used on each of these systems and, in addition, to show whether their use was seldom, steady or constant. These data support earlier points about the fall in the popularity of videotex and teletext as information systems in libraries. Not only has there been a fall in the number of authorities using the systems, but the number of terminals provided has also dropped—videotex almost to the level of 1985, teletext below it. Of course, mean numbers are just that, and the actual distribution shows that in a few authorities there are relatively large populations of terminals. Wiltshire, for example, reports 38 for videotex. In contrast, not only has the total number of authorities using private viewdata risen, but the mean number of terminals shows a 23.5% rise. Not surprising since if private viewdata is the means of delivering community information, as it usually is, then terminals should be as widely available as possible.

Having descended from the level of total use, to penetration within a library system, we can finally consider how much the systems are used. The questionnaire invited comment on whether the use of each of the three system was seldom, steady or constant. We must exercise some caution. One person's steady is another's constant and we can only draw limited information from these data. Also, use is likely to vary from terminal to terminal so the single comment may not reflect reality where more than one is in use. Steady is the most frequently cited option, except for videotex where seldom is top. We do not think there is much value in a detailed analysis of these data since their objectivity is questionable, but we can give a personal opinion. Videotex is not used much since alternative sources of information may provide speedier access (and you have to pay to use Prestel). The cost of teletext is unaffected by use since it is broadcast with the TV signals. Leaving terminals lying about for people to play with, therefore carries no risk of large bills. Safe for the customer to come in and tinker with. Moreover, many customers will now know more about the resources available on teletext than the managers providing it they will have it at home. We see in private viewdata systems a locally tailored system more likely to meet customer information needs and it should be no surprise that respondents reported many more steady and constants (83% of the total) than its cousin videotex (45% of the total), and even more than teletext (75% of the total) which is free of use cost [private viewdata has a cost in use since remote terminals will be connected by a telephone line or wide area network].

Community Information

The automation of community information highlights one of the paradoxes of information technology. It is very easy to start—just buy a micro and printer, some database software and off you go—but it can be very hard to keep the data comprehensive and up to date. Anyone who has had much to do with computers knows that the data are the most valuable commodity, much more valuable than the hardware or software that can be replaced at the corner shop. Creating any database takes time, maintaining it takes time, and time is money. Community information has always been an attractive product to automate since so much of it is in the form that can readily be fitted into database software products. Clubs, societies, business organisations and the like are the lifeblood of the community information database and are maintained in some form or other by the vast majority of libraries. Indeed, comprehensive community systems are something unique to libraries; you certainly can't buy them at Smiths.

Not surprisingly then the number of libraries automating community information continues to grow. 1987 and 1989 has been matched in the past two years by a total increase of just over 19%. The rend which was apparent between 1985 and 1987, use of the micro and wordprocessor, has now changed. This time the micro, still the most popular medium, remains unchanged at 38 while use of the library management system shows the most significant growth, up by 75%. It is also not unexpected that private viewdata continues to increase since we have already noted in this chapter that the number of authorities providing the medium continues to rise. One question which comes immediately to mind, however, is if 40 authorities reported use of the system under the videotex/teletext section above, but only 18 report using it for community information, what are the other 22 doing? Just the same question had to be asked in the last survey and suggested that the problem was one of interpretation—that the authorities might not be managing the private viewdata system and therefore thought that it should not be reported under the community information banner. Whether that is true one cannot say. Certainly the prime purpose of private viewdata networks is to deliver information of relevance to the community. Finally, while considering the method of processing, it should be noted that a further five libraries indicated that they were actively investigating the automation on their community information files, and by now they may have done just that. That gives a potential total of 102 authorities who use IT for community information or 60% of the 167 country wide. Micros and wordprocessors have been around for so many years, have at least 40% of the libraries in the country not started to automate the community information files which they certainly must have. With common sense, transferring manual files to a micro can save time and make the product much more useful. Mail merge makes remainders easier and with multiple indexing possible, more variety of presentation is not a problem. A micro/printer setup is not pricey and there are so many examples of applications that not to try seems swimming against the stream. To see whether there was any pattern to this reticence we looked a bit more closely at the 66 libraries without automated community information. An interesting fact emerged—that nearly half of the 66 were authorities of the same type. Twenty seven of the 41 Scottish authorities (66%) have yet to do anything about automating their community information; only one of the four Welsh Non-Mets has done so and none of the Northern Ireland libraries has started. Elsewhere, the most likely authority type to find automated systems is the English county where 85% have automated their community information. London, the Mets and the Welsh counties range from 74% uptake down to 63%. You will remember that Scottish authorities were also behind on the library management system front and one can only repeat that perhaps they have set different priorities or lack of resources places severe restrictions on the acquisition of technology. Conversely, English counties are large organisations with disparate service points and the benefits of using IT for community information has clearly been recognised. Lastly, the questionnaire sought details of how the information is actually made available to customers. There are three possibilities—online, hardcopy and a mixture of both—online in some places, or for staff use, hardcopy elsewhere, or for the customers. The trend which was reported in 1989 was towards more data to be presented online rather than in printed format and the 1991 data confirm that this trend has continued during the intervening two years.

Online as the only means of delivery has increased by more than a third and online/hardcopy has also edged up. On the other hand hardcopy has fallen by something over 10%, having remained unchanged for the two years before. It is a pity that ten libraries did not give any indication of dissemination format since, had they, the data might have looked different. Nevertheless, from what we have it seems hat progress towards direct public access for customers continues. Hardcopy should not be dismissed as an anachronism just yet since there are many occasions when it is useful to send the customer away with a list to browse through-doing that online in the library has implications for the number of terminals provided. The benefits of online access include the freedom of the customer to search in their own way without an intermediary and sometimes the opportunity to search the database from the comfort of the office or the front room.

This chapter has considered a number of IT applications all of which are linked by their role as deliverers of information to customers. The options available to library managers deciding what applications to use are not limitless. The choices to be made within each application area on the other hand can be very confusing. Whether it is the selection of CD Rom databases, online hosts or a database management system for community information, care is needed to ensure that the users benefit from the development. It is hard to argue that any of these applications is irrelevant to public libraries since so many are using them. Yet there remain many places where a customer is unlikely to find IT-based information systems and as we move towards maturity in their use—they are common and have proved their worth—it is worrying that pockets of non-use remain. Perhaps worrying is the wrong term-managers have obviously made choices—but there are differences which cannot yet be explained objectively and that should be of concern to the profession and those involved in information policy nationally.

❐

7

Online Information Service

The computer, if properly programmed, permits both Markey and Demeyer, for example, confirm the wellknown fact that the alphabetical and the classed search approaches complement each other frequently and, together, lead to richer results than either method by itself. Computers also encourage a third helpful approach, by keyword, that is, by uncontrolled terms. These may well be terms that a user may think of but that are not in the controlled vocabulary. For example, the title of a work on library buildings might be Library Interior Layout and Design. There is little doubt that efficient subject retrieval systems of the future will employ all three methods: classed approach, controlled alphabetical vocabulary, and uncontrolled keywords. One of the problems to be faced is the optimum interrelationship among the three methods within one system. Additional methods designed to help users refine a subject search until it meets their needs are being investigated.

Among the various known subject retrieval methods, the use of classification has strong advocates, such as Cochrane, Richmond, and Mandel. Much research has been and is being undertaken to examine the suitability of classification systems in general, and of the DDC and LCC in particular, for subject retrieval. Following are three major studies:

1. In 1968, one of the earliest major studies demonstrated that it is possible to use a, classification system like the UOC as a search tool in the then-newly developed interactive online retrieval system. It also called attention to the need for system designers to consider user needs and preferences.

2. After a hiatus, during which primarily word-based retrieval systems were investigated, the Dewey Decimal Classification Online Project was completed in 1985, under the direction of OCLC's Karen Markey. It showed that the use of DDC class numbers and of terms from the schedules and the relative index expanded the range of searching strategies then possible with alphabetical vocabularies, and permitted greater precision.

3. Finally, in 1984, a team led by Nancy J. Williamson of the University of Toronto began a series of studies designed to examine the suitability of the LCC for computerization, so that the schedules could be edited and used for assigning class numbers and for searching in an interactive online system.

The scope of a term like Tubs can only be understood if it is read in the context of the hierarchy, in this case:

Building construction (and in particular construction of)

Plumbing and pipe fitting (which includes plumbing of)

Bathrooms and similar rooms (and in particular of) Tubs.

In other words, the concept is of bathtubs as part of buildings' plumbing and construction. To the reader of the index to the LCC, the scope of the term Tubs is not clear if the index entry merely indicates

Tubs TH 6493

Likewise, the scope of notations like TH 6491-6496 can only be understood if the caption or notation or method of presentation on the screen makes it clear that this group of numbers refers to the various fixtures that are called baths, while the activity of baths in the sense of bathing is classed elsewhere, including RA 780 for the hygienic aspects (that is, bathing for the sake of cleanliness) and RM 819 for the medical aspects (that is, bathing as part of a cure).

Users Must Understand Notations' Meanings

Regardless of the classification scheme a library employs, users have shelf browsed for generations with no, or only very limited, understanding of the meaning of specific notations. They could move with fair success along the shelves and inspect works with notations like

515.25	Mathematical equations
515.3	Differential calculus
515.3077	
515.4	Integral calculus
515.4076	
515.52	Eulerian integrals

without having to know that the 077 in 515.3077 meant "A programmed text in differential calculus," or that the 076 in 515.4076 meant "A workbook with problems in integral calculus." The titles on the book spines usually explained the books' topics. OPAC searchers, however, must be far more sophisticated, even if the programme will lead them automatically to some answers. To mention only truncation as one example: OPAC users must know at least what truncation is, what it is supposed to achieve, where it can be applied, how it can be applied, and what to do when it does not bring desired results. For example, to-truncate a notation like 83?34 in order to retrieve all types of German-language literature of the Reformation period, the searcher must either know the structure of DDC's literature section, or must be instructed by the computer in how to truncate this particular type of notation, or the notation must have a built-in device that causes truncation to occur at the correct spot in the notation. While the computer can be programmed to do much of the work, probably *via* menus or directives, the OPAC user must clearly be better informed about classification principles than the casual shelfbrowser.

Components of Online Classed Retrieval Systems

Ignoring, for purposes of this chapter, requirements of subject heading and keyword access, a system that permits sophisticated access by classification requires three to four basic units. Essential are a file of document surrogates (entries); the classification schedules as authority; and an index to the class numbers. Highly desirable (and essential if keyword searching of the actual documents is desired in addition to keyword searching of the subject headings, classification captions, and titles) is a machine-readable file of the actual documents. Users should be able to enter the system with a known class notation or with an alphabetical term that describes the concept represented by a class notation.

Desirable Features of Online Classed Retrieval Systems

The quality of online subject retrieval *via* a classification scheme depends on the computer hardware and software capabilities, and on the structure and notation of the classification scheme. Among the latter's essential qualities for this purpose are a logical structure; a definite, standard and Communicable way of handling material that relates to more than one field (such as city planning or the influence of religion on art), and a notation that is expressive and therefore permits truncation and hierarchical searching relatively easily.

Following is a list of some of the features that an online classed retrieval system should contain. At this time, such computer wish lists cannot be final or finite, since demands increase as experience is gained. L'appetit vient en mangeant ("Good food increases the appetite"). The following list goes far beyond the current abilities of such systems, but it reflects the opinions of several experts in the field and of the authors.

1. **Access to individual entries by a known class or call number.** Many systems already permit this, but typically only as a follow-up to bibliographic retrieval through alphabetical subject terms, in order to obtain circulation status or other item-level information.

2. **Full-schedule browsing;** that is, display of the classification schedule. Either a display of as many contiguous class numbers, with their captions, as the screen will hold including instructions and crossreferences contained in the schedules, or a display of a range of notations, such as DDC's 337 (International economics) and its immediate sub-divisions or, if preferred, all levels of its sub-divisions is desirable, Along with this feature, backward and forward scrolling should be permitted. Scrolling permits moving from a notation to the next notation and, through further scrolling, to broader or narrower notations, as if the user were looking at a classification schedule. The phrasing of the instructions and cross-references that are in most typical classification schedules would need to differ for retrieval use and for input use. Example of an instruction intended for cataloguers that should be rephrased for retrieval use: "[333.9102] Surface water: Number discontinued; class in 333.911)".

This, like most other suggested features, demands that the schedules exist in machine-readable form. The DDC schedules do; the LCC schedules not yet, with some very limited exceptions. Experts in the field generally agree that it will be a major undertaking, fraught with difficulties, to put the LCC schedules online.

3. **Shelflist browsing;** that is, display of as many contiguous brief entries in shelflist order as the screen will hold. One line per entry may suffice, but again the user should be able to scroll forward and backward to permit pinpointing a search. Instructions and cross-references should be included in this display as well. This amounts to an enhanced shelf-browsing feature.

4. Since points 2 and 3 are intended to permit pinpointing a search not only for retrieval but also for input (that is, for assigning call numbers), it is important that the display of entries in call number order (point 3) be available in two formats: *(a)* consolidated order, in which all items in a collection are shown in call number order regardless of where the individual item is located; and *(b)* shelflist

order, in which the entries are shown in the shelf order of individual departments or branches.

5. **Hierarchical display of class numbers with their captions is needed.** The system should display a requested class notation as part of a hierarchical structure showing different levels of arrays, the notations as well as their captions. This is important in case nothing appropriate, or too little material, is available in a specific class number sought, and because many people tend to begin searches under terms that are broader than what is actually wanted.

6. The notation should permit left, internal, and right truncation in order to permit broadening a search. As is discussed later in this chapter, this would usually consist of broadening a search within a discipline. If the notation does not permit truncation, as is true in some instances with DDC and in most instances with LCC, other devices must be employed at considerable effort to achieve the same result.

7. Access to the schedules by the captions in the schedules and by terms in the index. These terms, however, are often cryptic. Various devices have been suggested to overcome this obstacle to precise recall.

8. With the hierarchical display should come menu ability, that is the ability to select from a hierarchical display one option and, when that option is displayed, to see how it is broken down, or how it can be broadened, and to keep on selecting options until the search has been refined or broadened sufficiently. The system thus would permit a combination of command functions (such as in point 1) and menu functions.

9. Ability to switch from one class or call number to another, to permit following up on the instructions and cross-references in the schedules. This should permit pinpointing a search, including sometimes moving to another discipline.

10. Access to the schedules by equivalent subject headings or descriptors. Since a concrete topic can often be distributed among

various disciplines and 7.11, this will often involve a reference from one subject heading or descriptor to several class numbers.

11. Boolean search capability of many kinds is essential. For example: between keywords in the description, such as the title, and a class number; between class number and subject headings; between author's surname and subject heading. This capability helps to make retrieval more precise.

12. Since a keyword approach has been shown to be helpful, captions, index terms (point 9), subject headings, and descriptors (point 10) should be accessible by keyword as well as by their complete terminology.

13. Experts also desire additional features (some of which already exist in individual cases), all designed to help users refine their searches or to forgive misspellings or the use of too-broad or "wrong" subject terms. Since computers are likely to access ever-increasing catalogues of whole groups of libraries, rather than of just one library, information overload is a very likely problem of the near future. The result of a fairly precise subject search may still be two hundred entries. Attempts are being made to develop intelligent systems which will, for example, match these entries against the searcher's interest profile or against previous checkouts by people in the searcher's field of interest, or some other automatic technique that will present these two hundred entries in order of the searcher's likely interest or expressed need.

This is primarily a wish list, and most existing OPACs can do none, or only very few, of these things. Moreover, this wish list is limited to features useful to notational retrieval. Other features that are useful for alphabetical retrieval can be added. In the above list, points 2, 3, 5, 6, 7, and 9 are related to the classification scheme and its notation rather than to the computer programme or hardware. The DDC and LCC will, therefore, be examined in the light of the following points:

(a) **Points 2-3.** Relationship of concepts as expressed by contiguous class notations

(b) ***Points 5-6.*** Hierarchical structure of the scheme; expressiveness of the notation

(c) ***Point 7.*** Truncating ability of the notation

(d) ***Point 9.*** Suitability of caption and index terminology as access points.

Finally, the system must be hospitable to accepting new concepts logically, where the resulting structure still makes sense.

Characteristics of the DDC

The Dewey Decimal Classification (DDC) was first published by Melvil Dewey in 1876. It is now in its twentieth edition. It is basically a theoretical scheme, designed to contain room for all knowledge, without attention to the subject emphases of the holdings of any one library. Although its use in North American libraries, especially academic libraries, diminished during the 1960s and 1970s, it is the most widely used library classification system in the world. It is used by over 85 percent of all types of libraries in, the United States and Canada, including almost all school and public libraries, and about two-fifths of all acadertuc libraries. It has been translated into thirty-four languages, from German to Gujarati. The DDC uses a pure notation based on numbers, and is divided into ten main classes:

000-099 Generalities, including Knowledge, Library science, Bibliographies

100-199 Philosophy; Psychology

200-299 Religion

300-399 Social sciences, Statistics, Customs, Etiquette, Folklore

400-499 Language

500-599 Pure sciences

600-699 Technology, Manufacture

700-799 The arts; Recreation and performing arts

800-899 Literature

900-999 History, Biography, Geography

Further sub-divisions are again in groups of ten:

300-309 Social sciences in general

310-319 Statistics

320-329 Political science

330-339 Economics

340-349 Law

350-359 Public administration

360-369 Social problems and services

370-379 Education

380-389 Commerce, Trade

390-399 Customs, Etiquette, Folklore

Still further sub-divisions are also in groups of ten:

370 Education

371 Generalities of education

372 Elementary education

373 Secondary education

374 Adult education

375 Curricula

376 Education of women

377 Schools and religion

378 Higher education

379 Education and the state

Numbers divided beyond three figures become decimal numbers:

378 Higher education

378.1 Organization and administration of institutions of higher education

378.11 Personnel administration

378.111 Academic personnel

378.14 College year

378.142 Summer school

Like any classification scheme, the DDC has advantages and disadvantages when examined with automation in mind. Among the positive characteristics that make it a possible candidate for, use in automated subject retrieval are:

— It obeys many logical principles of a well-designed classification scheme, for example, that the whole of a subject should precede its parts.

— It has, with some exceptions, an expressive notation in decimal form. These three facts (logic; expressive notation; decimal numbers) facilitate hierarchical search and permit truncation. The truncation technique is commonly found in keyword retrieval systems. When it is applied to notation, it makes the notation an even more powerful retrieval tool with which the depth and breadth of a search subject can be quickly and easily amended.

Truncation-in this case, right truncation (that is, truncating the right side of a notation) applied to an expressive notation allows a search to be extended or broadened, with more material to be retrieved. A search that began with the notation for bowfins (597.41) could be extended by using the notation 597.4? so that the documents with class numbers 597.42, 597.44, 597.46, etc., could be retrieved, allowing items relating to the scientific study of not only bowfins but also other related species such as sturgeons.

The search could be further expanded by using 597?, allowing all Items relating to fish to be matched. While 59? would retrieve everything on zoology, and 5? would retrieve everything on the pure sciences, the quantity of material on such broad subjects suggests a need for sõme way of preventing such searches from being performed, probably by limiting the number of items that can be retrieved in response to a truncated-notation search.

— The DDC uses standard sub-divisions, whereby to each subject, broad or specific (Social sciences, Education, Secondary education, Teaching French in secondary schools) can be added generally consistent symbols that indicate the format in which the subject is being treated or the geographic area with which it is concerned.

For example, -0977583 added to a topical number always means "in Madison," -097758 always means "in South Central Wisconsin," -09775 always means "in Wisconsin," -0977 always means "in North Central United States," 0973 always means "In the United States," and so forth. -06 added to a topical number always means "An organization in that field," and -0207 always means "Humorous treatment of the topic." The use of consistent numbers with the same meaning throughout the schedules is a mnemonic or memory-aiding device.

500	Natural sciences and mathematics
510	Mathematics
520	Astronomy
530	Physics
540	Chemistry
550	Earth sciences

550.21	Statistics of earth sciences
560	Paleontology, Paleozoology
570	Life sciences
580	Botanical sciences
590	Zoological sciences
591	Zoology, general aspects
591.021	Statistics of zoology
591.0941	Zoology of Great Britain
592	Invertebrates
593	Protozoa and other simple animals
594	Mollusca and molluscoidea
595	Other invertebrates
596	Vertebrata (Craniata, Vertebrates)
597	Cold-blooded vertebrates, Pisces (Fishes)
597.0021	Statistics of cold-blooded vertebrates
597.00941	Cold-blooded vertebrates in Great Britain
597.2	Agnatha (Cyclostomata)
597.2021	Statistics of agnatha
597.20941	Agnatha in Great Britain
597.3	Chondrichthyes (Cartilaginous fishes)
597.4	Chondrostel, Holostei, Sarcopterygii
597.41	Amiiformes (Bowfins, River dogfishes)
597.41021	Statistics of amiifornes
597.410941	Amiiformes In Great Britain

597.42	Polypteriformes (Fringe-finned ganoids)
597.44	Acipenseriformes (Cartilaginous ganoids)
597.46	Crossopterygii (Lobe-finned fishes)
597.47	Sensionotiformes (Gars)
597.48	Dipnoi (Lungfishes)
597.5	Teleostei (Fully-boned fishes)
597.51	Elopomorpha (Morays and true eels)
597.51021	Statistics of elopomorpha
597.510941	Elopomorpha in Great Britain

Fig. 1. Selections from DDC class 500, with emphasis on class 597.

In the online catalogue, standard sub-divisions permit broadening a topical search while retaining the limitation "in country X," or "in the form of." This is desirable if the more limited notation does not provide sufficient material. The technique used is internal truncation. For example, the notation for bowfins in Britain is 597.410941, where the 0941 represents the British aspect.

The user may want to broaden that topic without eliminating its British aspect. Middle truncation, as in 597?0941, will expand the topic to Fish regardless of species in Britain. Another example might be that of somebody who needed statistical information on bowfins. The notation for that topic is 597.41021, where 021 represents statistics, tables, etc. This Inquiry can be extended to, for example, 597.4?021, to retrieve statistics on bowfins and related species and then, if necessary, to 597?021 for statistics on fish in general. It would also be possible to use left truncation and enter ?0941 to retrieve information about books that deal with a large range of subjectsrelative to Britain.

While this particular example may be unlikely, because an excessive quantity of material might be retrieved, left truncation could be of use to the person interested in some less well-known or smaller part of the world, such as Angelina County in Texas. It would be interesting and useful, for example, to be able to go into a national library and to retrieve all indexed information about one particular region regardless of the subject.

By using truncation in these ways, one broadens recall (that is, retrieves more items) at the expense of decreasing precision; fewer of the items retrieved will be appropriate to the needs of the inquirer. However, the overall assessment of this technique is positive.

— The DDC uses mnemonics even in some of its topical numbers, particularly in Literature (800-899) and Geography, Biography, and History (900-999). The DDC literature symbols are composed of the following elements:

	Discipline of literature	*Language of writing*	*Literary genre*	*Period of creation*	
Examples:	8	2	1	.7	: English poetry of the early 19th century: 821.7
	8	3	2	.6	: German drama of the classical period (17501830): 832.6
	8	91.44	3	7	Bengali fiction of today: 891.4437

The numbers for the literary genre are consistent, while the numbers for the period of creation vary with the literature. Internal truncation thus permits queries like the following:

— 83?34 for all types of German language literature of the Reformation period

Internal and right truncation permits, for example,

— 8?1? for all poetry in the collection, regardless of language or time period

The DDC history symboJs are composed of the following elements:

	Discipline of history	*Continent*	*Country*		*Historical period*
Examples:	9	4	4	.082:	History of France during the Fourth Republic, 1945- 1958: 944.082
	9	4	4.36	082:	History of Paris during the Fourth Republic, 1945-1958 :.944.36082
	9	4	9.4	06:	History of Switzer-land during the 19th century: 949,406
	9	4	9.47	06:	History of the Swiss Alpine regions during the 19th century: 949.4706

This historical time periods of a country and of its sub-divisions are the same. Internal truncation thus permits queries like

— 944?082 for the history of the various regions, towns, etc. of France during the Fourth Republic

— The DDC is maintained by a well-funded, well-administered organization and is, therefore, a live scheme that, within limits, keeps pace with progress, creating with each edition new class categories or adapting existing ones, as needed

— The scheme's decimal notation permits the addition of new concepts as needed. The scheme is hospitable

— There is considerable quality control in the revision and updating of the scheme, based partly on advice and reactions from practicing librarians.

These three factors (willingness and ability to update in an effective manner) give searchers reasonable certainty that even relatively new topics can be searched in the spots where they can be logically expected, since provisions will have been made for them.

— The DDC symbols can be found in many MARC records

— The DDC is at least comparatively familiar to many librarians and information specialists and, to a lesser degree, to the public. Its decimal notation makes it relatively easy to be directed to specific topics, and to remember favourite topics for future use

These two factors (availability and familiarity) make it relatively inexpensive for an information facility to use the DDC, because the facility can copy existing numbers for many of its new acquisitions, and because the staff can direct the public orally to pertinent sections of the shelves or of the various classed records.

Disadvantages for Online Catalogues

In spite of its many excellent features, the DDC has disadvantages. It is old, having been created over a century ago and then for a library that by today's standards would be regarded as very small. Originally designed for filing entries (document surrogates) in paper-based files, the DDC was developed primarily for use in shelf arrangement, not for use in a computer.

A classification scheme, especially one that is to be used as a retrieval device in an online catalogue, should be consistent in structure and notation, although inconsistencies can sometimes be circumvented by sophisticated algorithms or retrieval programmes. While the DDC is in some respects a remarkably consistent scheme—far more so than the LCC—it also contains some inconsistencies that make the creation of menus, the display of arrays, and the use of truncation not only less than automatic, but often difficult to achieve. Also, while it has In several places a structure that resembles the more versatile and precisely structured faceted classification schemes, it is overwhelmingly enumerative, with the typical limitations of enumerative schemes.

DDC and Online Catalogue Features

Following is an examination of the DDC in the light of the features previously listed as desirable in an online classed retrieval system.

Age, Notational Base, and Logical Structure

Since the DDC was created over one hundred years ago, its basic structure reflects the knowledge, attitudes, emphases, and political situation of that time. One example is the topic of Psychology (150-159) which is still placed in the middle of Philosophy (100-149, 160-169) instead of with Medicine and health (610-619), to which it belongs according to current thought.

The use of arrays and scrolling is not aided by this structure. Since the DDC was created before many of today's scientific and technical achievements were invented, and before many of today's social concepts were developed, the scheme originally devoted proportionally far less space and detail to the social, pure, and applied sciences (300s, 500s, and 600s) than today's state of knowledge requires. New fields can be, and are being, inserted, thanks to the DDC's hospitality. However, because of the limited notational base of ten, the resulting numbers are often quite long (581.10428, Plant roots) which is more of a problem for humans than for computers.

The notational base, however, also causes some new topics to be inserted in ways that cause problems in logical relationships and, therefore, online classed searching ability. The DDC notation has a numerical base of ten. Therefore, if the notation were to be truly expressive, each topic could be divided into no more than ten subgroups. Unfortunately, nature does not work that way. Among the more obvious areas where the subject has broken the bounds of ten are:

— Life sciences (570-599): conceptually, Botany (580589) and Zoology (590-599) are sub-divisions of Life sciences, but the notations do not read that way.

— Manufactures (660-689): conceptually, this is one broad unit, sub-divided into different types of manufacture, but the notations do not express, for example, that 685.22 (Leather goods manufacture) is a subdivision of 660).

While such situations cause problems when the actual numbers are used to produce arrays, the problems can be relatively easily solved through the use of menus.

Relationship of Concepts Expressed by Contiguous Class Notations

While one can always quarrel with the logic of any classification scheme, the DDC is generally considered to be reasonably logical and effective for a general library in its grouping of related concepts and in its separation of unrelated ones. However, while it breaks down each major topic reasonably, the relationships among the major topics themselves are often tenuous. This is true for any classification scheme. For example, while the concepts of Education (370-379) and Commerce (380-389) are broken down more or less reasonably, there is little obvious logical connection between the last notations in the 370-379 group and the first few notations in the 380-389 group: 379.982 (Government control of public education in Greenland) and 380.1 (Commerce) are hardly logically connected.

Scrolling of class notations or of entries in call number order can, therefore, be limited to searches within anyone major topic, such as Education. In the desired displays of hierarchical arrays, the standard divisions mentioned may cloud the overall picture for the person who is trying to learn where in this network the desired topic is located. In other words, a clearer picture of the classification scheme may evolve if the display excludes, at least in some subjects, those notations and, therefore, arrays that indicate forms of presentation or geographic location. In subjects in which the geographical aspects are major elements, such as history, geography, or trade and industrial laws in various countries, such arrays should, of course, be kept.

The reader may by now suspect that decisions such as how much scrolling is helpful, or what should be included in an array, are not always automatic or easy, but often require judgment and individual decisions. The rest of this discussion should confirm that impression.

Like any enumerative scheme, the DDC suffers from Inability to assign a class number that truly reflects works relating to more than one field (such as "Effect of gasoline prices on automobile travel"). By tradition, if only one call number is assigned to such a work as a shelf location number, the work is classed under the topic affected, In the above case under 388.342 (Automobile travel). If the searcher looks, however, under 338,2328 (Prices in the oil and gas industry) for such a topic, or scrolls about it, the work will not be found, in spite of the DDC's basically logical structure. This is not a flaw in the DDC, but in the policies with which it is applied. The solutions to this problem depend on the total configuration of an OPAC' s retrieval possibilities. Possible solutions range from multiple classification (assigning both class numbers, which would then be no longer shelf location numbers but retrieval numbers) to reliance on subject headings to reliance on keywords in the title or subject headings.

Hierarchical Structure, Expressiveness of Notation, and Suitability of Captions as Index Terms

In an online system that permits broadening and narrowing a topical search by moving up and down the hierarchy, and that permits broadening a topical search through truncation, two of the most important features are a consistently logical structure and a consistently expressive notation. This requires that topics at anyone level in the consistently logical hierarchy have a notation that has at least one more symbol at the end than the notation for the topic at the immadiately more general level. While the DDC does fairly well both with respect to logical structure and expressive notation, there are quite a few exceptions that make truncation and hierarchical display based solely on the notation less than automatic, and that affect hierarchical online searches negatively.

Missing Links

In some places in the schedules, a step in the logical hierarchy was originally left out. It is difficult, especially in an online catalogue, to move in a search from a specific concept to the next broader one if that concept has no notation symbol. In the language of faceted classification specialists, this is the problem of the missing link. In the sixteenth edition of the DDC, published in 1958 (DDC 1958), the concept "Statistics on deaths caused by accidents arid crimes of violence" was broken down directly into five sub-categories: one category for "Crimes of violence," and four for specific types of accidents.

There was no middle-level category for "Statistics on deaths caused by accidents." With the seventeenth DDC edition, published in 1965 (DDC 1965), the editors wished to introduce a more logical theoretical structure. To do this, they had to add a new hierarchical level for "Statistics on deaths caused by accidents," to balance "Statistics on deaths caused by crimes of violence." But they also did not want to disturb the meanings of the existing numbers, possibly to save libraries from having to reclassify works already in their collection. They invented the concept of "centered headings" with a range of numbers, and marked with the symbol → in the margin (> in the twentieth edition)

This creates a logical structure and permits effective display of arrays, but it does not permit right truncation to reach the next broader level. For example, dropping the second 3 in 312.273 will not lead to the next broader array, but will cause a move to the second broader array. Also, because they are technically difficult to use in spite of their logic, the centered headings notations are never assigned and therefore cannot be used in recall at present. It would be far better if the notation were consistently expressive, rather than only most of the time.

Unsought Links

Unsought links, again, is a term used by faceted classification specialists. These links occur when the notational chain involves a link whose terms should be ignored in the compilation of an alphabetical index because the terms do not lead to a recognizable or useful concept.

One example is notations with captions for which no single natural language term exists. Such notations are often created for the sake of a logical hierarchical structure, and are therefore useful for displaying arrays, but the caption is not useful as a retrieval device. Another example of an unsought link is the notation that has a caption consisting of two terms, each of which has its own notation.

False Links

False links can cause misleading hierarchical searches if the notation is used as the basis for arrays and truncation. A false link occurs when the notation indicates that one topic is subordinate to another when, in fact, this is not the case. Use of the notation to produce an array thus results in wrong answers. In these examples, Reptiles (597.9) appears to be a sub-division of Fishes (597), and Portugal (946.9) appears to be a sub-division of Spain (946). Use of the notation as a searching device for the question "Produce the array of 946, Spain," shows Portugal erroneously as a region of Spain (DDC 1989).

The indentions of the captions show correct relationships; the notations do not. Use of the notation as a searching device for the question, "Produce the array for 597," shows amphibians and reptiles as types of fishes. While the situations described as missing links, unsought links, and false links are problems, they can be solved by various means such as menus, improved terminology in captions, and careful use of terms in the index.

Inconsistent Symbols and Meanings

In a faceted scheme, the notations for different facets use unique symbols. The operations facet may use symbols beginning with A, such as A17; the materials facet may use symbols beginning with B, such as B17. When these symbols are combined into one notation, they keep their uniqueness. Since this is impossible in an enumerative classification with a base of ten, identical DDC symbols sometimes carry different meanings.

For example, although the symbol group 0941 always means "in Britain," and 021 always means "statistical form of presentation," other combinations may have the same meanings:

372.941 (instead of 0941) : Elementary education in Britain

335.033541 (instead of 0941) : Military policy in Britain

338.43000941 (instead of 0941) : Prices for secondary Industries in Britain

666.321 (instead of 0941) : Statistics on pottery

629.450021 (instead of 0941) : Statistics on manned space flight

Conversely, the symbols -41 and -21 do not uniquely and invariably represent Britain and Statistics.

629.41 : Space flight

631.41 : Soil chemistry

635.221 : Diseases caused by environmental factors

821 : English poetry

Circumventing DDC Inconsistencies

One way in which the problem of varying lengths of notations for standard sub-divisions might be solved is to divide the DDC notation into sections that are more detailed than the current MARC format, and to mark each section with a tag or indicator that indicates the type of information provided.

Subfield indicatoring might indicate geographic sub-division:

385 g 0941 : Railroad transportation in Britain

372 g 941 : Elementary education in Britain

Sub field indicator h might indicate form of presentation:

384 h 021 : Statistics of railroad transportation

629.45 h 0021 : Statistics on manned space flight

While the above suggestion "parses" the notation for a synthesized number, it does not by itself put the notation into the context of a hierarchy and thus permit hierarchical searching. For example, it does not list 385 as a sub-division of 380, nor does it refer to the array of 385 sub-divisions such as 385.1. Wajenberg suggests a much more complex and complete method of expanding the current MARC code, which will consistently not only analyze synthesized DDC numbers but will also encode their hierarchy.

While he visualizes this encoding to be done continuously for each work as it is catalogued and classified (that is, for each call number), the system could also be employed with slight modifications more economically for the class number alone (that is, for the classification schedules). The DDC Office and the Library of Congress are currently working on similar techniques.

Usefulness of DDC for OPACs

The DDC is not particularly useful for automated retrieval. It was, after all, created for human use at a time when inconsistencies weighed less, because humans are flexible. Actually, the DDC is an excellent tool for online retrieval, and the question is now how to adopt or adapt it for online retrieval. There are good reasons for using DDC as a searching tool in an OPAC environment:

1. DDC's flaws are the exception rather than the rule. They are far outweighed by its advantages.
2. As previously mentioned, the DDC is well-designed; has an expressive notation which permits arrays and hierarchical searches; permits right, internal, and left truncation to permit broadening a search automatically; is a living scheme kept up to date; is hospitable; Is available on many MARC records; and is relatively familiar to many library users.

3. Forest Press, the publisher of DDC, has put the DDC online to produce the twentieth edition, and is undertakng several projects that should make DDC more effective in online use.

4. The DDC has strong advocates among researchers and experts in the field. For example, Cochrane and Markey stated: "Automatic [display of arrays] is only possible because the DDC notation usually expresses the broader, coordinate, or narrower relationships among class numbers". Mandel pointed out, "The hierarchical structure of the DDC is particularly powerful for browsing and refining concepts".

5. OCLC recently purchased the Forest Press. OCLC has supported, and is supporting, many research projects designed to improve online access, including projects investigating the usefulness of DDC for online catalog retrieval. Examples are Markey and Tolle. It can be expected that this association will facilitate DDC's general conversion into a completely successful online retrieval tool.

6. The DDC is already being used successfully for online retrieval. The "Librarian" software package for microcomputers enables searching on DDC numbers, allows truncation, and allows users to enter words in order to find class numbers. Pemberton, who acquired it for use in a small university library, gave it a very enthusiastic appraisal.

7. The DDC is quite suitable for producing menus, thus permitting the menu approach for inexperienced users while also permitting the command approach for experienced users. In particular, the expressiveness of the notation makes it possible to derive menus automatically from a machine-readable version of the DDC schedules, although initially much editing of the results of this process will be necessary.

The use of menus also brings problems. For example, whenever a library acquires a book that has a class number that has not appeared on any previously acquired book, an addition must be made to one of the menus. This might well make it worthwhile to have available a complete electronic version of the schedules in a form suitable for use in menus.

Numbers created by synthesis might be enumerated in the file, or some software might be created that would enable the automatic lookup of constituent parts of synthesized numbers. A more costly, approach would be to include the necessary menu information in an additional field in MARC records, allowinb them to be selected by the originators of those records.

In general, one can conclude that with some editing, the DDC is likely to become a useful online subject retrieval tool that will permit and speed searching techniques that were heretofore all but impossible.

Relocations: A Problem for any Living Classification Scheme

For users of any living classification scheme, like DDC or LCC, a big obstacle to consistent retrieval is that, over the years, the locations and notations for many concepts were changed (although Dewey promised in the second edition of the DDC that, once a notational symbol had been used for a topic, it would always represent that topic and, conversely, the topic would be represented only by that notational symbol). This principle of the integrity of numbers had great appeal, partly because it was made at a time when librarians who used an older method of shelf-bound classification had to reclassify their collections from time to time to accommodate growth.

Integrity of numbers has two effects. First, once a work has been given a symbol, that symbol will not have to be changed, because it will continue to appear in later editions of the classification scheme and will, therefore, be used for new books on the same subject. Second, patrons who search for a topic will find both old and new material on that topic in one place. The problem with this principle is that knowledge does not stand still. Therefore, notational symbols may have to be changed if a helpful and current arrangement of the schedules, of the books on the shelves, and of the entries in a classed file is to be achieved.

New discoveries and changing relationships within agriculture, or astronomy and astrophysics, or sociology, provide several examples of how much topics and relationships can change in the course of a few decades. However, if the notational symbols are changed in new editions of a classification schedule, old and new books on a topic will not necessarily be shelved or listed together. For example, some numerical changes between DDC editions involve only single numbers, such as moving Manufacture of sweaters from 687.38 in DDC's eighteenth edition to 687.146 in the nineteenth edition. There were 1,600 relocations in DDC 16, only 341 relocations in DDC .19, and approximately 900 relocations and about 400 "reductions" (shifting a topic to a number shorter than the old one, but not otherwise differing from it) in DDC 20.

LCC, for example, introduced in 1987—3,698 new class numbers and deleted 452 class numbers. In 1988, it introduced 3,872 new class numbers and deleted 457 existing class numbers. The introduction of a new class number means either that a new concept is introduced, or that a concept that formerly formed part of another notation now has a new, separate spot. The relocations of individual topics, the introduction of new notations, and the deletion of old notations have a profoundly negative effect on the thoroughness of subject searches, both manual and automated. Since libraries cannot reclassify substantial portions of their holdings whenever a new DDC edition is published, or whenever a new quarterly issue of LC Classification Additions and Changes appears, they either reclassify very selectively or not at all.

Although most patrons are not aware of it, this means that a searcher who finds a suitable class symbol has a fair chance of finding only recent material, or only older material, or only part of the topic that is being searched. This is not conducive to thorough, or especially to historical, research. Especially invidious are partial relocations' that is, changes in which the notation remains but part of its meaning has been altered, so that the user who looks at the shelves, or at the entries in a classed file, does not realize that the total number of entries under one class number really represents two different subject concepts.

Users doing a subject search must be unusually sophisticated and alert to recognize such scope changes in a class notation. The problem has existed for over a century. Online catalogues are likely to show it more clearly but can, if properly programmed, also provide the necessary linking between old and new notations. This will involve an enormous amount of historical research, and will probably be economically feasible only if the linking is done once and for all by the organization responsible for the classification scheme, on the basis of its schedules, rather than individually by each library on the basis of its own classifications decisions (which are hard to trace in any case). This means that the wording linking old and new notations must be cautious, because a library may or may not have reclassified its older works, or may or may not have used the new notation for newer works. For example:

> 134 (Hypnotism) changed in 1965 to 154.7. Works published after 1965 are likely to be classed 154.7.
>
> 154.7 (Hypnotism): Prior to 1965 classed as 134. Works published prior to 1965 are likely to be classed 134.

Situations in which a concept is transferred from one notation to more than one new notation are even more tricky. For example, 656 (Transportation and railroading) became with the fifteenth DDC edition the range of 385-388. A similar example, in reverse, is LCC notation HF 4653.E75.

The LCC began to be developed some twenty years after the DDC was introduced to the public in 1876; most of its schedules were developed between 1898 and 1910. Unlike the DDC, it was not designed as a theoretical scheme suitable for all general libraries, but as an inhouse scheme designed to reflect the emphases and purposes of the Library of Congress, As a result, it devotes proportionally greater space to the social sciences, especially history, political science, and law, and relatively little space to philosophy, religion, and the humanities. The Librarian of Congress was rather astonished when, soon after the scheme began to be developed, other libraries began to express an interest in it. Like the DDC, the LCC is an enumerative scheme but, unlike the DDC, LCC has no synthetic features whatsoever. It is probably the most enumerative general scheme ever published. Its enumerativeness and detail are shown by the fact that all of its schedules together take up about three and a half feet of shelf space, whereas the twentieth edition of DDC takes up only slightly more than five inches.

LCC Arrangement Pattern

The LCC uses a mixed notation of letters and numbers, and is divided into 21 classes.

A	General works
B	Philosophy; Religion
C	History: Auxiliary sciences
D	History: General and Old World
E-F	History: America
G	Geography; Anthropology; Folklore, etc.
H	Social sciences
J	Political science
K	Law
L	Education
M	Music
N	Fine arts
P	Philology and literature
Q	Science

R Medicine

S Agriculture

T Technology

U Military science

V Naval science

Z Bibliography; Library science

Each class, with the exception of classes E, F, and Z, is divided by a second, and sometimes also by a third, letter into subclasses. Class Q for example, is divided into:

Q Science (General)

QA Mathematics

QB Astronomy

QC Physics

QD Chemistry

QE Geology

QH Natural history (General)

QK Botany

QL Zoology

QM Human anatomy

QP Physiology

QR Microbiology

The sub-class CC (Physics) consists of the following major divisions:

QC 1-75 Physics in general

QC 81-114 Weights and measures

QC 120-168	Descriptive and experimental mechanics
QC 170-197	Atomic physics., Constitution and properties of matter
QC 221-246	Acoustics. Sound
QC 251-338	Heat
QC 350-467	Optics. Light
QC 474-496	Radiation physics (General)
QC 770-798	Electricity and magnetism Nuclear and particle physics. Atomic energy. Radioactivity
QC 801-809	Geophysics. Cosmic physics Geomagnetism
QC 851-999	Meteorology, Climatology.

Further Sub-division by Sequential, Cardinal Numbers

Further sub-division is by cardinal (not decimal) numbers from one to approximately 9999. When the notational base gets squeezed over the years by insertion of too many new topics, the system sometimes employs decimal numbers, but not in a hierarchical sense. In other words, CC 815.2 is not viewed notationally or conceptually as a sub-division of CC 815. Sometimes the decimal numbers happen to be in a location where they could have hierarchical value, as with CC 825 and CC 825.1-QC 825.7, but this is purely accidental, and CC 825.75 is conceptually hardly a sub-division of CC 825.7.

Further Alphabetical Sub-division

Still further sub-division is not by classification principles but alphabetically. Depending on the context, alphabetical sub-division may be by topic, geography, language or nationality, or other attributes.

LCC and Online Searching

The preceding list of LCC characteristics and problems may have seemed long, but it is still incomplete. Nevertheless, it indicates that the LCC notation is much less suitable to direct use for retrieval than an expressive notation like DDC's. By "suitable" is meant not just the ability to reach a notation *via* a subject heading, author, title, or keyword, but the ability to use the notation itself as a scrolling device; as an indicator of subject scope, subject hierarchies, and subject inter-relationships; and as a retrieval device either by itself or through the use of Boolean formulae that combine a notation with a subject heading, name, keyword, or other term.

Disadvantages

Like the DDC, the LCC suffers from the disadvantage of age. It too was not designed for use in a computer. It is a completely enumerative scheme with the typical limitations of such schemes. Miksa (1984) discusses the various new ideas which LCC introduced in the development of classification practice, but unfortunately most of these ideas make it extremely difficult, if not impossible, to use LCC for real information retrieval in a computer, other than just for browsing in the shelflist, without editing or computer-coding virtually every notation. The factors that affect adversely LCC's use for online information retrieval are:

- — A structure that is sometimes illogical in not grouping some topics and their sub-divisions together
- — A structure that often omits hierarchical levels and thereby makes hierarchical searches via the notation difficult or less effective
- — A structure that is often illogical in grouping topics related only in a superficial way (such as by the fact that they are treated in caricaturistic fashion), and that thereby often makes use of the notation as a collocative device difficult, if not impossible
- — Extensive use of alphabetical rather than logical sub-division
- — A none-xpressive notation that does not make it possible to narrow down or to broaden a search automatically via the notation, and that can also cause problems in scrolling

— Lack of a unified index (the existing commercial one is outdated, incomplete, and not coordinated)

— Printed schedules that have not yet been converted to machine-readable format, except for some experimental work. This conversion is going to be a major, problematic undertaking.

— Additional factors which, however, do not affect the online use of LCC directly, are its age and the fact that it is institution-bound rather than general.

Advantages

From an online information retrieval point of view, LCC's advantages are less compelling than DDC's advantages:

— It is maintained by a well-funded, leading organization, the Library of Congress. It is, therefore, a live scheme that, within limits, keeps pace with progress, adding new topics as needed, and changing others as needed

— It is hospitable

— As Chan pointed out, it uses in some subjects very specific notations which should help to pinpoint a search. For example, some literature notations provide unique locations for individual authors and even for some individual works; geography numbers for individual cities and even some city districts exist (DDC has specific notations for only some cities)

— The LCC notation can be found in almost all MARC records

— The LCC is at least somewhat familiar to many users of academic libraries. They tend, therefore, not to be in awe of it, although they typically do not know it well enough to take real advantage of it, or to circumvent its pitfalls

— People whose interests involve only very few highly specific LCC notations strongly support its use.

Plans for Using LCC On Line

It will be obvious by now that the LCC notation cannot be encoded automatically, number by number, in order to make the schedules readable and manipulable by computer. In one way or another, each notation must be shown in context, as part of the total hierarchical structure. As Cochrane and Markey pointed out,

> Encoding the hierarchy of LCC unit records is a requirement [original emphasis] in the conversion of printed LCC schedules to machine-readable form.... The hierarchy-encoding process in LCC has to be a manual task and must precede the production of machine-readable LCC unit records. This task must be completed when the LCC schedules are entered into machine-readable form for the first time.

Several possible techniques have been suggested. Basing their decision on earlier research, Cochrane and Markey suggest the nesting technique, which consists of recording, in the authority record for a notation, that notation with its caption, as well as the range of each subsequent broader level in the hierarchy until the letter level has been reached.

An authority record would permit display of the hierarchy and permit users to broaden or narrow down their search as desired. Chan suggests a different technique for encoding hierarchical structure in a classification authority record. In the LCC schedules, the breakdown of a topic into narrower subtopics and sub-subtopics is indicated by various levels of indentions in the schedule captions. The indention levels could be coded numerically, and the code recorded on the classification authority record for each class number. A third technique, which incorporates the nesting technique, is most likely the one that will be carried out, because it is part of an actual programme. The Library of Congress has established a set of long-range goals for the computerization of its classification schedules. It is LC's intention to design an Integrated system which, eventually, will:

— Enable LC to edit and update its classification schedules online

— Permit classifiers at LC and elsewhere to classify and shelf-list online

— Permit production of LCC schedules in a variety of physical formats: paper volumes, CD-ROM, etc.

— Enhance subject retrieval from online catalogues.

As part of this programme, LC is developing a MARC record format for each class number's authority record. Among the data elements which have been tentatively identified as necessary in a typical authority record are:

— Classification notations (from schedules and tables)

— Captions for topics and concepts (from schedules and tables)

— Notes (identified by function, *e.g.*, scope notes, "class elsewhere" notes, sub arrangement instructions, etc.)

— Preceding hierarchy

— Index terms

Since authority records must be established for literally millions of numbers, and since for each of them the hierarchical structure must be discovered and incorporated in the authority record, the caption and index terms examined, revised, and perhaps expanded, and a good deal of additional work done, this will take many years and enormous sums of money. Whether this type of expense is feasible remains to be seen, even in an age when the profession has gotten used to spending millions of dollars on special projects: in the 1960s and 1970s, by converting many academic libraries from DDC to LCC; in the 1980s by "retrospective conversion" to AACR2 style; and at present in purchasing ever-newer and ever more ambitious computer equipment.

A potential danger is that this very project, designed to make LCC a more effective subject retrieval tool, will calcify the LCC structure and make change, development, and improvement virtually impossible. A viable classification system, coupled with alphabetical subject headings and uncontrolled keywords, will provide more effective subject access to bibliographic files than has been available heretofore. However, their combined use still does not solve another problem. Whether one works with the DDC-Sears subject headings combination, or with the LCC-LC subject headings combination, the scope of quite a few topics is not the same in the vocabulary that is arranged in alphabetical order and in the vocabulary that is arranged in classed order. For example, that the subject Field artillery exists in LCC, but not in the LC subject heading structure, where it must be sought under the broader term Artillery, Field and mountain.

Some of these differences may be due to differences between alphabetical syntax and classed groupings, or to the limitations imposed by an enumerative classed vocabulary. It is more likely, however, that most such differences are caused by the separate and largely uncoordinated creation and development of both schemes, originally even by separate Library of Congress departments. The DDC and Sears subject headings were, of course, also created quite independently, of each other, without any formal coordination.

While some prefer to regard these differences positively—one system complements the other—the differences can also be viewed as unnecessary obstacles, since they cause problems to searchers who must know or discover when one or the other approach is more likely to be fruitful. No overall rules seem to exist to make this learning easy. For example, there seems to be no logical reason why the subject Colour in cartography can be retrieved precisely *via* the alphabetical approach but not *via* a class number and its captions. One way to solve this problem is to coordinate the Library of Congress class number structure with its subject heading structure, somewhat in the form of a thesaurofacet; that is, as a system in which a concept has a definite scope that remains the same regardless of whether it is expressed through controlled words or through controlled notation.

There are signs that LC is moving, very gradually and on an ad hoc basis, in this direction. As yet, however, the Library of Congress subject heading list does not answer this particular suggestion. While it has taken over some of the terminology of a thesaurus, its structure is still not entirely logical, and it does not take the LCC into account.

While amalgamation and restructuring of LCC and the Library of Congress subject headings into a combined structure may be desirable, it is probably at this time not politically feasible. Development of detailed authority records for each notation seems to be the most realistic way of incorporating LCC into a truly effective subject retrieval system. There can be no doubt that a combination of alphabetical and classed subject labels enhances retrieval effectiveness. It has been shown more than once that different subject retrieval systems often complement one another. For example, while LCC can be especially effective in known-item searches, because it tends to use very specific notations, DDC is usually much more effective for broad subject searches.

Moreover, LCC and DDC do not break down every topic in the same way, and thus can be used to serve different retrieval goals. While subject headings tend to retrieve many aspects of a specific topic, class numbers improve precision, if desired, by retrieving only one aspect of that topic. While use of uncontrolled keywords tends to increase recall at the cost of precision, it can also introduce users to previously unknown subject headings or captions. It has also been demonstrated more than once that overlapping, but still pertinent, groups of records can be retrieved from one database when searching with class numbers as well as with alphabetic subject headings. In other words, the combined use of both systems improves recall.

Furthermore, the advent of the online catalogue presents the opportunity for still another development, namely, multiclassification for multitopical works. Heretofore this has been done only for classed catalogues, whereas, in the alphabetical catalogues typical of

North American libraries, the single class number served primarily as call number, and subsidiary topics could be expressed only through subject headings. Assigning of several pertinent class numbers and subject headings to a multitopical work should enhance the retrieval of that work for all of its content rather than for just the predominant part.

In order to tackle the ease of interaction in OPACs, we will look at the possible contributions of the field of human-computer interaction (HCI) research to the study of user interaction in online catalogues. OPACs will not be discussed specifically as computerized catalogues but as interactive online systems. The aim is to go beyond the professional concern with the notion of catalogue. OPACs will be considered first as systems belonging to a growing group of machines being used by the general public on a self-service mode, almost as casual machines. Secondly, OPACs will be envisaged as information retrieval (IR) mechanisms in a broad sense, *i.e.*, machines which must help users in their retrieval tasks; by providing them with support and power as they formulte an information need and discover and learn new information as well as recognize already known information. This part of the study will include a short description and evaluation of existing OPACs and of the methods previously used for evaluating their interfaces and their ease of use.

Basic features to improve their usability and user interaction will be summarized (*e.g.*, traditional IR aids such as weighting and ranking; subject access aids such as the use of classification and dictionaries; and linguistic aids such as spelling and automatic stemming). Next will be discussed why and how advances in the theory of HCI apply to the design of online library catalogues, and which general concepts and findings in the study of HCI are useful for improving the understanding of the needs and problems of users as they interact with computer catalogues.

Interface issues are not solved solely by the appearance of more powerful hardware and/or software. For example, expert systems specialists have recently realized that even the best expert system will not be used if its interface is poor. This will not be a state-of-the-art review of the HCI field. It is a new, fast-growing area, exploring many conceptual avenues. Particular solutions depend on the specific application, and HCI specialists themselves stress that they cannot give definite answers. What we can find in the HCI research area is some idea of how to improve systems from the user interaction point of view (not necessarily from the point of view of the specific task at stake, *i.e.*, the IR task in our case).

Keeping an eye on how the HCI field evolves is a salutary exercise. It should make us aware of user interaction problems and how these are being analysed and understood. By doing so we can broaden our expectations and be more critical of current systems; and we can ensure that our design ideas evolve in the right direction. This part of the study will briefly include the following areas:

(a) general interface mechanics, WIMPS (Windows, Icons, Mouse, etc.), nature of HCI and direct manipulation;

(b) expert systems and intelligent knowledge-based systems; user psychology and individual differences, user modelling and cognitive aspects (conceptual/mental models, users' understanding).

More recent research in information science of relevance will also be mentioned: this includes the design of expert intelligent retrieval systems and the cognitive modelling of what expert intermediaries do when searching online databases. OPACs are IR systems used by end-users.

Potential OPAC users form a very large population with extremely varied needs and backgrounds. As designers of computerized IR systems, and as specialists in information handling, processing and retrieval, we must be aware of the problems users encounter when interacting with our systems. We should shift our interests from catalogue use studies to catalogues as IR public systems: their usability and ease of use; HCI aspects; end-users; and, ultimately, user information seeking behaviour.

There is now a well-known history of OPAC design developments and Hildreth has classified them into three generations. "The initial OPAC generation was derived from circulation or cataloguing systems, and gives rather limited access to the bibliographic information. It is essentially based upon pre-coordinate IR principles. Their interfaces simulate traditional catalogues in their forms of access by providing mainly phrase access to separate indexes (subject headings, titles, authors). This is appropriate for known item searching. The interfaces are usually menu driven. The second-generation OPAC systems are more similar to the commercial IR systems; they provide keyword or free-text access, corresponding to post-coordinate IR principles.

The indexes to be searched have to be specified by the user in the search formulation. The first kind of design improvement found in third generation OPAC systems was to combine the features of the first two OPAC generations by providing both phrase searching and keyword searching. In terms of interface this is often achieved by a simplified command language which facilitates user interaction. It leads users through menus and question/answers as well as commands; the interface has improved help screens and instructions and operations are simplified. This is typified by recent developments of a few systems, such as MELVYL, LCS/ WLN at the University of Illinois, and CARL, which now also provide access to other kinds of bibliographic information through their OPAC: accessing monographs as well as journal articles becomes more integrated. MELVYL gives access to the Medline files, CARL searches newspaper clippings, and LCS/WLN uses a PC front-end interface to traditional online systems. This latter system assists users in the use of the command language; it helps them to build a search strategy offline, with a wealth of help screens and detailed instructions; it executes the resulting search strategy online; it downloads the retrieved references on the PC; and it offers to locate the journal titles in the Illinois University library catalogue. Obviously, offering command languages (and their powerful features, even if simplified) to OPAC users is a long-awaited and welcome trend. Nevertheless, it still presents problems with lack of ease and simplicity of use for a large proportion of users.

Many end-users would not necessarily want to plough through the lengthy text of LCS/WLN University of Illinois front-end's numerous screens. Other systems, either experimental or operational, are trying to overcome these problems using such means as retrieval, linguistic and semantic aids. Some of these improvements are also referred to by Hildreth. These will be reviewed briefly, starting with 'mechanical' devices and moving towards more 'semantically oriented' devices.

Whilst the former try to improve the mechanical matching processes, their interface design does not employ knowledge of the subject area. The latter, however, make use of subject knowledge actively to offer contextual and semantic support in order to assist user interaction.

There have been a few attempts at incorporating the knowledge learned from IR research and experimentation to improve conventional Boolean retrieval systems. The most well-known systems are CITE and Okapi. They have implemented implicit Boolean searching on natural language input, weighting and ranking techniques, and relevance feedback from the user. Thus, they enable the user to search without necessarily being knowledgeable about Boolean search formulation and reformulation. Okapi also offers 'intelligent search sequencing'. This follows automatically various search trees, which combine phrase and keyword access and search various indexes simultaneously or consecutively, particularly for author/title searches.

It therefore goes beyond an initial matching between the user input and the database indexes. Okapi attempts various further matches using all the information available from the system and the user. The system retrieves as many references as possible without the user having to reformulate his search.

More recent work done at the Polytechnic of Central London consisted of implementing automatic spelling correction and stemming.

The automatic spelling is achieved using sound-matching algorithms and corrects miskeyings and other misspellings by mapping orthographically related words. The sound-matching algorithm reduces words phonetically by representing them by their most significant characters. The automatic stemming links morphologically related words, hence providing a form of implicit truncation. The Okapi '86 team went some way into considering to what extent a word should be stemmed: keeping the longest possible suffix to start with, then stemming further.

Both 'strong' and 'weak' stems are generated and a combinatorial method is used for term weighting so that the output is ranked. Weak stems get higher weights than strong stems. Spelling variations (*e.g.*, UK and US forms) are incorporated into the weak stemming procedure. When a word does not stem to anything in the index, it is then sound matched and looked up in the index for the nearest match. These design features are basically mechanical devices to improve the system matching processes. They are intended to provide the users with as much and as good retrieval as possible, without them having to learn the search mechanics (*e.g.*, truncation) to do it. The burden of the search interaction has therefore shifted from the user to the system. Some of these features have semantic implications; for example, the implicit truncation may bring in semantically related words, although the underlying mechanism uses morphological principles. Other design improvements are more definitely aimed at improving the semantic aspect of the searching process. They are described below.

LCS/WLN at the University of Illinois has implemented a way of leading users from retrieved information to related information that was not initially formulated by the user. It does this by linking relevant records retrieved with free-text words to other records, using their subject headings. It is an interesting attempt at relating free text to controlled vocabulary. This assists the user in navigating through the natural words and the subject authority entries of the database. CITE, implemented at the National Library of Medicine, also has the same feature: from the user natural input it gives a list of the relevant medical subject headings (MeSH) to be 'weighted' by the user (rather than by the system, as in Okapi). However, the system assumes that the user will be familiar with the medical terminology and the structure of MeSH.

Well-known suggestions by Pauline Cochrane Atherton and Irene Wormell are to add the back-of-the-book indexes, tables of contents and chapter headings to enrich the subject description of monographs. These have not yet been implemented. Another area for subject access and semantic improvements is the use of classification schemes. A very interesting experiment was carried out by Karen Markey and Anh Demeyer at the Online C= Library Center (OCLC). Using the Dewey Decimal Classification (DDC) Schedules and Relative Indexes machine-readable file provided by Forest Press, they tried: *(a)* to enrich the vocabulary of the database, and *(b)* to provide for systematic access through the DDC Schedules. By means of a rigorous experimental set-up they proved that the classification schemes and indexes did enrich the database vocabulary and retrieved records not found with the control OPAC system.

With the DDC-based experimental OPAC, the user input is related to the class number(s) under which it appears; the system also displays the context of the search input within the classification scheme, emphasizing different 'perspectives' under which that topic is classified. The class number of retrieved and relevant records could also be used for expanding and retrieving other records, as a search 'pivot' (in the same way, LCS/WLN at Illinois University uses subject headings). This design idea has not been implemented. Work is also currently being done on the use of PRECIS (PREserved Context Indexing System) as subject authority or online thesaurus by Juliet Congreve at the Middlesex Polytechnic. Without actually implementing a full online thesaurus, it is possible to improve the semantics of the system. Okagi '86 does it in a simple way, using look-up tables which handle semantically related words.

A semantic tool can range from a simple stop-list of words to a full subject authority control list. Okapi '86 look-up tables contain three types of entries: stopwords; terms to be treated as equivalent (child' and 'children'); and certain compound words to be treated as single terms (*e.g.*, 'industrial relations' and 'Great Britain'). This was found to provide more precise and unique matching than stemming. Other semantically oriented work has been done by Michael Lesk, using the eighteenth-century short title catalogue database at the British Library. He uses various dictionaries [*e.g.*, The Oxford English Dictionary (OED), Collins and specialized dictionaries] to expand the user query.

An inverted file of dictionary definitions is kept, along with the number of overlapped words and their frequencies to enable a weighting procedure. The point of using and linking dictionary definitions is that it gives a large quantity of words which a thesaurus would not offer, and also a wide range of different meanings for the words. The dictionary definitions are called in if the user word(s) do not appear in the fie, and 'bring in related 'words. H the user input retrieves only a few references, the system gets relevance feedback from the user and expands the query, using the dictionary definitions, to suggest other records to the user.

Hildreth states that, librarians should learn about *(a)* the potential of online retrieval, *(b)* catalog access issues, and *(c)* user-system interface problems and promises'. The possible OPAC design developments presented above should help them visualize the various directions that future systems can take. It might also extend the debate beyond the traditional catalogue access issues' by introducing categories such as mechanical matching devices and semantic-oriented features.

Any attempt to avoid putting the burden on the user to reformulate and re-enter searches until satisfactory results are obtained is well worth pursuing. Most IR systems still do little to help the user transform an information need to the explicit descriptions understandable by the system. To optimize retrieval results in subject searching, more than one search approach may have to be employed in the overall search strategy'. This quotation from Chan, referring to the use of various subject aids (*e.g.*, DDC, keywords, Library of Congress Subject Headings, Library of Congress Classification) seems very appropriate: the process of seeking and identifying information to assist with a problem typically follows a more circuitous, cyclical and unstructured path than the one provided for by strictly matching devices.

The remaining research quotation is, How do we choose among all these numerous design features? A way of illustrating this problem is to refer to a recently designed operational OPAC system. This system features Boolean searching on keywords, relevance feedback based on free text, mixed with Universal Decimal Classification (UDC) numbers. It seems that the design features mentioned above are now taken into account and being incorporated into operational systems. But which, or which combination, is the best and for what purpose? Any improvement in design must also be accompanied by an evaluation of its use and success or failure with the users. Furthermore, any design decision should stem from an understanding of user interaction problems. We have seen many information system which a panel of experts would undoubtedly rate technical successes however, upon talking to users in the organisations, we hear different story ... products should be more carefully matched both users' skills and their psychological needs.

Evaluation of OPACs has in the past chiefly concentrated on impact studies, public usage, technical and IR performance and use patterns. Impact studies look at how well users react to and accept these new computer systems as compared with traditional catalogues, and if they prefer them or not. Public usage studies are concerned with which types of users use or do not use the OPAC and the reasons why. These two types of studies are usually carried out using the traditional methods of data gathering, *i.e.*, questionnaires, surveys and focus group interviews.

Technical performance studies look at the computer workload, the response time or the required number of terminals. IR performance studies compare search keys versus keyword searching, title searches in OPACs and in card catalogues, or retrieval results using different features. Use pattern studies monitor the number of known-item versus subject searches, the utilization and success of various search criteria by users, or the pattern of users' errors in searching the OPAC. These studies use the transaction log analysis method and controlled experiments. The transaction log analysis enables us to monitor real usage and gives data on use patterns. Many case studies of individual systems can be found in the literature. Some cover several of these aspects; see Mitev and Efthimiadis, for example. However, on the whole, they tend to be specific to a system and to a library context.

A few studies compare the use of two systems in an experimental manner, in order to support the choice of a system by a particular library. Of special interest is a recent study: which compares keyword subject searching on six operational British university OPACs available through JANET (Joint Academic NETWork). Two specimen subject searches were carried out on the six OPACs. The number of items retrieved on each were compared, together with whether they were retrieved using title keywords or Library of Congress Subject Headings (LCSH) keywords. The various searching features are surveyed and conclusions are drawn on their merits (*e.g.*, nesting and truncation at Hull, LCSH indexing at Cambridge, phrase searching at Sussex, set creation and truncation at York, reverse chronological display and LCSH at Newcastle). In terms of evaluating the user interaction, several areas have been explored: ergonomic studies (screen displays, legibility, typing), ease-of-use studies (ease of searching, usability, search satisfaction), and studies of information seeking behaviour (cognitive aspects, mental processes, search strategies for subject searching and browsing in particular).

Work on the comparative ease of use of two types of user interface has been done. A menu-driven user interface giving access to a hierarchical classification scheme and a command-driven interface were compared in a natural setting. It was concluded that users would rather employ their own, words than go through several screens of classified data to choose their topic. This last group of evaluation studies has made use of controlled experiments, protocol analysis and talk-aloud methods. This area is by far the least explored.

HUMAN-COMPUTER INTERACTION

First of all, it is worth pointing out that, 'we know that any system architecture has significant and widespread implications for user friendliness, but we know, very little about how to make fundamental architectural decisions differently as a result of an emphasis on human factors.' On the whole, HCI research has only touched upon a few aspects of the user interface design. It has looked at hardware problems (keyboard and screen design) and at the very surface of software problems (*e.g.*, command names and menu formats). Beyond the description of these aspects, HCI is not so much concerned with artificial intelligence (AI) (the task of building a computer to reason as we imagine people do) as with what might be called artificial personality (how to make the computer behave the way we want it to). Ideally, the interface design should be dissociated from the rest of the system to allow for flexibility, adaptability and change. The design of many interactive systems is often influenced by our beliefs about the human mind as well as by the traditional (and still essential) criteria of functionality and efficiency.

The user interaction has been divided into (our levels by Moran: a task level (the IR task in our case); a semantic level (how the objects and the operations on these objects are defined and represented); a syntactic level (what the things are called); and a physical interaction level (how the users can act upon these objects, operations, etc.). The ease with which the user can interact with the system is also split according to these levels: how well the task is analysed and dealt with by the system and communicated to the user; how well chosen the objects and operations are in order to perform the task; how well expressed this choice is; and how easy it is to manipulate them. It is important here to stress the existence of the first two levels (task and semantic). These are often neglected.

The last two levels (syntactic and physical) are more often dealt with, perhaps because they can be seen. They are also more easily modified; one can experiment with them and compare them. Although less obvious, the other two levels (task and semantic levels) are just as c:ucial for a good interface, perhaps even more crucial than the syntactic and physical operation levels.

'The interface should be unobtrusive, not interfering or intruding. If the interface itself is noticed, then it stands in a third-person relationship to the objects of interest, and detracts from the directness of engagement. This idea of 'direct engagement' or 'direct manipulation' is related to (if not issued from) the recent WIMPS developments.

Users interact directly with objects represented graphically on the screen, instead of having a conversation about these objects in order to act upon them. The interface is itself a world in which the user can act, and which changes state in response to user actions. The world of interest is explicitly represented. The interface is not an implied intermediary between the user and the world about which things are said. Although this feeling of direct engagement is of critical importance, the actual requirements for producing it are little known.

The purpose of the system is to serve the user, not to use a specific technology and not to be an elegant piece of programming. The use of icons that look like waste-paper baskets is of questionable value if associated concepts are not supported (Can it fill up? Who empties it? Can things be retrieved?). 'Metaphor crucially depends on knowing enough about the attributes of the objects in both the central domain and the domain to which it is being likened, to determine what it could possibly make sense to import.

The computer is capable of using many arbitrarily complex mappings between symbols-including those displayed on the screen-and the objects, situations and events they refer to. The relationship between what appears on the screen and, for example, a file being edited, is non-trivial: if is a copy that is being manipulated (although this is not apparent). Failing to save it, a common mistake, may result in the loss of many hours' work. Such relationships become more sophisticated with the use of icons and customized direct manipulation workbenches. There is potential for confusion between actions performed on the object itself and its manifestation in one of several displays.

The relationship between what happens to an object and what happens to its screen manifestation has to be accepted by a novice user as arbitrary. One example of the use of icons in the context of OPACs is the system designed by Benest et al. at York University Department of Computer Science. In it, the user is first offered a picture of the indexes the user can search (Subject, Author, KWIC, Classmark, personal indexes). Each index is represented as a book on a shelf, and the user can select one with a mouse.

The chosen index is then displayed on the screen as an open book, two pages at a time, and the user can flick through these pages of index-entries alphabetically. There is a way of skipping to a particular letter if required, by selecting a letter among an A to Z sequence on the side. Once an index entry is selected, the book is located on a physically simulated bookshelf. The physical sizes of the books are related to the actual number of pages, format, etc. The authors envisage that the spine could be used for giving further information in the future.

The user can browse through the classified iterns on the shelf. If a book is selected, there is a book emulator, and pushing buttons will flick and jump through its pages. Pages may be annotated with a highlighting pen and book-markers can be inserted. References within the main text may be selected, causing the full reference to be displayed in a nearby window. Selecting a reference within the list of references causes the display of those page numbers on which the reference occurs. The use of icons in this system is based on the idea that the physical presence of a book, particularly its front cover design, provides the reader with an overall impression of its contents. Spatial awareness is seen as providing recognition clues. A first remark one can make about this system is that its form of access is phrase searching. Even if it offers sophisticated graphics, it is at heart a first-generation OPAC. It does not make use of the potential power of computer retrieval capabilities. Furthermore, one can question the use of these pictorial representations. Is it pertinent to the user to have books physically displayed on the screen? Is the traditional way of searching bookshelves in any way related to searching a computer? Is it a relevant way of representing and referring to the process of searching monographs online? It could be seen as a diversion from the primary aim of an IR system.

One could comment that it may be over-simplifying the issue of ease of interaction, as if ergonomists decided to paint telephone sets pink to make them more user-friendly. Users of such a system might very quickly get frustrated with its apparently simple representation of the IR task, and with the poverty of its retrieval features. This kind of approach is only tackling the representation of objects and operations on these subjects, *i.e.*, Moran's semantic, syntactic and physical interaction levels mentioned above under the heading Nature of HCI Moran's task level is not really addressed. To put it differently, the task is assumed to be of a certain nature.

The designers have a preconceived model of what the task should be (the traditional task of searching books in a library, reproduced exactly on the screen). This might not be necessarily related to the computerized IR task. Nevertheless, this system offers an unusual approach to reading full text and physically annotating pages. It also provides for browsing a classified sequence of books, whichever selection criterion was used to retrieve them.

With user interfaces and their quality of HCI, one has to be aware of the fact that the feeling of directness can depend on how much practice the particular user has. Users may adjust themselves to the interface and, with sufficient practice, may view it as directly supporting their intentions. This gives credit for the work the use has done. Nevertheless, this notion of direct engagement is of interest. One can see that for IR, the use of command languages is like having an intermediate layer between the user and the actual task. Command languages force the user to think about the mechanics of how to ask for something; they are noticed, distract from the task itself, render the interface 'visible' and suppress this sensation of directness.

What would be a feeling of directness for an IR task? The IR task is not a straightforward execution task, but a search/find/explore task. What could be manipulated, interacted with directly; and not just talked about, asked for, ordered or executed? Users often cannot formulate precisely what they are looking for. They should not have to get involved with specific retrieval mechanics (Boolean operators, field specifiers, adjacency limiters, truncation, etc.). Similarly, they should not have to understand fully record structures, search keys, indexes, thesauri, controlled vocabularies, etc.

One could envisage a direct manipulation of words and/or documents on the screen *via* joysticks, highlighters, touch-screen, etc., to negotiate a search formulation some interesting questions immediately arise. Should users have to go through a thesaurus or a subject authority file? Should they access and manipulate documents directly? Or should they be given both forms of access and manipulation? How should it be implemented? A list of subject headings, a classification scheme or a thesaurus could be seen as surrogates of the real objects (the documents). They introduce an extra layer between the desired outcome and the user. Another interesting notion found in the direct manipulation literature is the following the expression of a direct manipulation output language must be such that the user can assume that it, in some sense, is the things it refers to. Furthermore, the nature of the relationship between input and output languages must be such that an output expression can serve as a component of an input expression.

Input and output languages of the interface should be interreferential, allowing an input expression to incorporate or make use of a previous output expression . This is crucial to create the illusion that one is directly manipulating the objects of concern. This seems to apply immediately to retrieval systems. Parts of document(s), individual word(s), sentences or groups of word(s) displayed could be used directly as something to be input for another search. This could be done, for example, by pointing and 'picking' them on the screen and carrying them across another area of the screen. The user would not have to input them again. We can conclude here that although WDAPS do obviously offer considerable advantages, their automatic use should not go unquestioned. Nevertheless, it is important to recognize that the direction manipulation concepts and features do address some of the problems of HCI design, in particular its semantic level.

The possible contributions of AI to the design of online IR systems have already been examined for some time. AI first, then expert systems or intelligent knowledge-based systems, attempt to overcome barriers to database access by casual users; the AI approach tries to build a better database system with understanding of the user, his requirements and natural language communication. It tries to put all the load on the computer and make it clever enough to deal with the casual user.

The HCI approach, in contrast, attempts to remove as much of the load as possible from both human and computer and share what is left between them, through user-computer interaction or 'negotiation'. AI has not been extremely concerned with HCI and ease-of-use problems (natural language interfaces are often assumed to solve that problem). Rather it has concentrated on the issue of computer understanding of users' general reasoning processes, especially knowledge representation and inference mechanisms, in order to simulate them in the machine.

Expert systems have a more pragmatic approach. They concentrate on limited domains as opposed to general problem-solving mechanisms. They build specialized knowledge bases and inference engines; this knowledge is generally acquired from human domain experts using knowledge elicitation techniques. It is formalized using knowledge engineering methods, so that it can be implemented on a machine, often using an expert system 'shell'.

Expert system users still have HCI needs. Moreover, for some major practical applications the interface should be developed ahead of the reasoning part of the system. Berry and Broadbent even predict that; 'there will soon be more power associated with the interface of an expert system than with the knowledge base and inference engine'.

IR and Expert Systems Techniques

There have been various attempts at incorporating expert system techniques in IR systems, such as CAN search EXPERT, Expert System Assistant, etc. A recent paper by Brooks reviews the current developments in this area. There was a special issue of Information processing and management on expert systems in 1987. The reader is also referred to Belkin and Vickery for a thorough theoretical review of research into document retrieval and knowledge-based systems, within the conceptual framework of 'interaction in information systems'.

Expert front-end IR Systems

'The first category of intelligent IR systems might be more appropriate classified as 'frônt-ends'. These systems' interfaces assist users with search strategy formulation. They use improved retrieval techniques, *i.e.*, term weighting, document ranking and relevance feedback, techniques already mentioned above under the heading 'Retrieval aids'. These techniques are now being incorporated in OPACs. In other systems (*e.g.*, EXPERT) searches are carried out using a common command language which the system translates into the appropriate query language command.

EXPERT embodies a number of rules for deciding which database to search, how to select synonyms and how to combine terms. It enables users to represent their search topic; it assists users with selecting a database to search; it automatically constructs a search strategy from the topic representation and executes it; and it uses relevance feedback to reformulate the search strategy. So far; these interfaces are concerned with mapping the user's input into appropriate search terms, constructing a search strategy and carrying out the search automatically. This deals with the automatic query formulation.

The task of assisting with the online search itself, where the role of the interface is to monitor and advise the user rather than to do the search, has been neglected. For example, the problems with EXPERT are: it is unable to formulate database-dependent strategies; it is unable to suggest search terms; and, perhaps more importantly, it lacks sufficient user involvement in search strategy reformulation. Apart from its use of production rule techniques, EXPERT seems to be little more than a gateway plus relevance feedback retrieval system. With the exception of the construction of search statements and assistance with database selection, the intellectual effort is still largely on the user's side.

An exception is IIDA (Individualized Instruction for Database Access), developed within a training/teaching context. IIDA examines commands and responses, looking for errors or indications of problems and detecting faulty search patterns. However, it is more of an intelligent tutoring system, which trains inexperienced searchers in the use of Boolean command languages. These systems still envisage the IR task as a strict matching process, and the underlying dominant searching model is the Boolean retrieval model. The designers have a limited preconceived idea of Moran's task level.

Expert IR Systems

A second category of projects is trying to develop intelligent interfaces for online IR systems, based on expert system techniques. Expert systems try to embody and use some of the knowledge and skills of a human expert in such a form that the system can offer intelligent advice or take an intelligent decision about a processing function. The system, on demand, should be able to justify its own line of reasoning in a manner directly intelligible to the enquirer.

The domains to which expert system techniques have been successfully applied, though, are areas such as medical diagnosis and geological prospecting. These areas are of a very different nature from that of an interface to an IR system. Another critical difference is the very wide subject domain covered by most document retrieval systems. Little work has been done on expert systems which can cope with domains which are broad and not very detailed, and which involve large numbers of concepts and relations.

The successful use of expert system techniques in our field may not be possible until such techniques have been further advanced. Still, it might be useful to look into it, as we can gain insight into possible design developments. This could be helpful for several reasons: the interactive nature of OPACs, the complex nature of the IR task, and the fact that it is impossible to train the large population of OPAC potential users to the thorough understanding and manipulation of command languages. An interesting example is described in Shoval this system is designed to assist users with the selection of terms. It employs a knowledge base which contains the knowledge available to the human expert a thesaurus and additional knowledge of terms, meanings and associations.

The usual hierarchical and synonymity relations found in thesauri are enhanced by the addition of two other types of relation, generator and modal. Generator relations link the components of multiword phrases (*e.g.*, 'industrial' and 'relations' see under 'Semantic aids' above); modal links are used to express more general relations (*e.g.*, the relation between 'business' and organizational structure). The user decides which terms represent his query and enters them one by one. The system then conducts a search of its knowledge base and additional terms of probable relevance are selected.

An evaluation process is applied to distinguish terms which are most representative of the user's request. This system employs more powerful term selection heuristics than EXPERT, and does so as a co-operative effort with the user. Whilst the system 'knows' about the vocabulary of particular subject domains and some of the relationships between the concepts, it does not appear to embody knowledge about how these terms are applied by the indexers to documents in the database.

CANsearch enables medical practitioners to access directly the online databases which cover the cancer literature. The MeSH thesaurus is not easy to use and indexing policies are complicated

(CITE also tries to help the user with this problem-see under 'Retrieval aids' above). CANsearch helps further, by assuming that a cancer therapy search topic involves certain facets. It uses these facets as a framework, guiding the user through relevant sections of the MeSH thesaurus.

The user touches the screen to select the appropriate facets. The facet structure also guides the combination of terms with Boolean operators to form a sophisticated search strategy. CAN search incorporates subject knowledge (including facet metastructure), indexing knowledge, knowledge of the query language and knowledge about searching. In terms of IR for both these systems (Shoval and CANsearch), the domain is narrow enough to be well represented and structured.

These systems go a long way in terms of semantic or contextual assistance. Obviously that would be much more difficult with an OP AC and its large subject domain. In terms of HCI, Moran's task level is taken a step further than a straight matching process; the IR task is seen as involving semantic/contextual help as well. It is pleasant to use (touch-screen hardware), but users have to go through the same long sequence of facets to choose their topic from, every time they use the system. And, as we have seen under 'User interaction studies' above, users tend to like to use their own words rather than go through screens of facets or classification headings. Moran's semantic level (how objects and operations are represented) and syntactic level (what are the things called) are only touched upon.

The last IR system considered using expert system techniques is PLEXUS, designed under a British Library Research & Development Department grant at the Central Information Service of the University of London. PLEXUS was designed to help librarians to deal with referral queries about a particular domain, 'gardening'. It has a dictionary of terms, a database of referral resources and a hierarchical classification of the subject domain (by facets using the Broad System of Ordering (BSO).

The user is asked to describe what the gardening problem is about; the input is stemmed; and semantic categories, synonyms and pointers to the BSO classification are found. The system then displays concepts in the domain (a section of the BSO classification) from which the user can browse and select terms. If the model is incomplete, rules direct what questions should be posed in order to elicit the missing information (*e.g.*, 'Is it a plant?'). The search employs knowledge of search strategies and tactics to broaden and narrow the search if necessary (enter broader descriptors, exclude concepts, add synonyms). The result is a Boolean search strategy, which is modified automatically if the user wants more or less information.

Perhaps the most interesting aspect of PLEXUS is the fact that it constructs a user model: by a series of questions it assesses the level of experience of the user, his gardening experience, geographical location, previous searching habits, etc. It will use this information when giving results, for example, by giving introductory manuals if the user is non-expert at gardening. Again, this system deals with a very narrow knowledge area, and user queries are may be more of a problem-solving nature than of a strict reference retrieval nature. Nevertheless, it provides an interesting semantic/contextual approach to IR.

OPACs and Expert Systems

As has already been shown, OPACs have started incorporating some intelligent IR devices, classified above as 'expert front-ends' May be OPAC design should gain from the experience of providing a semantic/contextual intelligent approach, as illustrated in other IR expert systems in the previous section. This semantic/contextual approach should not merely aim at improving the retrieval process (recall and/ or precision). It should be envisaged as a means of assisting the User in his negotiation of a search, or task dialogue, with the system. In contrast to traditional IR systems, OPACs' coverage is very broad. Perhaps this contextual approach could be of prime importance. Our having borrowed design concepts from traditional

IR systems (Boolean post-coordinate matching) shouldn't make us lose sight of the contextual nature of our systems.

Broad subject IR systems such as OPACs, full text and mixed media databases are characterized by the fact that the structure of the information is not known a priori, unlike expert systems domains. This prevents advance knowledge of the types of questions that will be asked, unlike the situation found in hierarchical and relational data base management systems, or in narrow domain expert systems. It is much more difficult to explore and design expert systems for reasoning on open-ended domains.

Nevertheless, current efforts at using expert systems techniques for retrieving information, even on small domains, have shown that the semantic/contextual approach is vital. This should be borne in mind when examining OPAC designs. Eastman's recent chapter examines similar issues, although from the evaluation viewpoint (recall and precision). More specifically, she mentions the classificatory nature of online catalogues as opposed to other IR systems; how expert system techniques have been used for classification problem solving; and she even considers the problem structure of classification systems for catalogue selection to be a subclass of expert systems, and more so than traditional IR systems. 'The general architecture of the operation of a classification system is broken down into three major steps: abstraction of the problem data, heuristic matching of the abstraction in a specialization network and refinement into specific solutions.... The architecture of a number of expert systems can be viewed in this way.

Another interesting design effort although unfinished, is reported by Micco and Smith. Their goal was to explore the possibility of building an expert system that would serve as an assistant to the reference librarian by helping end-users to refine their search strategies before going online in the databases. This was to be accomplished by means of a sophisticated user interface. It would use a windowing process to build a user profile and negotiate at appropriate search strategy. It would include faceting and various other techniques for improving search precision. They also planned to experiment with a graphed display of appropriate subject headings showing how the literature was distributed over the subject area.

This paper describes the problems and issues involved in such an ambitious project. They soon realized that, to be effective at all, their system needed to be fully integrated: it had to provide access to all library databases (books, reference collection, periodical literature, Books in Print) and other tools such as the name authority list and a greatly modernized LCSH. They produced a limited system (in terms of the size and possibly the coverage of its database). It offers dictionaries, reference works and Books in Print as pop-up reference tools, and the display of subject headings and simulated databases, including the online catalogue. They developed a knowledge base and sets of rules, rather than producing an operational system. They looked into author and title searches, fiction/recreational reading, periodical literature and subject searches.

The 'search strategy negotiation screen' allows users to flip through two thesaurus windows: the first one is a series of concentric circles and permits the user to scan for broader and related terms; the second one permits the user to scroll across the hierarchy. The underlying classification system can also be superimposed, One problem the authors do point out is the integration of all these subsystems from a system design point of view. Although we wondered if the user's viewpoint was at a present in the authors' mind when producing all these pop-up screens, windows, etc., and these variously integrated retrieval tools, an interesting point is made: in order to design a system which assists a reference librarian, they analysed the task of the reference librarian. They found out that, the libraridn obtains a great deal of information about the clients, their background, interests, reading skills, knowledge of the library and the nature of their information need, before beginning to determine the most appropriate source of information'. They also state that their original expert system, which was intended simply to focus on the use of online databases, went back to the drawing-board. It was decided to focus on capturing and encoding the analytical techniques used by experienced reference librarians. This aspect will be covered further in the next section.

There has been a fair amount of work on the applications of psychological theory to the study of computer users in general, on the study of usability and ease of use; and on the study of users of IR systems and/or PACs in particular

Psychological Models of HCI

Fundamental work has been carried out by psychologists and HCI researchers on Psychological models and theories of human-computer interaction, in order to make predictions about aspects of the behaviour of the users of a device. There is a collection of complex and unrelated modelling approaches to be found in the literature. Each deals in some distinctions which may help to differentiate between different types of models. The first distinction is competence models versus performance models.

Competence models, such as the task action Grammars, are concerned with what the user needs to know and needs to be able to do in order to carry out the task. There is no performance element, so the dynamic aspects of the interaction are not covered. Performance models take into account the user competence, plus how the user carries out the task. There are many performance models, covering different behaviours to varying degrees of depth and breadth. performance models can also be process models, in that they cover mental/cognitive operations. An example of a performance non-process model is the keystroke level model. An example of a performance process model is ICS (interactive computer system developed at the MRC Applied Psychology Unit, Cambridge.

Interesting results regarding this latter work relate not to what the users didn't know, but to what they wrongly thought they did know; this type of error appears to be related to the number of opportunities for false inferences that the system provided. Users evidently do not patiently collect a bundle of facts, waiting for them to gel into a complete whole. They use inferences and actively build knowledge structures which combine observation, guesswork and inference. If we knew more about how knowledge is built, we could design systems to support the natural processes instead of misleading them. A further distinction to be made is whether the models deal with routine skills or problem solving. A routine skilis model deals with methods within a well-known task domain.

The main characteristics of user behaviour involve selecting between these methods. A typical task investigated with these models is text editing. This leads to building models of expert users' behaviour. A problem-solving model pays more attention to figuring out the user's next actions, based on user's knowledge.

A Psychology of OPAC users

Some of the sources of problems on the-users' side have been identified as being: *(a)* individual differences and demographic characteristics; *(b)* usage patterns and error behaviour; and *(c)* content of training and searching abilities. Individual differences and demographic characteristics refer to age, spatial memory ability, éducational background, personality types, achievement tests, academic status, etc.

Usage patterns and error behaviour correspond to the number of descriptors searched and of commands used, the connect time, the number of retrieved references, recall and precision, etc. This type of data is often gathered using transaction log monitoring. Training and searching abilities mean experience with OPACs and other computers, learning styles, symbolic reasoning, logical deductive skills, etc.

Researchers have tried to correlate these users' characteristics to their searching performance; overall, they found that users' cognitive attributes affected the search process but not the search results. They found that under laboratory conditions none of these measures explained much of the variance in any significant manner. This type of research, 'has done more to identify the range of performance and satisfaction than it has in identifying the variables responsible'. Furthermore, 'the degree of variance is perhaps the strongest user behaviour finding in Information Retrieval to date'.

One cold possibly argue that this direction of research is only substantiating the (probably previously held) insight that users search in extremely varied and different ways, even when they have to do pre-determined searches under experimental laboratory conditions. However, this should be seen as a reassuring fact! May be one of the problems with this approach to HCI aspects of OPACs, and of IR systems at large, is that the modelling technique used is definitely of a 'competence model' type. It might be linked with how users and their task are envisaged. Borgman and Bellardo are focusing on users' levels of competence and how these relate to a performance defined as retrieving a previously known document or not. There is no emphasis on how the search process takes place.

Borgman classifies the problems users encounter when using IR systems as 'mechanical' and 'conceptual' problems. The mechanical problems encompass things like typographical errors, command errors, term errors, quitting the system, no matches for wrong author names, etc. She concludes that users face more mechanical problems with OPACs than with other IR systems. The mechanical aspects of searching appear to be a problem in other retrieval systems only for infrequent and inexperienced users. Mechanical aspects are therefore the very first hurdle users have to overcome.

However, many people have noted that Boolean logic appears to be one of the most difficult aspects of IR for users, experienced or not, to grasp. It is an inherently difficult task and one that is not 'common sense' for most people. This is even more pronounced for OPACs since many online catalogue users probably remain permanent novices. Designing menu-driven systems for 'naive' users and command-driven systems for 'sophisticated' users might not be appropriate. Similarly, wanting to train all users to learn to use command languages might not be the answer. The belief underlying these approaches is that the IR task is a strict matching process (a routine skills task?), and that good searching is equivalent to mastering a Boolean command language.

Borgman focused on users' mental models through an experimental study of the use of a prototype Boolean logic-based OPAC Her research is based on the mental mod theory which proposes that people can be trained to develop a 'mental model' This mental model will aid users in generating methods of interacting with the system, debugging errors and keeping track of their place in the system.

A laboratory condition was set up in which users were subjected to two different modes of training, a procedural one (based on the mechanics of the system) and a conceptual one (based on an explanation of the system). The conceptually based training was based on an analogy with the card catalogue. The results seem inconclusive in that, although the training effects were not as strong as predicted, we did find the hypothesized interaction effect between training method and task complexity, indicating that model-based training is not always superior.

Other conclusions are drawn about the individual differences (especially educational background) and their related performance. It seems that this particular work is mainly concerned with teaching IR by giving a conceptual model to the subjects (assuming that their mental model of this particular task is inadequate or non-existent), and checking how well they perform with/without that model. It may not be surprising that the results are rather inconclusive, since this, work is not exploring how users conceptualize actively while interacting. It is not concerned with users' activities and understandings. This is highlighted by the choice of methodology: the subjects are given some pre-determined retrieval questions, hence may be suppressing some aspects of the IR task and only examining a straight matching process.

The task is equalled to a strict computing match routine. The result of this matching process is evaluated. The fact that the systems complexity might interfere with it by triggering some inadequate representations is not taken into account.

It could be argued that the model provided by the conceptually based training is also inadequate since it refers to card catalogue searching, which is very different from online searching. We could reflect that we were never totally able to teach our users to use traditional catalogues 'properly' anyway, and they coped with the catalogues' inadequacies by browsing through the shelves.

May be the most interesting results are:

(a) the fact that one-third of the subjects were unable to achieve a minimal level of competency; and

(b) that few of the subjects could apply Boolean logic effectively to the search tasks.

This should make us question OPAC designers who carryon implementing command languages. But, as Gould and Lewis put it, 'designers underestimate user diversity, don't appreciate the role of cognitive processes in system interaction... and don't put their faith in empirical data.

Borgman focuses on how to give the 'right' conceptual model for users to search with. The IR task is seen within a Boolean logic model to be taught to users, and it being the unique model for searching. The fact that, 'users seem to have a difficult time defining search strategies and executing them in an optimal manner' may be more of an argument for stopping to impose Boolean logic upon them than for trying to find such factors as individual differences to explain those difficulties.

Another area of investigation is illustrated by the work of Janosky *et al*. They used a 'think-aloud' data gathering technique on subjects having to perform standard searches (for example, difficult author searches, author/title searches with stopwords, subject searches for words in titles and journal searches). A detailed analysis of errors and associated verbal protocols provided insights into the design features and mental processes contributing to the commission of errors.

The main conclusions were:

(a) the profound influence that incorrect mental representations have on the viewing and interpretation of online/offline help and instructions; and

(b) the snowballing effect of a misconception as a user tries to seek and interpret additional information in attempts to recover from an error.

This analysis also served to illustrate the often severe problems that can Occur when the mental representations developed and/or activated by a computer system user are inconsistent with the actual system design. They mainly looked at manipulation of syntax and the use of commands. Not only could users not get the commands right, but there was also confusion about bibliographic elements. This work concentrates on Moran's syntactic and physical interaction levels, and does not include the task level. Nevertheless, its approach to HCI modelling is very much a user's performance and process model in that it covers mental/cognitive operations, applied to mainly manipulation and syntactic problems. They rightly conclude that the designer's goal should be to be consistent with those mental representations that the users will activate/ develop and use as a result of interacting with the system. This requires a great deal more understanding of cognitive processes in general than does simply designing to be consistent with the system designer's personal representation. It is unlikely that the system designer will predict all of the information processing sequences, errors and misconceptions that users are likely to generate. Empirical evaluations can be very effective in identifying the existence and causes of unanticipated behaviour.

User models can be based on stereotypes or prototypes (Rich has built such a system, called GRUNDY, which advises a user on the choice of a novel from a library fiction catalogue using stored stereotypes and feedback from the user), or they can be based on individual users. The information can be gained:

(a) through explicit interaction with the user through a short series of questions and answers about his level of expertise, preferences, interests, goals, etc. (PLEXUS, mentioned earlier, does this); or

(b) by implicitly inferring or abstracting characteristics through the actual user's interaction with the system.

The user models held by the machine can contain short-term and/or long-term information.

The area in which user models have been applied most success fully is intelligent teaching/ tutoring machines, where the user model generally feeds into the teaching strategy so that the system adapts itself as the student progresses. User models are beginning to be implemented in expert systems. Although the nature and purpose of user models have not been critically enough investigated... we should look at the extent to which user models contribute towards a systems effectiveness, efficiency and acceptability. For IR systems, there are some current attempts at exploring this user modelling approach. For a review on this see Daniels and Brajnik et al. More specifically, Brooks's and Daniels's PhD studies' at the City University Department of Information Science investigate this method. Their basic assumption is that IR systems do not have any understanding of the individual user or his problem. In order to gain some of this understanding, they start from the premises that the elicitation and use of information about users, their status, goals, intentions, beliefs and so on, during the reference/pre-search interview is something that reference librarians and human intermediaries do as a matter of course.

They therefore state that, 'the development of an intelligent interface which approaches human functional behaviour requires an understanding not only of what tasks are carried out by human intermediaries but also a model of functional interaction which will account for the complex patterns observed and which can be then incorporated into the design of the system.

Their raw data consisted of audio-recorded pre-search interviews between intermediaries and end-users, which they subjected to a functional discourse analysis. This was found to produce a wealth of detailed information about each interview, both with respect to the tasks of the intermediary and the knowledge he employs and also with respect to the process of negotiation between user and intermediary. From this they derived a set of functions, such as 'problem description,' 'retrieval strategy, 'user model', etc. They analysed and described them in depth; they formalized them in terms of tasks, sub tasks, plan building and knowledge resources used; they suggested how to implement each function in a distributed expert problem treatment system, using expert system techniques and a 'blackboard' architecture.

One function (the user model) was partially implemented but the results are not yet available. One very strong point about this current work is its extremely detailed analysis. It is going very far in the understanding and modelling of the actual task carried out by intermediaries in order to elicit knowledge from the user. It offers ways of incorporating this in system design, possibly including OPAC design.

One possible objection, with respect to its usefulness for the understanding of HCI problems which end-users encounter when searching IR systems, is that intermediaries are highly trained, specialized and experienced at searching online. One can wonder if untrained end-users would behave in the same way and if they should. Brooks concentrates on the performance and process aspects of intermediaries behaviour; focusing on intermediaries tasks might entail an analysis of a more routine expert skills task as opposed to looking at end-users' behaviour. This may lead to modelling expert users' interaction.

The outcome of a pre-search interview is a search strategy executed by an intermediary. This might not allow specifically for perhaps more interactive, negotiated, reformulated, exploratory general browsing, serendipity and discovery types of searches which end-users may need. Nevertheless, where systems are to be used by more than one class of users, some degree of tunability is obviously desirable. In many cases presenting users with a few simple questions at the start of an interaction could be sufficient to ascertain the necessary critical information', as illustrated in PLEXUS.

We have seen that OPAC design developments are beginning to offer: *(a)* improved retrieval and linguistic features which may help users overcome their difficulties with the use of Boolean command languages and the complexities of computerized matching; and *(b)* various semantic/contextual devices which may support them in finding contextual information, orienting themselves and browsing through files, hence enhancing the nature of the IR computerized task.

Recent interface features and expert systems developments also highlight this trend of offering various knowledge devices to help the user formulate and negotiate his information need.

Psychological research work which investigates users' interaction with IR systems from various viewpoints was also presented. This work is still fairly limited in that:

- It examines the human-computer interaction largely under its 'physical interaction' and 'syntactic' levels and often does not tackle its 'semantic' and 'task' levels.
- The HCI modelling techniques used are based on:
  - (a) A 'competence' model focusing on individual differences.
  - (b) A 'performance non-process' model which does not examine how the usel carries out the task.
  - (c) A 'performance process' model. This latter modelling approach can be further subdivided into: *(i)* a model which examines the syntactic and operational aspects of the interaction only; and *(ii)* a model which, by

focusing on intermediaries' expertise, treats the interaction as an expert skills task rather than an end-user problem-solving task (see under 'Psychological models of HCI' for further explanations of these models).

If we want to discover which design features are the best to suit our users' needs, we have to start investigating end-users' problem-solving behaviour while doing computerized IR. It was shown that confronting users with the use of a Boolean command language is probably forcing a model of IR upon them. Also, it might well load users in a cognitive sense: they are busy enough thinking about their search topic and should not have to think about complex computational IR principles.

Owen suggests that we should try to understand better what 'naive' theories of computation users hold (they do have some kind of pre-existing conceptual models and actively build and modify them), so that we can try to, 'resolve the trade-off between confusing users by swamping them with information and confusing them by concealing it'. This is even more crucial if we are to opt for interfaces using windows, mice, icons and the like, in order to provide for graphical/contextual IR features, as a recent project using hypertext software illustrates. These interfaces might be easy to use but one often needs four legs and three arms to press all the buttons and probably five eyes and two brains too! We know that people tend to use fairly simple classification structures and that elaborate systems are not maintained.

❐

8

Library Information Networking

Computer is a device used by many people all over the world for different purposes. Its use is increasing in our daily life. It is used in laboratories, hospitals, schools, colleges, houses, offices, industries, etc. Its use is multifunctional. It is used for computing, communication, designing, learning, etc. It helps to get things done at a faster rate with accurate results. Hqwever, the accuracy depends upon the programme or software used. Computer receives the data, processes and provides information as required by the user. To transform the data into information, a computer and a set of instructions are required. Use of computer means using physical device or hardware and a set of instructions or software.

French defined these terms as follows:

(a) **Computer.** is a device that works under the control of stored programme, automatically accepting and processing data to produce information that is the result of that processing.

(b) **Hardware.** is a physical device found in the computer system.

(c) **Software.** is a programme or a set of instructions used on a computer system for data processing.

(d) **Types of Computers.** Quantity of the data to be handled by the computer and processing depends upon the size/ capacity of hardware and the programme.

Computers are categorised into three types on the basis of hardware. The types are:

1. **Mainframes.** These are large general purpose computers with extensive processing, storage, and input/output facilities.

2. **Mini Computers.** These are physically smaller computers compared with the main frames.

3. **Micro Computers.** These are maintained and run with the help of a single integrated circuit known as chip. Large systems use main frames and large software system to handle the data as well as to provide the information.

Software

Software plays an important and decisive role in use of hardware. Computer access is controlled by the software. The same hardware can be used for different purposes by changing the software. The function of hardware changes on the basis of software. Additional facilities can be provided with the help of software system. It can be divided into two categories.

— Operating system (as);

— Application programme.

Operating System. Operating system is a programme used as a means of instructing computers to carry out operational tasks. It controls and facilitates other programmes to use the hardware in a safe and controlled way. It monitors and controls hardware use. It also aids and monitors application programme. French defines OS as a suite of programmes that takes over the operation of the computer to the extent of being to allow a number of programmes to be run on the computer without human intervention by an operator. Operating system is a system software.

Application Programme. Application programmes are developed to perform a specific job or application. They are developed in any language. They are also developed in sets, to be used in conjunction with one another. These programmes vary in size depending upon the job. These are either written by user himself or by a software specialist. The programmes are either general or specific in purpose. The general purpose programmes are useful to any user and specific purpose programmes are useful to specific users.

Large Software System (LSS): LSS uses computers to process large and complex data. Processing should result in production of information in different formats as required by the system managers. To deal with the complexity of problems, there is need for a LSS. Development of a LSS is difficult because of:

— continuous change;

— difficulties to predict;

— not distinct;

— difficulties to test and evaluate.

To alleviate the problem of a LSS, Rammurthy *et al*, suggested the support of automation, graphic aids, metrics and knowledge based system.

Development of a programme is a big task and it can be divided into stages. French had recognized the following six stages.

— Understanding the problem;

— Planning the method of solution,;

— Developing the methods using suitable aids;

— Typing the instructions into the computer using a programming language; Testing the programme; and

— Documenting all the work.

Development of the software can be broadly divided into four stages. They are:

— Understanding the requirements;

— Design;

— Implementation; and

— Maintenance.

The two stages, namely, understanding the requirements and design are the major activities. It may be difficult for a single individual to develop a LSS. Several programmers, managers and designers have to be involved in the development process. During the development process programme files, documents and test cases are produced. Rammurthy *cl al* stressed the need for resource and activity management to avoid inconsistencies due to high level concurrency in activities and to keep track of the project.

Programme Languages. To write the programme, programme languages have to be used. The languages used can be categorised into two types:

— Low level languages; and

— High level languages.

Low Level Languages. French defines low level languages as machine oriented languages in which each instruction corresponds to or resembles a machine instruction.

High Level Languages. These are machine independent and problem oriented. They reflect the type of problem solved rather than the features of the machine. They can run on different machines. The programme can be changed to another computer. Users can store or exchange programmes. They are portable and can be altered to meet the changes in technology. These languages are also used to develop the large software systems.

French listed the following general features of these languages:

— They have extensive vocabalary of words, symbols and sentences;

— The programme statements are translated into machine instructions. The translation is done by compiler.

— The programmer can work independent to that of machine.

— The rules must be obeyed while writing the programmes.

— Instructions in high level languages are known as statements.

French divides the languages into five types:

— Commercial;

— Scientific;

— Special Purpose;

— Command; and

— Multipurpose.

Gilbert categorized languages into four types on the basis of broad application areas. They are:

— Numeric/Scientific calculations (*e.g.*, ALGOL, BASI FORTRAN);

— Business data processing (*e.g.*, COBOL, PL/1);

— Military data processing (*e.g.*, JOVIAL, PL/l); and

— Computer science research in symbol manipulation and artificial intelligence (*e.g.*, LISP, SNOBO).

Language has to be selected to suit the application. The suitability can be determined by:

— Notational characteristics;

— Compilation characteristics, and

— Operational characteristics.

The programme style should direct the computer to execute the algorithm and should also convey the design and techniques to other programmers, who may want to change the programme. Relevant programme language is chosen to write the programme and there are certain other considerations such as qualities of programme, methods and IPSE.

Qualities of Programme. Yourden'listed the, qualities of a good programme as follows. A good programme:

— works.

— works according to specification.

— is flexible.

— is ready on time.

— or atleast can fix.

— has no bugs.

— is well documented.

— executes quickly.

— makes efficient use of memory.

Gilbert gave the aspects of quality as follows:

— correctness,

— robustness,

— performance,

— utility,

— reliability,

— ease of use,

— work capacity,

— response time,

— portability.

The programme should have as many qualities mentioned above as possible.

IPSE. IPSE means Integrated Project Support Environment IPSE and software engineering environment are synonymous. What is environment in this context? According to Sommerville, environment is used to encompass all the automated facilities (such as electronic mail, documentation support, etc.) that are available to the software engineer as an aid in the task of software development. Environment is divided into three classes. They are,

Langauge Oriented Environment. This environment supports programming in one particular programming language.

Educational Environment. This environment helps in learning the programmes by beginners.

Software Engineers Environment. This environment helps to develop the large software system, *e.g.*, ISTAR, ENCOMPASS. These are developed to support software process. The support is from feasibility study to operation and maintenance.

Methods of Programme. Different methods (main) used to develop programmes are:

— Modular programming (MP);

— Structural programming (SP); and

— Object oriented programming (COP)

Modular Programming. Yourdon defines the module as similar to that of programme, that is, it is a collection of instructions sufficient to accomplish some logical programme. It is considered synonymous to subroutines and sometimes defined in terms of physical constraints.

Encyclopaedia of computer science and engineering defines modular programming as a logically self-contained and discrete part of a larger system. A complete programme is a collection of modules.

While using this method, the programme is broken into smaller and simpler subtasks. These sub-tasks facilitate to write correct programmes. It is. comparatively easy to design, write and test each subroutine of a programme, which is equivalent to module. According to IBM users, the size of a module is 4096 (Max) bytes of memory. Every module accepts input, which is well defined set of processing actions and produces output that is well defined as to content and structure. Every module will have only one entry and only one exit point. After executing programme of the module, it always returns to the statement.

In this type, each module is independent of other. This method also facilitates to change any module without changing the rest of the programme and is useful when combined with others. Modular programme is easy to control, debug, write, maintain and change. It may need more memory space and also require a great deal of extra work.

Yourdon listed the following techniques to achieve the modular programme.

— Break programmes into small independent sub routines;

— Use decision tables;

— Use of symbolic parameters;

— Separate input and output functions; and

— Do not share temporary storage location.

This programming is ideal for large software systems as it can be divided into manageable pieces/modules. Each module can be distributed among the people and all the work done by them independently.

Structured Programming. Structured programming is a new approach in programming. It provides improvement over other methods of programming.

Yourdon defines it as a philosophy of writing programmes according to a set of rigid rules in order to decrease testing problems, increase productivity and increase the readability of the resulting programmes. Its technique is to eliminate GO-TO statement. It also includes concept of top-down programme design and programme restructure and conventions. Encyclopaedia of computer Science and Engineering defines SP as a methodological style whereby a computer programme constructed by concatenating or coherently nesting logical subunits which either are themselves structured programmes or else are of the form of one or another of a small number of particularly well understood control structures. SP is developed in a top down or layered fashion. The whole programme is considered as one module and it is broken into level one modules. Level one modules are decomposed into level two submodules. Decomposition is continued until small building blocks are left, which can be easily coded. Further sub modules can be tested independently.

According to Yourdon, the basic principles of SP are:

- Control structures;
- Modular composition;
- Programme format:
- Comments;
- Readability *vs* efficiency;
- Step wise refinement; and
- Programme verification.

Gilbert listed three important qualities of SP text. They are:

- easy to understand;
- easy to demonstrate; and
- easy to maintain or modify.

The benefits of structured programme are:

- more readable;
- intelligible;
- systematic verification;
- possibility of less bugs;

— clarity;

— easy maintenance; and

— easy to modify.

Cost of Software. Software packages (software and documentation) are available in the market. Any organization can buy such software if it is useful to their requirements. Few software companies do alter or modify the package to suit to the needs of users, provided the changes are not major. Otherwise, software has to be developed specially for the organization, which will be costly compared to that or readily available.

Cost of software is at two stages

— development stage; and

— maintenance stage.

Development cost is non-recurring and maintenance cost is recurring. Maintenance cost is several times more than development cost. A study by Boehm estimates that U.S. Air Force System cost $30 per instruction to develop and $4000 per instruction for maintenance in its life time.

Sommerville listed factors for maintenance cost:

Non-technical:

— Application domain;

— Staff stability;

— Programme age;

— External environment; and

— Hardware stability:

Technical

— Module independence;

— Programming languages;

— Programming style;

— Programme validation; and

— Documentation.

As the large software system is costly to develop and maintain, it is necessary for the organization to assess the returns in terms of:

— finance;

— time; and

— accuracy.

If the returns are satisfactory or beneficial over cost, the software can either be purchased or developed.

Development of Large Software System. Developing a large software system needs lot of effort, knowledge and work. The main steps for development and use of software could be grouped into three phases:

— Design;

— Implementation; and

— Maintenance.

Gilbert had given sequence of seven steps for development of software system. The steps are:

— Requirement analysis,

— Programme specification,

— Design including analyzing the specification,

— Coding of individual modules,

— Testing of individual modules,

— Integration of individual modules, and

— Validation of system performance.

The detailed description of each stage can be seen in next sections.

While developing the software, the support of Computer Aided Software Engineering (CASE) tools are necessary.

CASE. CASE provides support to software engineers with automated tools. The case tools are also known as CASE work bench. The work bench components are:

— Diagram editing system;

— Design analysis and checking;

— Query language facilities;

— Data dictionary facilities;

— Report generation facilities;

— Forms generation facilities;

— Import/export facilities.

Design

Design is a plan or scheme of action which outlines how a desired programme will perform its included function. Thirty percent of time is spent on designing a programme.

In this phase, important decisions are to be taken. Design phase also previews the characteristics of the intended programme. This phase includes planning, understanding requirements, identification of solutions, etc. Forethought, curiosity and quality are essential in design.

The principles of design are listed by Gilbert, as follows:

— Confirm requirements;

— Keep the future in mind;

— Divide and conquer;

— Evaluate for improvement.

Further according to Gilbert every design should answer

— What tasks must be performed.

— How can each task be done.

— How various solutions be connected to gather to form a system.

Various stages in design phase are as follows.

Requirement Analysis. To design the software, it is necessary to understand the problem. It is also necessary to know the intent of the system, possible modifications. The designer has to prepare a set of c questions, which must be posed to the system for which the software is being developed. The questions should answer the intent of each aspect, rules, etc. Ultimately, we should be able to derive the users, original requirements. Once the requirements are known, they may be summarized to prepare requirement document.

On the basis of requirements, precise specifications have to be formulated. Specification is the description of what the system is supposed to do in order to meet the requirements. To prepare specifications may be difficult as the requirements are specified by the user in one or two sentences, *e.g.*, automatization of customer services in a super market. To prepare specifications, whole concept of supermarket and its service are to be analyzed by the experts.

Rammurthy et al had suggested that at least three factors must be taken into account when users want to introduce a LSS. The factors are:

— Problem purification;

— Future characteristic analysis; and

— Safety analysis.

Problem purification is the analysis of the current solution to determine what are the real problems that have to be solved. Purification also includes examination of drawbacks and inconvenience of the present system. By decomposing the problem continuously until it is reduced to bare factors, purification is possible. It also gives clear idea of the requirements of the system and avoids misunderstanding. Future characteristic analysis is to examine and predict change of these problems in future. This phase needs lot of expertise in the subject.

Safety analysis is to prevent the destruction and malfunction that can be caused by the new system. In this-stage analysis of the problems by malfunction of the system are to be identified. The alternative ways have to be developed to cope with malfunction.

Specification Analysis. In this phase, the system data flow and algorithms are to be planned. Even the system has to be organized into modules. The designer starts searching for solutions in this stage. Gilbert had suggested following steps for large software system.

— Specification analysis to break down the desired functions to uncover inconsistencies in the specification;

— Improvement of specification by providing for modification and good communication facilities between user and problem., and

— Development of detailed final programme specification.

To design LSS, a specification model can be chosen. Specification generation is difficult to prepare on the basis of informal requirements. It is also difficult to do manually. The existing models that are similar to programme behaviour may be chosen.

Rammurthy *et al* listed the systems that emphasize or, models. For example, Data Structure System Design emphasizes on data flow oriented model.

Specification should also include

— non functional requirements such as performance, reliability, and user friendliness; and

— changing specifications which are common in the life time of the software.

The design also could be either knowledge-based or system. Knowledge-based is algorithm design and system design includes decomposition of the system into modules.

According to Gilbert every solution involves three decisions: What information must be stored for task;

— What use will the programme make of the stored information;

— What data blocks must be used and what is their form.

Further the author also stated that the design should answer:

— What tasks must be performed;

— How can each task behave; and

— How can various solutions be connected together to form a system.

This stage is important in design of software.

Data Flow. Data flow is the scheme of movement of data between programme's data objects and processing actions. On the basis of data flow, the software system can be categorized into the following:

Embedded System. In this system, inputs flow from another system and outputs to another system. In this format, data flow between systems is to be considered.

Updating System. In this, the data is kept for systems, use and updating the data at each execution.

Data flow techniques help designer to build iterations piece by piece. Additional objects are determined at each iteration. The objects can be linked by their appropriate actions. The data flow based design is used in both OS and software. On the basis of the data flow, data flow diagram has to be drawn. Data flow diagram helps in design of the system. Data flow diagram is defined by Gilbert as a diagram of a programme in terms of its data objects (such as files or arrays or flags and its processing actions, showing what data used by each action and where each action places data. It has to be developed by repeated considerations of what data objects are needed and what actions are performed on these objects.

Design Proposal. The designer has to achieve the design. In the process, the designer makes assumptions about

— Characteristics of inputs;

— Overall approach; and

— Analysis of critical actions.

These assumptions are to be documented. The documented assumptions are evaluated for further coding.

Coding and Integration. At this stage, coding can be made. It can be done for each independent module, if it is module programming. Once the coding is finished every module has to be tested. Testing is part of coding and at this stage the necessary changes could be made in coding.

In modular programming, after coding these modules have to be integrated into a cohesive system. After integration it is necessary to test. To integrate and test, top-down method is used. While coding and testing, the qualities of a good programme are to be incorporated. These qualities will help to maintain acceptable level of quality. Rammurthy et al had defined software quality as the totality .of features and characteristics of a product or service that bear on the ability to satisfy given needs. Further, the factors such as reliability, reusability and efficiency are to be taken care of.

Evaluation of Design. Every software should meet the quality parameters alid specifications. The deficiencies of the system could be identified by evaluation. The correctness can be evaluated either by the designer or a group of evaluators or reviewers. In this, the software is tested to know whether it can handle the situation and achieve tasks or not. The evaluation could be done phase by phase to identity the deficiencies and errors. At the end of each phase, necessary, corrections can be made.

Software Life Cycle. The software systems pass through many stages during their life cycle. Life cycle begins when someone gives the requirements and until it dies or becomes obsolete. Re phases of life cycle had been divided into two parts.

Development Phase. It includes all the activities from the point the need of the product is identified to the point when implemented product is listed and delivered for operation.

Operations and Maintenance Phase. This part includes all activities after delivery, such as fixing bugs discovered during operation and performance enhancements.

Various models of life cycle had been proposed to describe the activities during the development phase. Important models had been described by Rammurthy et al. They are:

Waterfall Model. It is the most traditional one. Life cycle is divided into requirements, design, coding, testing and maintenance. The software goes from one phase to another sequentially.

Rapid Prototype. This model is in two stages. Prototype development identifies the feasibility and ensures understanding between the customer and developer about the expected functionality of the system. Production quality software development phase is concerned with the actual system development.

Automatic Programming. It is in two stages. Specification development which includes maintenance changes and machine assisted.

Reusability Model. This model recommends searching of reusable components. These reusable components need not be developed again. More appropriate ones are picked and used. In this, the reusability factor is important. This model recommends to develop tools to make software reusable. The models help in designing the software and the software developed is delivered for implementation.

Implementation

The software development is developed by a team of programmers in consultation with managers. While development, several precautions art, taken to. meet the requirements. The software has to be implemented in real situation and has to be evaluated in terms of its performance. Implementation has to be followed by verification of the software.

Verification. While developing the programme, there is a possibility of errors. Elimination of errors is necessary. At least the errors may be reduced to acceptable levels so that the system operates as per specifications. Verification of the programme helps to identify such errors and their elimination is possible. Verification of the programme can be of two stages: Testing debugging.

Testing. Testing is checking the programme, whether it is correct or not and whether it can do what it is supposed to do. At this stage, the software is integrated and exercised. Testing is also determination of properties of programme by using sequence of experiments. Each experiment with selected input has to be presented to the programme. Programme is to be executed and the output has to be observed. This method of observation is testing. Each experiment may be known as test case. By repeating tests at every point the errors can be found out and the same can be eliminated. There is every possibility of bypassing the errors. Testing provides information about programme's behaviour in actual environment or real situation. According to Dijkstra testing shows the presence, not the absence of bugs. At this stage, software developer convinces the buyer, by demonstrating the software working. Elimination of errors at this stage will help to avoid future expensive and troublesome elimination process.

Debugging. French defines bug as a fault that causes a programme to fail during testing or after programme is commissioned. The process of finding and getting number of bugs is debugging. Gilbert defines debugging as a process of finding and repairing the errors. Debugging is inevitable as errors are found in large software system due to their complexities. The errors are to be detected while testing and the same should be isolated for elimination. Good design helps for debugging.

Yourdon suggested a technique known as anti-bugging, which refers to writing programmes in such a way as to make bugs less likely to occur. Whenever they occur, they should be easily noticeable by user and programmers. Testing and debugging are key factors in implementation of software system. The recent news in computing shows how the mistakes or errors effect organizations.

Computing reported that a computing error caused 0.1% mistake in the retail price index. This blunder costed the Government £12 millions in compensation to pension and benefit loosers, donations to charities and administrative costs.

Maintenance

Software is designed and implemented by the programmers. Once implementation is done, the user makes use of the software. To use the software, it has to be maintained. What is maintenance? Maintenance is continuing or retaining the use of software, to enable to achieve the specified objectives of using it. Further 50 percent of total programming effort is to maintain existing systems.

Generally maintenance includes:

— error correction;

— fulfilment changes in requirements;

— system testing;

— incorporating modifications; and

— minimizing programme corruption.

Categories of Maintenance. Somerville categorized maintenance into three types:

Perfective Maintenance. This includes the changes demanded by the users or the system programmer; which improve the system in some way without changing its functionality. Sixty five percent of maintenance comes under this category.

Adaptive Maintenance. It is maintenance due to changes in environment of the programme. This category constitutes 18 percent of maintenance.

Corrective Maintenance. It is correction of undiscovered system errors. This category constitutes 17 percent of maintenance.

Software maintenance can be categorized into four areas:

— General maintenance,

— Internal requirements,

— Additional requirements; and

— External influence.

General Maintenance. The programme performance may be effected due to power failure, errors, "bugs or operational problems. These are to be taken care if we are to use the software. They are general in nature. These can be managed either by software engineers or programmers.

Internal Requirement. in a large system there could be changes in its processes, procedures and input/output formats. The changes may occur over a period of time. To retain the software, the changes have to be incorporated.

Additional Requirements. Every dynamic system develops and new requirements are demanded. To meet the new and additional requirements of the system, software has to be planned.

External Influence. External forces such as virus influence on the software. These forces have to be controlled.

Computing reported that due to virus, the data in the European Community offices in Luxemburg was corrupted. This influenced the performance of storage calculations.

Networking and Resource Sharing

A Public Library System is an important organ of the state, entrusted with the responsibility of maintaining organised collection of books and other reading, material in the service of the public. The system is designed to serve the twin purposes of providing educational support to the under privileged in the society as well as a means of continuing education for the. working class who have no opportunity for formal schooling and education. It is, therefore, apparent that the public library system has a major role to play in propagating literacy, in supporting formal education of the weaker sections, and in providing facilities for continuing education for the working class. It is a pity that nearly half a century after the nation became independent our country has a very poor system of public libraries, even in those states where formal library legislation has been introduced and public are levied of a library cess. The resources so accruing to the state combined with the matching grants made by the Government are too meagre to sustain the existing public library services, not to speak of promoting a healthy growth in their acquisitions.

The economic scenario prevailing in. the country at present makes it abundantly clear that no enhanced allocations to the public library sector will be coming forth from the Government and the libraries themselves will have to find the ways and means of augmenting and supplementing their resources. One way of doing this is to arrive at a satisfactory arrangement of pooling and sharing their available resources, both men and material, first at the local level, then at district level, next at the state level and finally at the national level. Such a system pooling of the resources would enhance the information resources of the public libraries indirectly, at the same time preventing avoidable duplication.

Resource sharing may then be defined as a mode of operation whereby, functions are shared in common by a number of participants having the same objective or goal in mind. In the context of public libraries, resource sharing means the sharing of the information resources available in one library by the clientele served by other libraries, when they are unable to get their requirements met from the local library. Resources here connote reading/audio visual material that is of information value. In fact the modem concept of resource sharing overflows the boundaries as defined above and encompasses other spheres of activities like cooperative acquisitioning, cataloguing and classification; cooperation in the training and development of the professional workers in public libraries and cooperative acquisitioning of equipment and machines which, are extensively employed in the activity of information dissemination and which are too expensive for individual libraries to acquire on their own. While resource sharing activity has at its heart, the goal of maximising the availability and utilisation of information resources and services at minimum cost, some of the essential prerequisites for effective resources sharing are: *(1)* Possession of sharable resources by the participating libraries; *(2)* Willingness to share the resources; *(3)* A planned mechanism of sharing; *(4)* Precise understanding of the use and information potential of their respective collections; and *(5)* A common bibliographic access to the collections of the participating libraries.

No library would be financially strong enough to be self sufficient as far as information resources are concerned. Hence, the concept of resource sharing becomes the central theme of any networking system. The. rise in the cost of publications, lack of adequate manpower to organise the same and the location of libraries at distant and remote places have necessiated the need for networking. The networking of libraries then is one way of achieving maximum results with minimum input.

Although evolving the lasting and permanent arrangement for a mechanism to foster resource sharing among libraries is an ideal and long term goal, there are some immediate factors which make it necessary for libraries to enter into an arrangement for resource sharing at various levels. The most important among them is a resources crunch, *i.e.*, non-availability of funds for non-plan expenditure. With the main thrust of budget allocation by the Government being in the direction of industrial and agricultural development, the libraries are obliged to plan their acquisitions, keeping in view the resources available in other libraries in the area, so that they can get maximum number of books and publications that are not available in other libraries in their geographic proximity. The everincreasing cost of books and publications coupled with the exponential growth in the publishing of books and other reading material, has been the immediate factor in compelling libraries to enter into arrangements for resource sharing. Other factors like increasing needs of the user, easy accessibility of reprographic facilities to the libraries, and the general awareness among the public of the need to share the resources are the other factors which help resource sharing in an indirect manner.

Rapid advances made in the information technology have ushered in a number of advanced information products, technologies and services that can be conveniently harnessed by the librarian community for achieving the objective of networking. These are the computers, the vast communication network developed in the country with STD facility and the T.V. with its own national hookup via satellite and microwave links.

Development of Network

Networking of libraries/information centres using computer and communication facilities became a reality in 1970's. Networks of all types, *i.e.*, local, national, regional and global are operating in the world today. Though the computerisation of information activities started in India in mid 60's, the development of computerised library networks did not gather momentum till recently.

National Network. Over the last ten years the country has successfully seen the emergence of a number of networks like I-NET, NICNET, INDONET, ERNET, INFLIBNET, etc., and some local area networks like the CALIBNET, DELNET, MALIBNET, HYLIBNET, etc. Brief particulars of some of these networks are given below:

I-NET. The Department of Telecommunications has introduced a network called "I-NET". This is the new packet switched public data network. It provides cost effective services to the Government as well as private organisations. The X28 dial up mode is the cheapest connection that many public libraries in the country would be able to afford.

INDONET. In India, the CMC Limited has setup INDONET which is a national computer network with main frame computers being setup at Bombay, Calcutta, Delhi, Hyderabad, Madras, Bangalore and Pune with distributed data processing facility. Databases available at any of these INDONET nodes can be accessed on-line from remote terminals.

NICNET. This is a computer network setup by the National Informatics Centre (NIC), Government of India, for providing information to central and state government departments to draw plans for efficient utilisation of resources thus ensuring uniform socioeconomic development throughout the country.

It is being expanded as a dedicated network covering 22 state capitals and 400 districts to address the rapidly growing awareness to computerisation in different sectors of the Government. Its headquarters is at New Delhi with regional centres at Pune, Hyderabad and Bhubaneswar. Although NICNET is principally meant for use by Government departments, it does have the potential for use by the library and information community.

ERNET. ERNET is a computer network for academic and research community in India.

INFLIBNET. INFLIBNET is envisaged as a computer communications network linking libraries in universities and colleges in the country and libraries in institutions affiliated to the CSIR, ICMR, ICAR, DRDO and Government departments. When full-fledged it is envisaged that INFLIBNET will network 184 universities and 23 institutions deemed to be universities, 7200 colleges and 200 libraries affiliated to other organizations. INFLIBNET is designed to operate at four different levels, viz., national, regional, sectoral and local.

DELNET. DELNET will network 35 libraries in the Delhi area.

CALIBNET. CALIBNET will network 38 science and technology libraries in the Calcutta metropolitan area.

International Networks. Apart from the above national networks, the apex body of the public library network namely the National Library can have access to the number of specialised international databases like INIS, AGRIS, MEDLARS, INSPEC, etc. through some of the international and regional networks like the TELENET, TYMNET, DIALNET, ESA/IRS, BLAISE, EURONET, etc.

In India, among the various types of libraries, the public libraries are the most neglected ones. This is in spite of the fact that they are. the oldest ones in terms of existence. Of late, there is a growing recognition of their services not only in eradication of illiteracy and promotion of adult literacy programmes but also in socioeconomic development of the nation. Public libraries cover a wide range of user groups: illiterates, neo-literates, children, disadvantaged groups like the blind, housewives, students, artisans, labourers and many others engaged in a variety of professions and vocations. To put it in a nutshell, all individuals residing in the area of jurisdiction of a public library may be either its actual users or potential users.

In the earlier days, public libraries were thought to be self-sufficient in terms of acquisition and preservation of all the documents that are required by its user communities and also for provision of free and easy access to its literature/collection. But, of late, it is being felt that no public library can afford to operate in isolation; it has to join the mainstream along with academic and special libraries and go in for modernisation and networking to provide effective and efficient services to its varied and demanding clientele.

The present state of Indian public libraries is deplorable. While other types of libraries such as academic and special libraries are in the process of modernisation through use of computers and communication technologies, the public libraries are lurching. It appears that there is no perceivable impact of modern technology on Indian public libraries. The possible reasons for this sad state of affairs are many. Some of these are:

— lack of realisation of the benefits of modernisation of public libraries;

— lack of political will for public library development.

— under-estimation by the political leadership of the potential of public libraries in nation-building process.

The term 'Network' is used in the present times in place of 'Resource Sharing' or 'Cooperative Systems'. It is because of two important reasons: Potential improvement of library and information operations by interconnecting individual library systems with the more recently developed facilities for data and information transfer; and The significant role played by the computers, telecommunications and new reprographic techniques.

Networking and modernisation are becoming very important in all types of libraries as they enable the users to have access to the resources of many other libraries in addition to their own one. The public libraries are also likely to benefit themselves by participating in networks. The benefits that accrue from networking of public libraries are:

(i) Preparation of union catalogues;

(ii) Provision of cataloguing data/catalogue cards for the publications available in the network libraries;

(iii) Provision of bibliographies;

(iv) Optimum utilisation of rare collections;

(v) Cooperative acquisition of documents;

(vi) Cooperative exchange and distribution;

(vii) Cooperative storage of documents;

(viii) Savings, both of technical work and collections; and

(ix) Minimises cost of the library services in the long run.

Above all, networks offer provision of more number of materials, that is, comprehensively, at less cost and quickly.

With rapid advancements in the various technologies such as telecommunicatjons, satellite communications, microprocessors, computers, etc., several networks are either presently functional or in the formative stage in India. They can be grouped into:

A. **General Networks.** NICNET, INDO NET, VIKRAM.

B. **Subject Networks.** VIDYANET, BTISNET, SIRNET INELIBNET, ERNET.

C. **Specialised/Business Networks.** BANKNET, COALNET, RAILNET, TOURNET, SAILNET.

D. **Geographical Networks.** CALIBNET, DELNET, HYLIBNET, PUNENET, BONET, etc.

A brief note on the purpose and participating libraries of each of the above networks is given below:

NICNET is a Government of India network aimed at providing information to support planning, decision-making and monitoring Government schemes and programmes. It links all the districts and states with the headquarters at New Delhi.

INDONET is a commercial computer network developed by the Computer Maintenance Corporation Ltd. (CMC), New Delhi. It is expected to have about 100 centres in several parts of the country like Calcutta, Bombay, Madras, Bangalore, Ahmedabad, Bangalore, Pune, Hyderabad, etc.

VIKRAM is a packet switched public data network being developed by the Department of Telecommunications, Government of India. The network's main centre is located in Delhi and would link to 8 switching modes. While NICNET is meant solely for the use of Government departments, INDONET and VIKRAM are public networks.

SIRET is a computer communication network of CSIR aimed at linking about 40 CSIR laboratories spread throughout India.

BTISNET, set up by the Department of Biotechnology, Government of India, is a specialised network linking the information centres in genetic engineering, cell culture, biology, etc.

DESINET, developed by the DESIDOC for the DRDO units, covers the defence scientific and research information, and connects all the DRDO laboratories, scattered throughout India.

ERNET is a network meant for the academic and research community. It links 5 IITs, IISc, NCST and DOE.

INFLIBNET (Information and Library Network), being developed by the UGC, will link the institutions of higher learning covering all disciplines, R & D institutions and other national organisations like CSIR, WAR, DRDO, ICSSR, etc.

VIDYANET links several research institutions and laboratories, universities and higher education institutions, research centres of industrial and other commercial organisations.

CALIBNET (Calcutta Library Network), DELNET (Delhi Library Network), HYLIBNET (Hyderabad Library Network), PUNENET (Pune Libraries Network) and BONET (Bombay Libraries Networks) are the library networks linking the library and information centres located in their respective geographical regions.

CALIBNET is a metropolitan network linking 38 libraries in the Calcutta metropolitan area. The libraries or the institutions linked in this network are either scientific research institutions like Bose Institute, Saha Institute of Nuclear Physics or the higher learning institutions like Jadhavpur University, etc.

DELNET links All-India Institute of Medical Sciences, DESIDOC, DST, India International Centre, IIPA, INSDOC, JNU, NPL and NASSDOC.

It is clearly evident from the above that in none of the networks mentioned including the geographical area networks, not even a single public library has been included.

In fact, no sincere and worthwhile efforts have been made in India for public library networking. Recognition of the importance of resource sharing among the public libraries can be traced as far back as to 1919. Shri Suri Venkata Narsimha Sastry, a pioneer in the library movement in Andhra Pradesh, had emphasised the importance of resource sharing among the public libraries at the VI Annual Conference of the Granthalaya Sangham held at Madras in 1919.

No library can be entirely self-sufficient and selfreliant. Therefore, libraries in any region have necessarily to develop interdependence and depend on each other. In the matter of acquisition of a collection, it may be appropriate for a library to concentrate on one or more disciplines or areas of knowledge by building up a strong and comprehensive collection supported by some books generally recognised required in other areas. Occasionally when need arises one could draw on the book stock of another library strong in another field. Such an arrangement results in available resources being utilised more economically and a larger book stock being used by readers in the region.

All the libraries within a state should form part of a network extending from the community library of the village through intermediary levels to the district and to the state central library The state network should eventually connect with the national level.

But, unfortunately, this report is lying in cold storage for the past 8 years. As a result, we do not still have a national policy on library and information system even after 46 years of attaining Independence. This has seriously affected the modernisation and networking of Indian public libraries.

Computer Aided Instruction is a powerful tool in instructing students. CAI has not made much impact in India, in subjects other than Computer Science where we come across many such packages in the form of 'tutors'. As the capabilities of CAI are not restricted to the field of Computer Science and Computer Applications alone, there is wide and promising scope for its application in general education. CAI can be classified as one of the audio visual materials in education. It can be used both in formal and non-formal education.

Metaphorically, they can be called 'Electronic books'. In fact, there is a class of books called 'programmed text books' designed on the lines of CAI packages, which use basically a non-linear model of presentation of lessons. Further, CAI could be used by libraries and information centres in orienting the library users. Use of CAI can be enhanced by providing it as an on.line service in any of the proposed networks. S.M. Rawlines observes that, "Results of the recently conducted surveys indicate that on-line computer assisted instruction is equal or superior to traditional method of training new student library workers. While costing the same, the system frees staff members for other duties. Students response to CAI has been favourable. Staff members have welcomed the free time CAI permits for other projects and more individual attention to students."

According to K.L; Zinn, "Computer Assisted Instruction refers to the use of computers to present drills, practice exercises, and tutorial sequences to the student, and perhaps to engage the student in dialog about the substance of the instruction. A CAI (tutorial) dialog is achieved between computer programme and student when the responses derived from the programme are highly responsive to the questions, answers, and directives given by the student, while at the same time the dialog advances the goals and merns established by the author of the curriculum materials. He further adds that the most visible use of computers in instruction is to provide direct assistance to learners and to assist teachers, administrators and educational technologists in helping learners. The users may work individually or in groups using a device directly connected to computer.

The types of CAI material could be classified into the following:

Drills

Skills practice

Programmed tutorials

Testing and diagnosis

Dialog tutorial

Simulation

Gaming

Information retrieval process Computation

Problem solving

The following guidelines have been identified after examining a few CAI (packages and also with the experience gained in developing one such software called SOCRATES. In fact, these guidelines could be used as bench marks in selecting some of the available CAI software or shells. The selection basically depends on the user requirements and affordability.

Shells *vs.* Prepackaged Lessons. One of the advantages of tutorials with builtin lessons is that the teachers need not worry about lesson preparation and presentation design. However, they are rigid and closed systems. On the contrary, CAI shells offer much desired flexibility and allows teachers to tailor the lesson depending on his evaluation of the students and the feedback. Once the lessons are prepared, they become as good as tutorials with prepackaged lessons, Yet they offer flexibility to update the lessons periodically in tune with the changes in curricula, method of presentation and feedback.

Novice-Friendly. The phrase 'novice friendly' is preferred to the widely used phrase 'user friendly'. We personally believe that user friendly software should offer powerful functions with case of use. Many user friendly software trade off power to simplicity. If a software does not demand prior knowledge of computers, it could be categorized as novice friendly, which may not mean less powerful. One of the widespread notions about UNIX operating system is that it is not user friendly. However, we feel, UNIX is user friendly and provides so many facilities for the user to accomplish varied tasks, though it requires effort on the part of the user in learning the usage of its utilities. In other words, UNIX is user friendly and perhaps is not novice friendly. Many of the so called user friendly software provide layers of menus. But once the user is familiar with the software, he may consider it tedious to reach a particular menu, if it is not one of the first few menus. This prompted many software developers to give options for both menus and command driven functions. Menu driven programmes need not be user friendly programmes but definitely be novice friendly. In the case of CAI packages, it is normally expected that the user might not have prior exposure to the computers and it should be novice friendly. In conclusion, it is ideal to have option for command driven and menu driven.

System Configuration. It is ideal to have a CAI package which runs on a system with minimum configuration. However, this may limit the programmer introducing many beneficial audio, visual effects, especially in the case of graphics presentations. CAI packages in general (exception being Hypertext) do not require much computing power. But the presentation of pictures poses a different problem, as there is no unanimity in the choice of display adopter cards. The adopter cards come in monochrome and in colour modes and in colour with different screen resolutions. However, this problem could be solved if the software provides install able device drivers, so that only the relevant driver is loaded at the time of installation of the package. It is suggested that a fairly good CAI software could be brought on an IBM PC compatible with the following configuration: IBM PC or its clone with 640 KB main memory; 360 KB Floppy disk drive; CGA/HGA switchable card; preferably a colour monitor. However, for a CAI package to be used on an online network, the package should have provision for multi-user access.

Audiovisual Effects. It is attractive if the presentation of lessons are sugared with audiovisual effects. Graphics image presentation, animation sound bring any CAI package near to the video presentation with an added advantage of the interaction with the system. In video presentation, the user becomes a passive observer and his presence or absence makes no difference. An intelligent CAI software can interact with the user and will not proceed further, unless the user wishes so. This could be best achieved by hypertext technology. However, the required hardware configuration and software may cost more.

Evaluation. Presently, only a few systems have the capability of assigning scores to the students. It is desirable if the system could evaluate a user on the basis of certain criteria, like the number of correct answers, the number of times the user has attempted to get the correct answer, the time taken by the student to answer a question. In such cases, the software should have some way of identifying the user so that it keeps track of his usage or discourse with the system.

Keeping these guidelines- the authors have developed a CAI package called SOCRATES (Software for Computer Assisted Teaching System). Socrates is a CAI shell and is distinct from the tutors that are in wide use. One of the important problems with these tutors is that the lessons are prewritten as a part of the source code and compiled. In order to alter or modify or add a lesson, one should have access to the source code, which is not the case normally, as we get only an executable modules and overlay files which are binary files. This problem prompted the design model of Socrates to separate the executable module from the lessons and the lessons are ASCII flies. The basic model design is that of 'Learn' package of the UNIX system.

Unlike 'Learn', Socrates is menu driven. It displays horizontal menus of two modules, one for student and the other for teachers. The student is shown a popmenu of subjects on which the lessons are provided with. Once he moves the cursor on to the desired subject and presses return, he will be shown the list of lessons. He can either start with the first lesson or choose a lesson which he left off in his previous interaction with Socrates. The student is asked a question on the lesson he read with multiple choice answers. These answers are presented in window, and the student can choose the likely answer by moving a scroll bar and pressing the return key. Depending on the choice of the correctness of the answer, the student may be presented the same lesson or a previous lesson or the next lesson. Socrates has provision for teachers to modify, add., delete and even change the sequence of lessons. In order to perform these operations, Socrates offers a Screen Oriented Word Processor. This word processor is distinct from the common word processors' which we prefer to call 'Printer Oriented Word Processors'. The word processor of Socrates is programmed for Colour Graphics

Adapter (CGA) and Extended Colour Graphic Adapter (EGA) cards. Although, the software could be run on monochrome and Hercules Graphics Adapter (HGA) cards, its visual effects could only be realized with CGA and EGA cards. The word processor allows teachers to present definitions or technical terms, etc. in distinct colours and colour backgrounds. However, graphical presentation and music are not provided in Socrates. It is the responsibility of the teachers to prepare lessons and design the sequence of presentation. They can present questions with multiple answers and can direct the system to present another lesson depending on the choice of his answer.

Current Technology in the Library

CD-ROM is a growing and advancing technology that holds great promise for libraries and as an alternative for both online database and printed sources. It permits the lowest cost for information provision, that is, to distribute information in bulk and at a comparatively low cost. CD-ROM is an up-and-coming technology in the library world. Librarians must understand and appreciate CD-ROM if they are to make informed decisions regarding its place and application in the library. There is no doubt that CD-ROM can work very well for large static databases. One thing that would like to say with certainity concerning CD-ROM products is that there is constant developments taking place continuously. As librarians, we must have to identify the potential and worth of this new information product.

The history of CD-ROM has recently begun. Philips and Sony the patent holders for basic compact disc (CD) technology established the specifications for compact disc in the Red Book Actually, CD-ROM has been built on the success of CD. Philips and Sony later produced the Yellow Book with a set of licensed standards for CD-ROM.

The two companies first exhibited CD-ROM players at COMDEX (The Computer Dealers Exposition) in November 1984. Later Microsoft proclaimed the importance of CD-ROM in 1985 and sponsored the Microsoft First International Conference on CD-ROM in March 1986 in Seattle, Washington. Microsoft also published the

book "CD-ROM: The New Papyrus" Microsoft's first real CD-ROM product, Bookhelf came to market in 1987. The first commercial CD-ROM product was marketed only to libraries.

The first CD-ROM product produced by the Library Corporation contained MARC (Machine Readable Catalogue) records. Silver Platter delivered CD-ROM products to the library reference market. The Educational Resources Information Centre (ERIC) database was introduced in mid 1986 by Silver Platter, in late 1986 by Dialog and in early 1987 by OCLC. At present a number of interesting developments are under way which make the product more effective and efficient to use the number of published CD-ROM, titles and drive installations has grown dramatically over the last two to three years. A recent survey claimed that 3,88,000 CD-ROM drives were installed worldwide by March 1990. It is predicted that it will increase to 4.3 million by the end of 1993. According to IMO Statistics the United States produced approximately three quarters of all CD-ROM products.

CD-ROM stands for Compact Disc Read Only Memory. The Information Technology Handbook describes CD-ROM as follows:

"CD-ROM, short for compact disc read only memory, refers to the use of audio compact disks for computer storage. Like a laser vision disk, information on a CDROM disk is read by bouncing a laser beam off its surface. Unlike a laser vision disk, the information is stored in digital form. The pits are very small, and the function of the laser beam is merely to detect the presence or absence of a pit, indicating a binary 1 or a binary 0.

The Dictionary of Computing explains CD-ROM as:

"The predominant form of read only (ROM) optical disk. Both disk and drive are based on the compact audio consumer product. The disk is 120 mm in diameter, single sided and holds upto 660 megabytes of data. The data is enclosed in the form of a spiral of minute bumps impressed into the surface of the disk at the time of manufacture, and cannot subsequently be altered. Many commercial databases are now available on CD-ROM, often as an alternative to an online service."

Squeezing 660,00 bytes on to a single floppy disk using the nine tracks per inch format of a standard MS-DOS 360K diskette would require a diskette approximately 800 feet across. Therefore, one CD-ROM is equivalent to ten COMPUTER MAGNETIC TAPES, hundreds of pages of microfiche or million of pages of text.

Now let us look into some details about the critical elements that make up the CD-ROM optical disc medium. The CD-ROM disc is a simple circle of a plastic made of bullet proof polycarbonate of the size 4.72 "in diameter with a center hole of 0.59". One side of the plastic is embosed with pattern of recessed pits. This side is metal coated with Aluminium which is approximately 1000A thick. The Aluminium metal is coated with a transport lacquer for protection.

How CD ROM Works

Data is stored on the disc as a spiral track of microscopic pits. Machine readable information is stored on the disc as a series of pits. When inserted into a CD-ROM drive, these microscopic pits appear as bumps from beneath the disc and scatter the light from the laser beam. Lands, that is, the areas between the pits, reflect the light from the laser. This is called the translation of "pits to bits". Intermittent busts of light are deflected into light-detector laser diodes through light polarization techniques that convert the light into electronic signals and decode them as one-off binary bits-ones and zeros. CD-ROM drives read the information contained on disc by focussing low-powered laser beams on the microscopic pits. An optical unit measures the pit's reflectivity and the CD-ROM drives semiconductors translates that reflectivity back into a binary signal that can be read by a computer. CQ-ROM spins at a constant linear rate of 75 data blocks per second which yields a 150 k byte/second data transfer rate. The rotation speed of disc varies as the head moves from inner to outer tracks, so that a constant number of blocks are read every second during reading.

The International Standards Organisation (ISO) 9660 Volume and File structure of CD-ROM Information Interchange (ISO 9660 CD-ROM standard), has originated from a proposal to the ISO by the High-Sierra Group which is an adhoc group of computer vendors

including DEC, Apple, Hewlett Packard, Philips, Sony and in cooperation with NISO (National Information Standards Organisation).

CD-ROM drives are computer peripherals. They can be attached to an installed base of host computers or supplied as part of a complete work-station package comprising a host computer, the physical and logical interface and the CD-ROM drive. CD-ROM installations are all based around the IBM/PC/XT/AT and compatibles. Mainframe and minicomputer suppliers are distributing user manuals and documentation on CD-ROM. The performance of the drives is also set to improve as smaller, lighter read laser and better drive motors are employed. The first CD-ROM drives offered average access speeds of 1 second to 2 seconds. In the latest drives this average access speed has come to 0.5 seconds to 1 second. As the size of the CD-ROM drives comes' down, the prices also come down. The Multimedia PC Marketing Council has set a standard for connecting CD-ROM drives to IBM compatible PCs. This eases the customers' fears about incompatibility.

The host computer's operating systems determine the design of the device driver and file server software needed to control a CD-ROM drive and handle it as a peripheral of the host computer. Mostly MSDOS and PCDOS (Disc Operating Systems) are used at present. The file structure creation programme is used to structure and build the directory on the CD-ROM. The device drivers act as a link between the film server software and the CD-ROM controller. Regarding application software, the High Sierra Group's standard is widely adopted for new versions of PC. The application software communicates with the lower system component through 'system calls' defined by the host operating system. System calls allow the application software to tell the system software to do such things like input from the keyboard.

The importance of information in decision making has been recognised by the service organisations, which use it as a vital raw material. It is only recently that information is being recognised as a valuable, saleable commodity. With the availability of CD-ROM, users and producers of information products are confronted with a new information delivery medium and CD-ROM challenges current practices of publishing and integrating information in a fundamental way. Considering the potential of CD-ROM, its feasibilities are limitless. Its high storage capacity is a major advantage, which offers the potential for considerable consumable savings when compared with large microform or paper publications. To quote a few examples, it could be useful for interacting with huge paper collections, for tapping into the world's data banks without the cumulative charges, and for supplying pictures, graphics and other non-text information also with text. It is being used in-house by a range of public and private organisations for data distribution, distributing procedures manuals, reference works, technical manuals, etc. It is also used in a wide range of technical publishing applications in the aerospace, aircraft, automotive, shipbuilding and many more manufacturing environments and to distribute graphic database in the CAD (Computer Aided Design), Desktop publishing and scientific computing fields. The commercial database previously available online are now being distributed through CD-ROM. The Independent, the Times and The Guardian have launched their discs. The Times and The Sunday Times are now fully searchable (full text and retrieval) on CD-ROM which is an emerging alternative to multiple microfilm reels or openended online searches. The software for the CD-ROM edition of The Times and The Sunday Times also permits Boolean searching of all articles. Compton's New Media and Grolier have already come out with CD-ROM encyclopaedias, while the IBM-National Geographical joint venture has released kid targeted disks about mammals and the Presidents of the US.

CD-ROMs being based on CD-audio discs, are rugged, portable media and they are capable of being transported via postal services. Its drive and media costs can be kept low. The more the sales the lower the per unit production costs. Therefore, the most popular material can be produced very cheaply. CD-ROM being a digital storage medium, data can be searched interactively and data can be downloaded into other programmes for processing.

Once a reference material is available on CD-ROM, fully integrated system can be developed. It offers much more flexibility than print does, because of more access points, multi-year access, user friendly software, etc. With networking (Local Area Networks-LAN) and remote access, CD-ROMs can be available to many more users. CD-ROM can provide value added information that is not possible with print, if it can include hybrid indexing /Full-text products which allow increased search access. As we become proficient with optical disc technology and its creative and competitive applications to recent information products, we must also decide on how these products can be best positioned and utilised. Recently the "Magneto Optical" (MO) disc has been developed which not only stores millions of words, pictures, computer data like CD-ROM but it is also capable of erasing and rerecording fresh information over and over again, by the user rather than the manufacturer. The International Serials Data Systems, (ISDS) Register, the world register of International Standard Serial Number, (ISSN) is now available on CDROM under the title ISSN COMPACT. Therefore, more variables may be introduced as users and producers gain experience and confidence with the medium.

CD-ROM in the Library

The largest number of CD-ROM products in the market are aimed at the Library and Information Centres. From the libraries point of view, it requires a more detached perception of our purchasing decisions and smarter buying, we need to develop a built-in bias in favour of change, that is, change of technology and change of service objectives. The first commercially available CD-ROM product, namely, The Library Corporation's Biblio File, was designed and developed specifically for the library market. When first introduced at the 'American Library Associations' (ALA) midwinter meeting in January 1985, Biblio File was a great success. Biblio File contain the complete Library of Congress (LC) MARC (Machine Readable catalogue) database of more than 1,500,000 records. This database includes LC holdings both in English and in foreign languages of books, serials, Government Printing Office publications, maps, fjlms and music scores, It is stored on a minimum of two CD-ROM discs. By 1988 the company reported more than 1000 systems in operation.

This growth was due to its low price and its ability to replace costly automated systems. Other companies such as OCLC, Inc., EBSCO Electronic information, etc. market similar cataloguing systems. Silver Platter Inc. and H.W. Wilson Company market different databases, on CD-ROM. Silver Platter markets topically aligned databases such as MEDLINE and Ca-CD and Compu-index and Software CD. H. W. Wilson Company has their 'Wilson Disc'. Pre Quest Systems from UMI has CD-ROM database packages like 'Periodical Abstracts Ondisc, Newspaper Abstracts Ondisc' and Full Text Newspapers. Laser Quest contains 6.9 million MARC records to meet current as well as retrospective cataloguing needs. Engineering Information Inc., publisher of 'The Engineering Index' and (Ei compendex Plus' now offer a line of disc services on DIALOG On Disc as well as Ei Disc. Meridian Data, Inc. markets Meridians V.R. Publisher which handles premastering needs, that is, we have to prepare any database for preview and test variables before commiting to the final mastered disc. Once the disc is mastered, with Meridian's CD-NET, any CD-ROM is also made available to every one linked with Local Area Network (LAN). CD PACs (CD-ROM Public Access Catalogues) is an inexpensive alternative to Online PACs. Susan K. Charles and Katharine E.Clark conducted a research product to evaluate the feasibility of providing an online updating service to end-users searching . CD-ROM databases. They have found out that end-users are interested in the availability of a low-cost, hybridized CD-ROM / Online updating system. The Aslib survey, The Use of Information Technology by Information Services revealed that a majority of Aslib members were considering searching database on CD-ROM. Grolier Electronic Publishing Inc., has brought out (The 1988 Academic American Encyclopaedia (containing 21 volumes and 9 million words) on a single compact disc with full-text access, which is a valuable addition to libraries. Other notable entrants are Bowker's 'Books in Print' and Silver Platter's 'Library and Information Science Abstracts' (LISA).

ROMARIN is a new CD-ROM, just launched by the World intellectual Property Organization (WIPO). It contains information on all trademarks registered under the Madrid Agreement concerning the international registration of marks in the International Register maintained by WIPO's International Bureau, and which are currently in force.

The ROMARIN CD-ROMs (ROMARIN stands for 'Read-Only-Memory of Marid Actualized Registry Information") have been available since June 1992; they were developed jointly with Jouve Systems d' Information in Paris, France. The CDROMs contain such information (on each mark) as: the serial number of its registration, the mark, itself, the name and address of the owner, and data on exclusions or limitations.

In India, the National Information System for Science and Technology (NISSAT) has established Sectoral Information Centres (SICs) with the object of creating information awareness and to meet the information needs of scientists, technologists, academicians, entrepreneurs, management executives and decision-makers. Out of the ten SICs, 'NICDROM' caters to the information professionals and institutions providing information on CD-ROM, a reference collection of books and journals on CD-ROM, technical specifications, choice and cost of the CD-ROM equipment, CD-ROM database and services. NICDROM services are national in character and the host institution is National Aeronautical Laboratory (NAL), Bangalore.

Compact Disc India Limited is setting up the country's first facility for manufacture of compact discs (CDs) in technical and financial collaboration with Neststal and First Light Technology Inc. of USA.

Compact disc is the new revolutionary recording medium for storing sound, data and video images. Although CDs have worldwide market of more than 900 million discs per annum, India does not have any manufacturing facilities for them.

The main benefits of CD-ROM for the library are:

(a) CD-ROM offers on-disk access to bibliographic database without connect time costs and telecommunication fees.

(b) CD-ROM is physically portable and can be even mailed.

(c) No telecommunication facilities essential.

(d) The physical specifications are standardized. (ISO 9660 International Standards).

(e) Less storage needed for print products because of its high storage capacity.

(f) More service to the end user with all search options and brows ability. It is user friendly (search indexes are available).

(g) CD-ROM databases are more cost effective.

(h) Premastering is possible.

(i) Printing and downloading to hard disk or floppy disk is feasible.

(j) CD-ROM networking helps to share resources through Local Area Networks.

CD-ROM systems resolve many of the retrieval issues of preservation, access, storage and security of libraries and information centres. Since these systems are expensive and beyond the budget of individuals, libraries must make it possible for people to use and become familiar with this media. Libraries must aggressively identify and prioritize those databases that should ideally be converted or created an CD-ROM. Antony W. Brewerton an audiovisual librarian has said that "We should be praising CD-ROM not burying it". David 1. Rait and Ching-Chih-Chin conducted a survey under the auspices of FID (Federation International d' Information et de Documentation) on the use of CD-ROMs and other optical products in public, special, academic, government and other types of libraries in eighteen Western European countries. They feel "on the whole, users completing the FID questionnaire found many CD-ROMs easier, faster, more flexible and more convenient to use than corresponding print and online products. Many CD-ROMs were considered better than print products and were often more comprehensive in coverage." For CD-ROM products to be successful in libraries it is necessary to remove the obstacles for the libraries as well as to guarantee the Information providers a return on their investment.

❐